THE MASSIVE™
RAGNAROK

BRIAN WOOD
STORY

GARRY BROWN
ART

JORDIE BELLAIRE
COLORS

JARED K. FLETCHER
LETTERING

J. P. LEON
COVER ART

DARK HORSE BOOKS

MIKE RICHARDSON
PRESIDENT & PUBLISHER

SIERRA HAHN
EDITOR

SPENCER CUSHING
ASSISTANT EDITOR

JUSTIN COUCH
COLLECTION DESIGNER

Published by **DARK HORSE BOOKS**

A division of Dark Horse Comics, Inc.

10956 SE Main Street, Milwaukie, OR 97222

DARKHORSE.COM

First edition: June 2015

ISBN 978-1-61655-652-5

1 3 5 7 9 10 8 6 4 2

To find a comics shop in your area, call the Comic Shop Locator Service toll-free at (888) 266-4226.
International Licensing: (503) 905-2377

Library of Congress Cataloging-in-Publication Data

Wood, Brian, 1972- author.
The Massive. Volume 5, Ragnarok / story, Brian Wood ; art, Garry Brown ; colors, Jordie Bellaire ; lettering, Jared K. Fletcher ; cover art, J. P. Leon. – First edition.
pages cm
Summary: "The Crash was only the beginning. What remains of civilization is being obliterated by a series of cataclysmic events. The truth about Mary's identity, which began as a faint signal, grows louder–and she's seemingly connected to it all. The secret of the Crash and the location of the missing ship The Massive get answered here, in the final arc, Ragnarok! The Massive careens into its final climactic chapter as Brian Wood and Garry Brown pull back the curtain on the mysteries of one of the most thought-provoking comics series of the last decade!"– Provided by publisher.
Summary: "The final chapter of The Massive comic series"– Provided by publisher.
"This volume collects the comic-book series The Massive #25-#30"
ISBN 978-1-61655-652-5 (paperback)
1. Graphic novels. I. Brown, Garry, 1981- illustrator. II. Bellaire, Jordie, colorist. III. Fletcher, Jared K., illustrator. IV. Leon, J. P., illustrator. V. Title. VI. Title: Ragnarok.
PN6727.W59M39 2015
741.5'973–dc23

2015006276

This volume collects the comic-book series *The Massive* #25–#30 from Dark Horse Comics.

ASSIVE ™

"It's a testament to the exceptional work of Wood, Brown, and Bellaire that they are able to take us on a journey with such surprising twists and turns that end up being deliberate and appropriate. With darkness ever-present on the horizon, the tale of *The Massive* is one of hope and rebirth; out of such horrendous abuse that we inflict on ourselves and our world can come a healing."

— Multiversity

"THE WRAP OF THIS SERIES HAS BEEN PHENOMENAL."
—COMIC BASTARDS

"*THE MASSIVE* CONTINUES TO BE A THRILLING READ."
—UNLEASH THE FANBOY

"Wood's silent act of heroism is poignant; just as we'd expect from a groundbreaking character. All hail artists Garry Brown and Jordie Bellaire."

— Geeks Unleashed

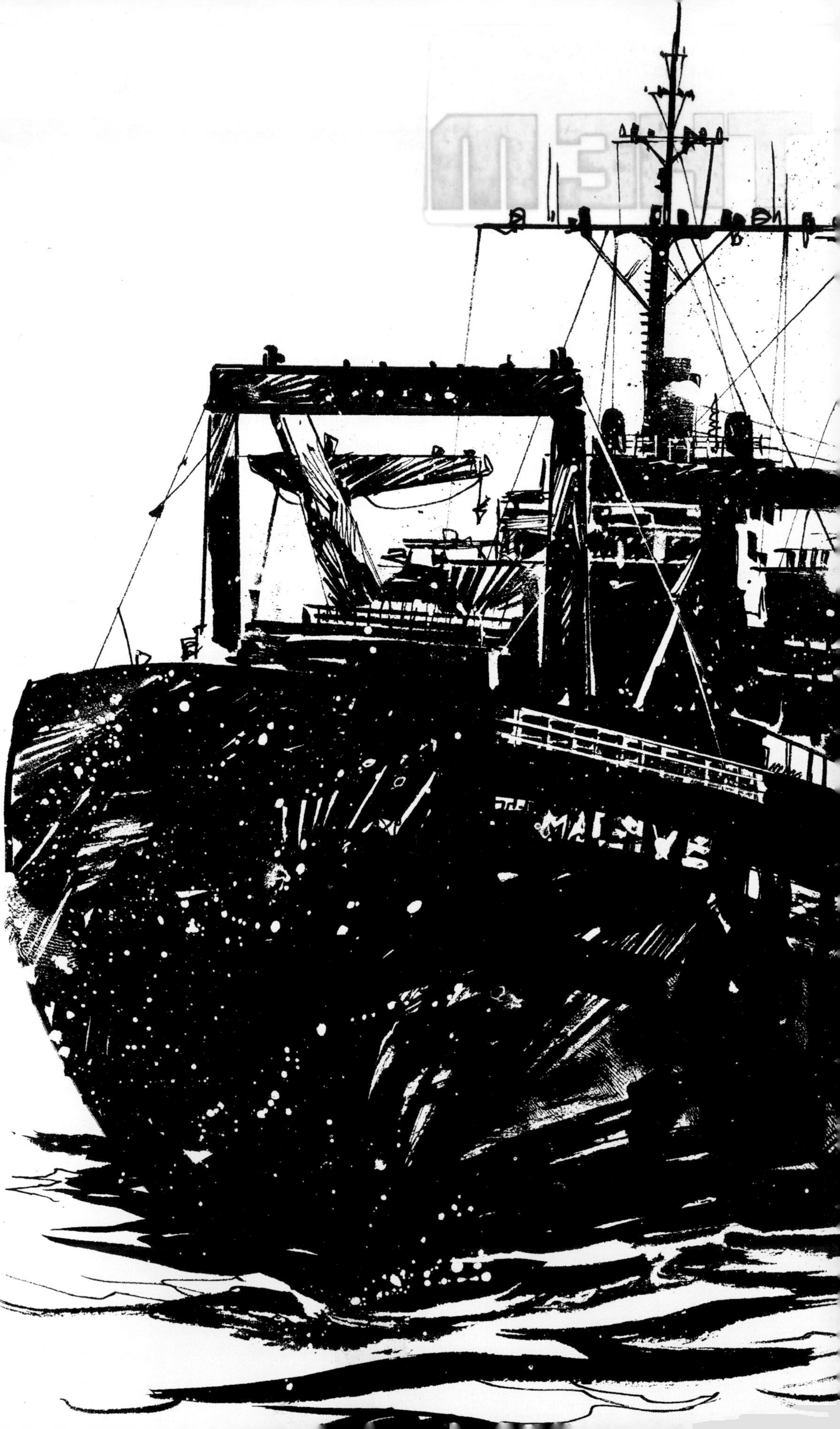

WHEN OBSOLESCENCE GETS PASSÉ OR, RECOURSE TO ESCHATON
BY KEITH PHILIP SILVA

Once humans begin to push off from muddy banks in dugouts and rush canoes, the watchkeeper steps to the fore. Oh, sure, watchmen have always stood on terra firma as lookouts or sentries, but in the watery part of the world, to keep the watch becomes sacred and vital for survival. There's a clinical term for what happens in its absence: drowning.

A ship's watch implies safety, specifics, and above all else, bearing witness. The women and men who keep watch act as analysts, chroniclers, and interlocutors of information; life aboard a ship means becoming synonymous with data, with interpretation and explanation. Open water breeds writers.

The same can be said for the hangers-on after Armageddon. Hold fast. Except for those trained in small arms, who's more important than some scrivener who can plot the postapocalypse? For the survivors of a blasted, sunken, or collapsed world, a postplanet, the pen matches the sword. Eschaton places equal value on prior military experience and literacy. The only ones left when that seventh trumpet sounds will be the detail oriented and the dead.

The Massive is an empty vessel for writer Brian Wood, cartoonist Garry Brown, colorist Jordie Bellaire, letterer Jared K. Fletcher, and cover artist John Paul Leon to fill with castaways and cutouts, codes and ideologies. The bones of *The Massive* are built from a set of detailed schematics—writerly stuff. It may take intelligent design to create a world, but it takes a different type, a circumspect soul, to dismantle a world.

As a comic book, *The Massive* uses a team approach to reckoning. Storytellers have to answer a very specific and eternal question: "Now what?" The answers the creative team of *The Massive* find in their self-made, drowned world—a limitless Gehenna, a Gethsemane asea—speak to the joys of destruction and the art of salvation. As above, so below . . .

For the crew on the *Kapital* the question of "Now what?" shapes characters more than worlds, forming interiors instead of exteriors. Callum Israel, the *Kapital*'s captain and leader of Ninth Wave, a marine-conservationist direct-action force, asks himself a similar question: "What does it mean to be an environmentalist at the end of the world?" The rhetorical nature of Cal's query casts (disguises) him as an optimist in a pessimist's pea coat— imagine a protagonist whose sole purpose equates to an unanswerable question. Do ends justify means, even at the end? What happens when obsolescence becomes passé, postdated? Cal's rhetoric, shady nihilism, and captain's bearing leave little room for redemption or mercy. Call it Cal's fatal flaw, his personal mark of Cain. And so along comes Mary, the anima to his animus.

Mary, the most mindful of *The Massive*'s prime movers, represents an ur-text, the *prima* watchkeeper, a sharky character, full of mystery and full of grace. Unlike Cal, she transcends (so-called) earthly needs and desires. Whereas Cal's pragmatism leads him in a straight line from one challenge to the next, Mary looks to the horizon, to beyond, sunrise to Cal's sunset. As often happens, these opposites attract, and as also often happens, one and one become one: Yeva, Cal and Mary's daughter. Like her mother and her father, she becomes a scrupulous observer of people and . . . a writer. Where one mystery ends and another begins, Mary tells Cal that Yeva "needs to witness this." Like mother, like daughter. Watchkeepers remain eternal.

The specificity of its characters reflects in the precision of *The Massive*'s creators. Details like the Swedish *Star Wars* poster Garry Brown draws on the wall of Lars's cabin attest to the authenticity of the work. Look at the emotion Brown evokes when he composes a page so a character's face dominates the frame, the thickness of his lines, how they cut across chins and cheeks to carve out desperation and fatigue, dedication and pride, with the exactness of portraiture, inky accounts of open enigmas. Consider how Jordie Bellaire works the color palette to find the exact, polarizing shade of citrine for Cal's aviator sunglasses or her blue-sky approach to the turbulence of seawater and steady skylines. Bellaire works in moods the same way roughnecks work in oil—viscous, but satisfying.

The Massive is Brian Wood's redemption song, a spiritual of (re)creation: proof life is worth the unbroken fight. As a writer, Wood courts conflict. He's drawn to it because he knows when the stakes are at their highest; nature, human or otherwise, always finds a way. A writer discovers the world word by word or, as Wood says in the final issue, "grid by grid"; tedium leads to escape or emancipation. Hope—audacious, no?

How else to describe the watchkeeper, whether witness or writer? Each one allows the story to keep going and the question to keep being asked: "Now what?"

Keith Philip Silva earns a living by asking questions and making sure to listen while the camera rolls. He writes about comics and pop culture for Comics Bulletin, Psycho Drive-In, and Loser City. These endeavors have made him an inveterate caffeine addict with an increasing taste for stronger vices, like Kentucky bourbon and single-malt Scotch. He does not need his hand held, unless it's by his wife or daughters.

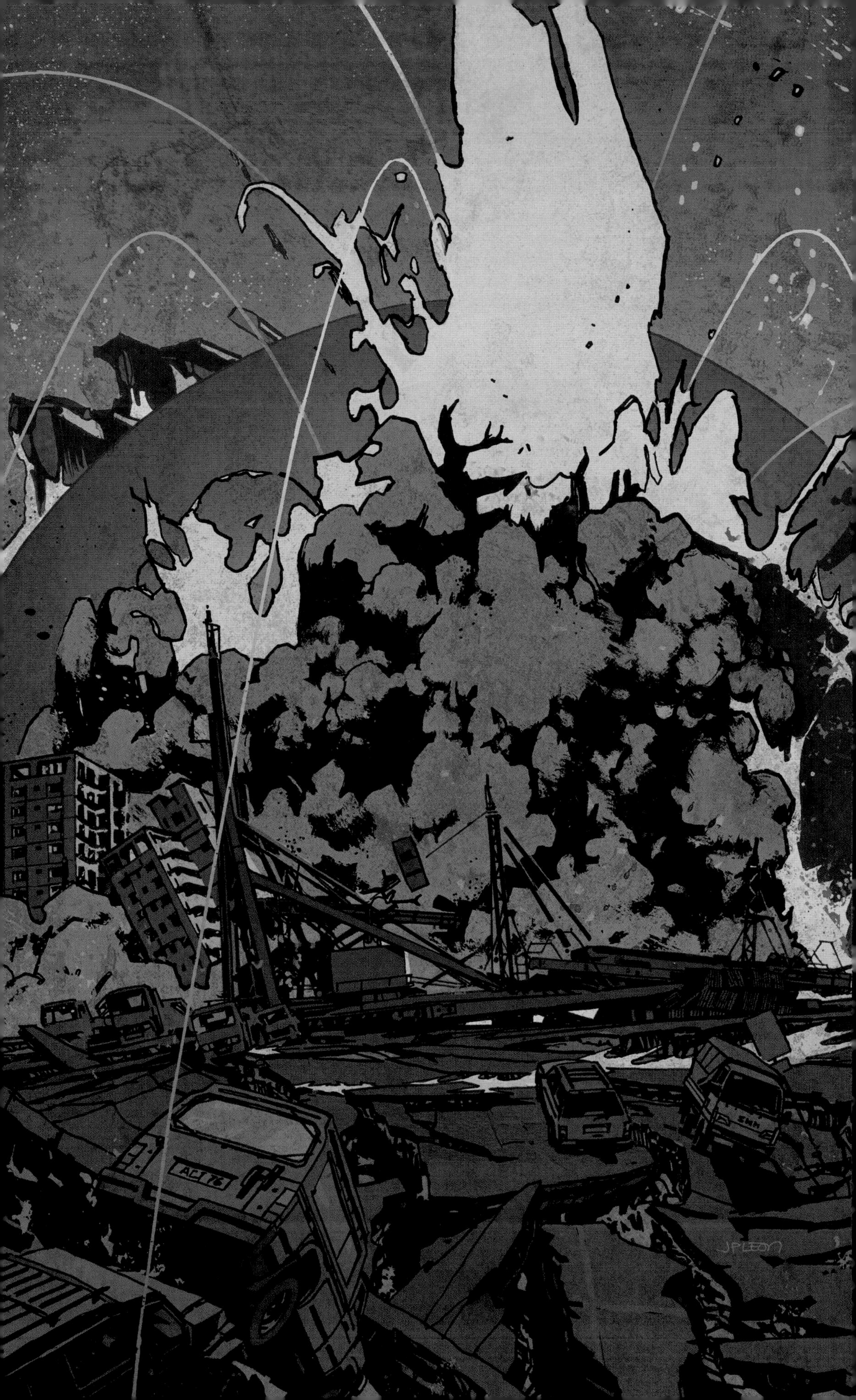
AC1 76

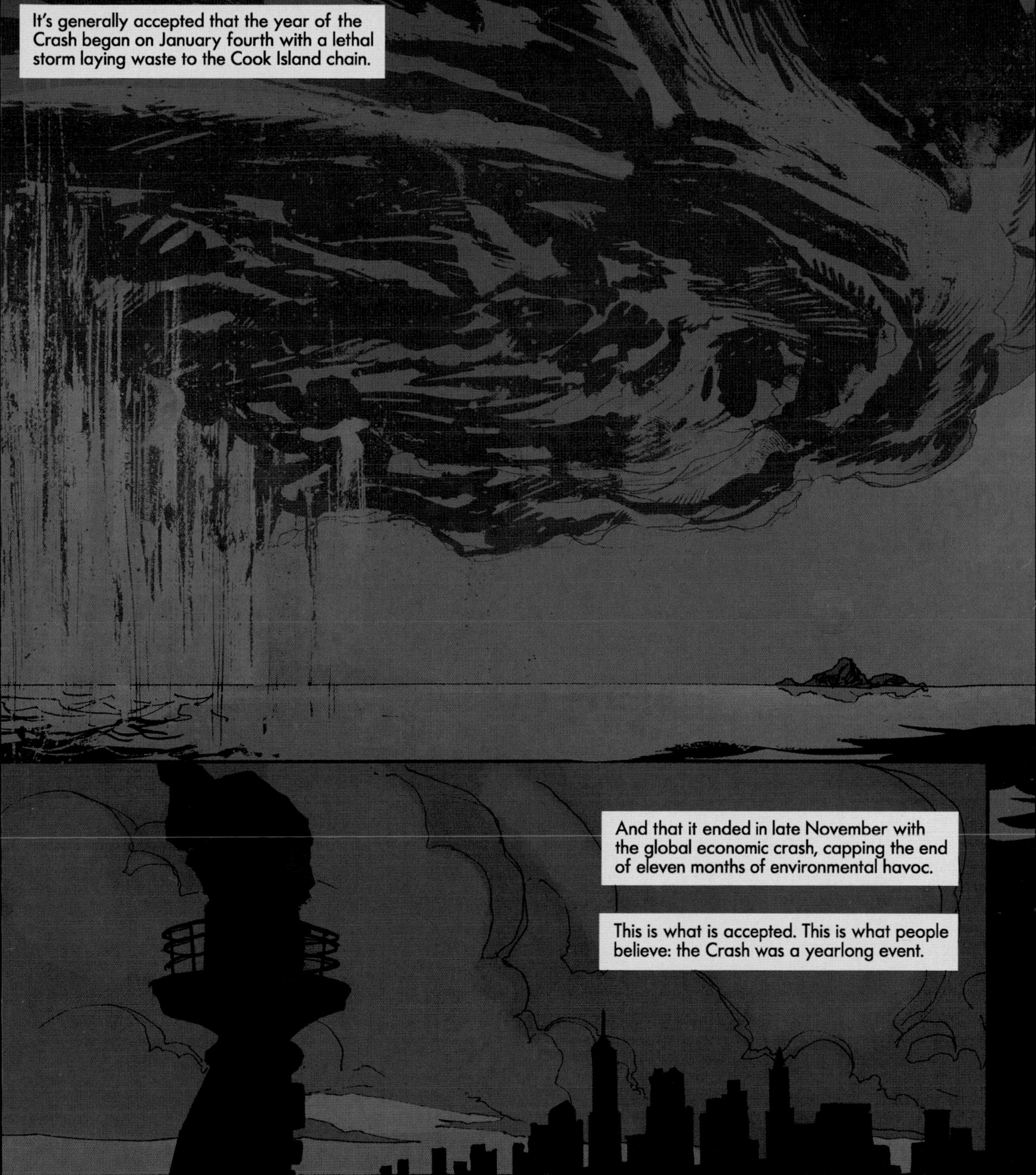
It's generally accepted that the year of the Crash began on January fourth with a lethal storm laying waste to the Cook Island chain.
And that it ended in late November with the global economic crash, capping the end of eleven months of environmental havoc.
This is what is accepted. This is what people believe: the Crash was a yearlong event.

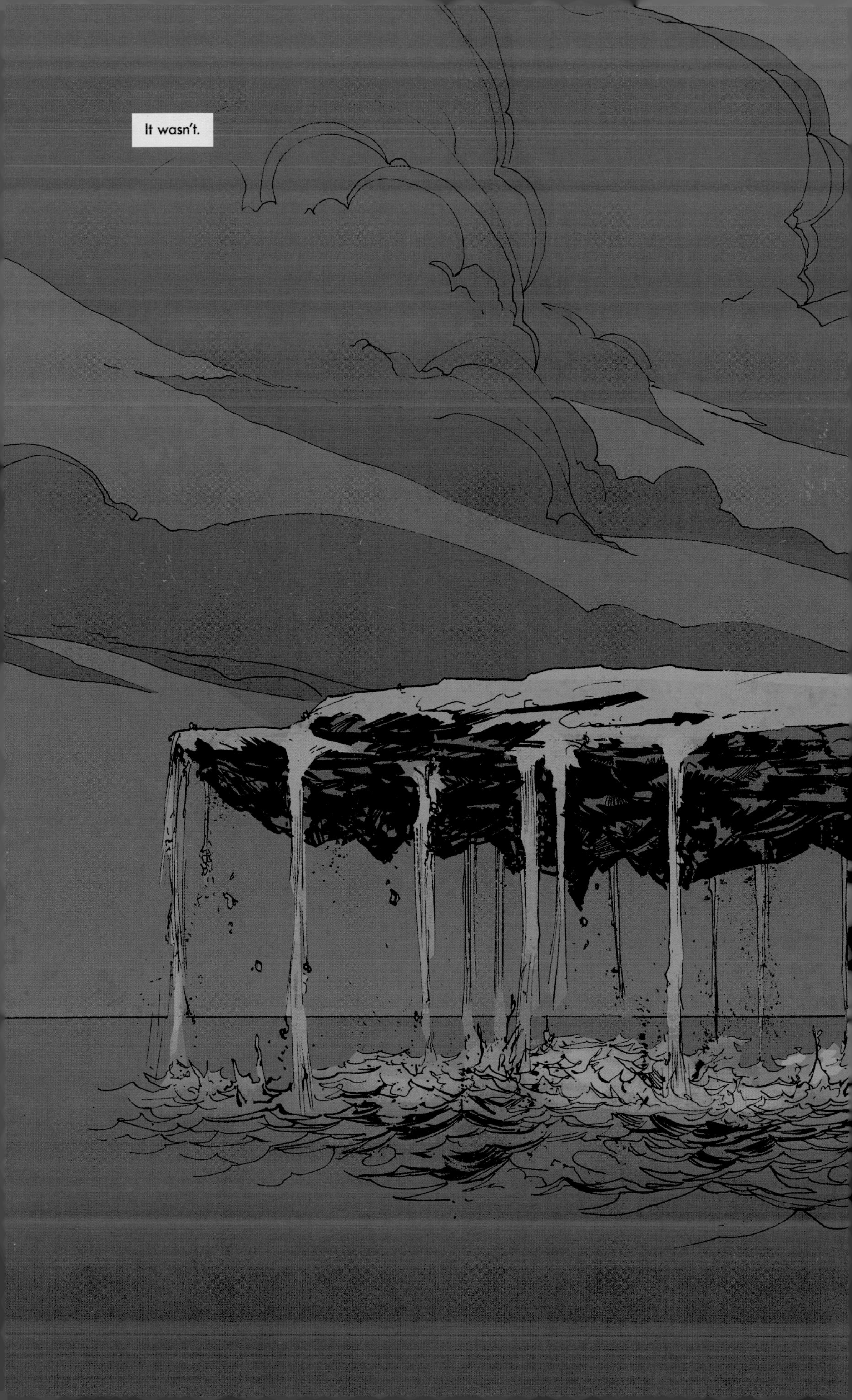
It wasn't.

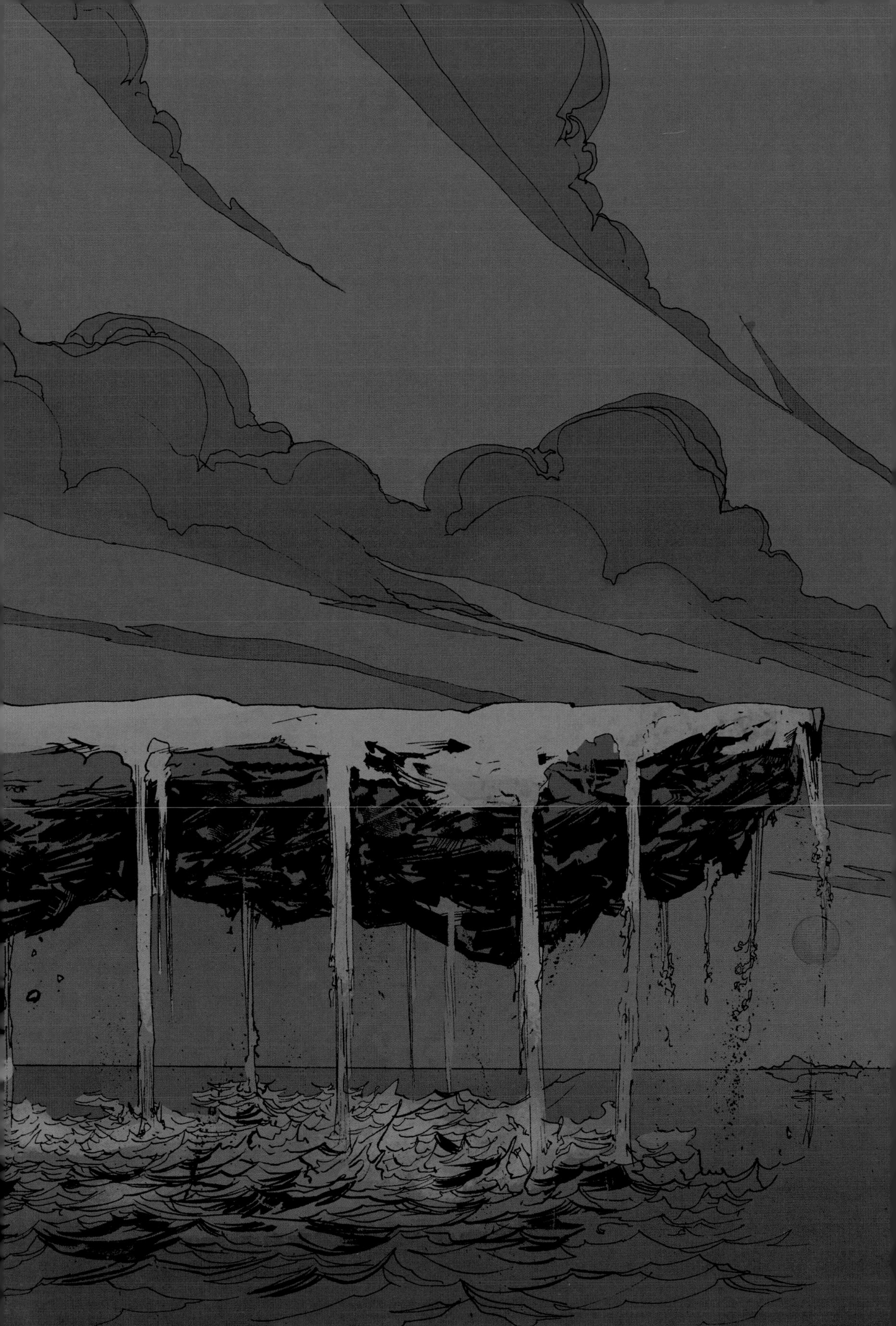

THE MASSIVE
RAGNAROK: PART ONE

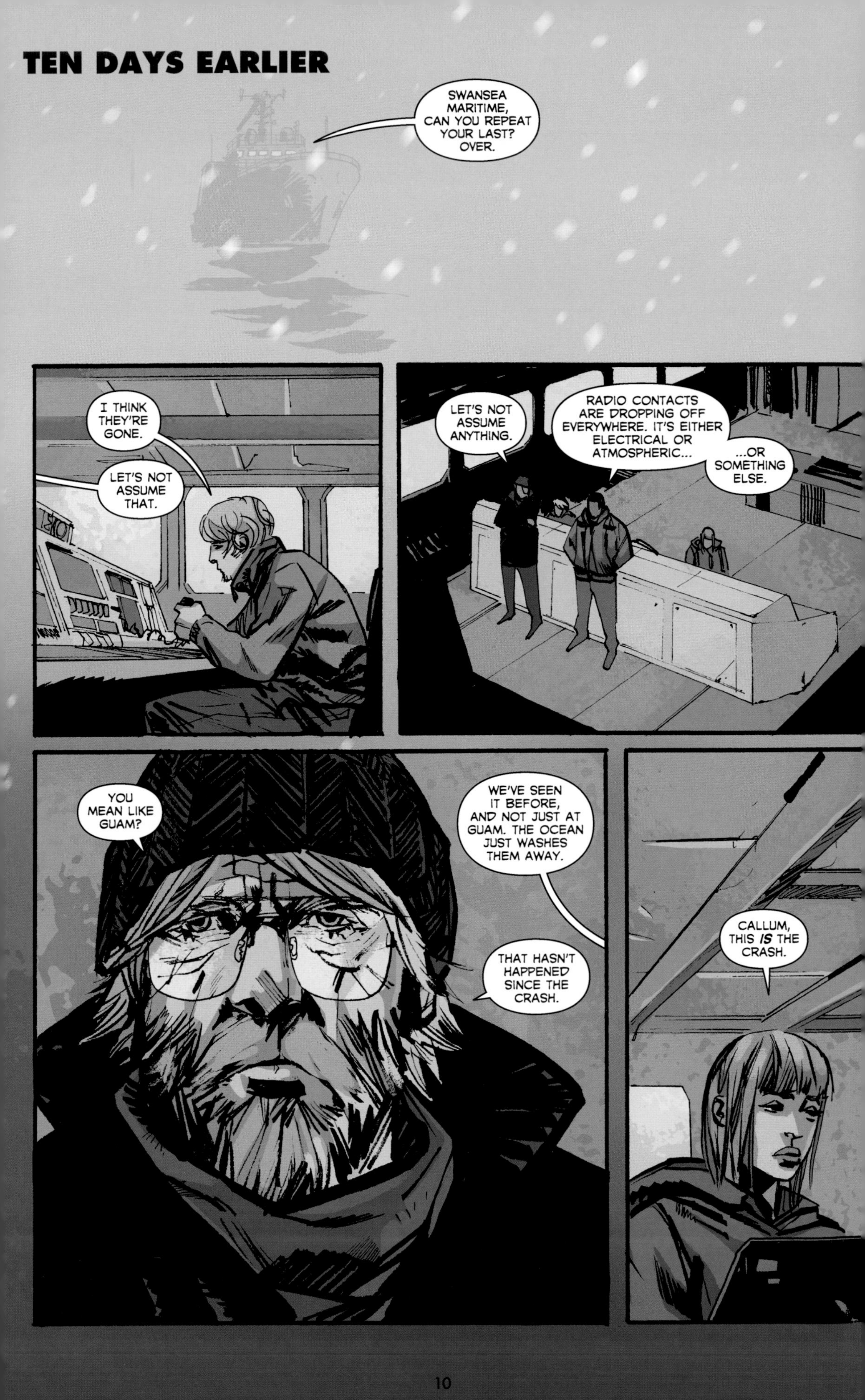
TEN DAYS EARLIER
SWANSEA MARITIME, CAN YOU REPEAT YOUR LAST? OVER.
I THINK THEY'RE GONE.
LET'S NOT ASSUME THAT.
LET'S NOT ASSUME ANYTHING.
RADIO CONTACTS ARE DROPPING OFF EVERYWHERE. IT'S EITHER ELECTRICAL OR ATMOSPHERIC...
...OR SOMETHING ELSE.
YOU MEAN LIKE GUAM?
WE'VE SEEN IT BEFORE, AND NOT JUST AT GUAM. THE OCEAN JUST WASHES THEM AWAY.
THAT HASN'T HAPPENED SINCE THE CRASH.
CALLUM, THIS *IS* THE CRASH.

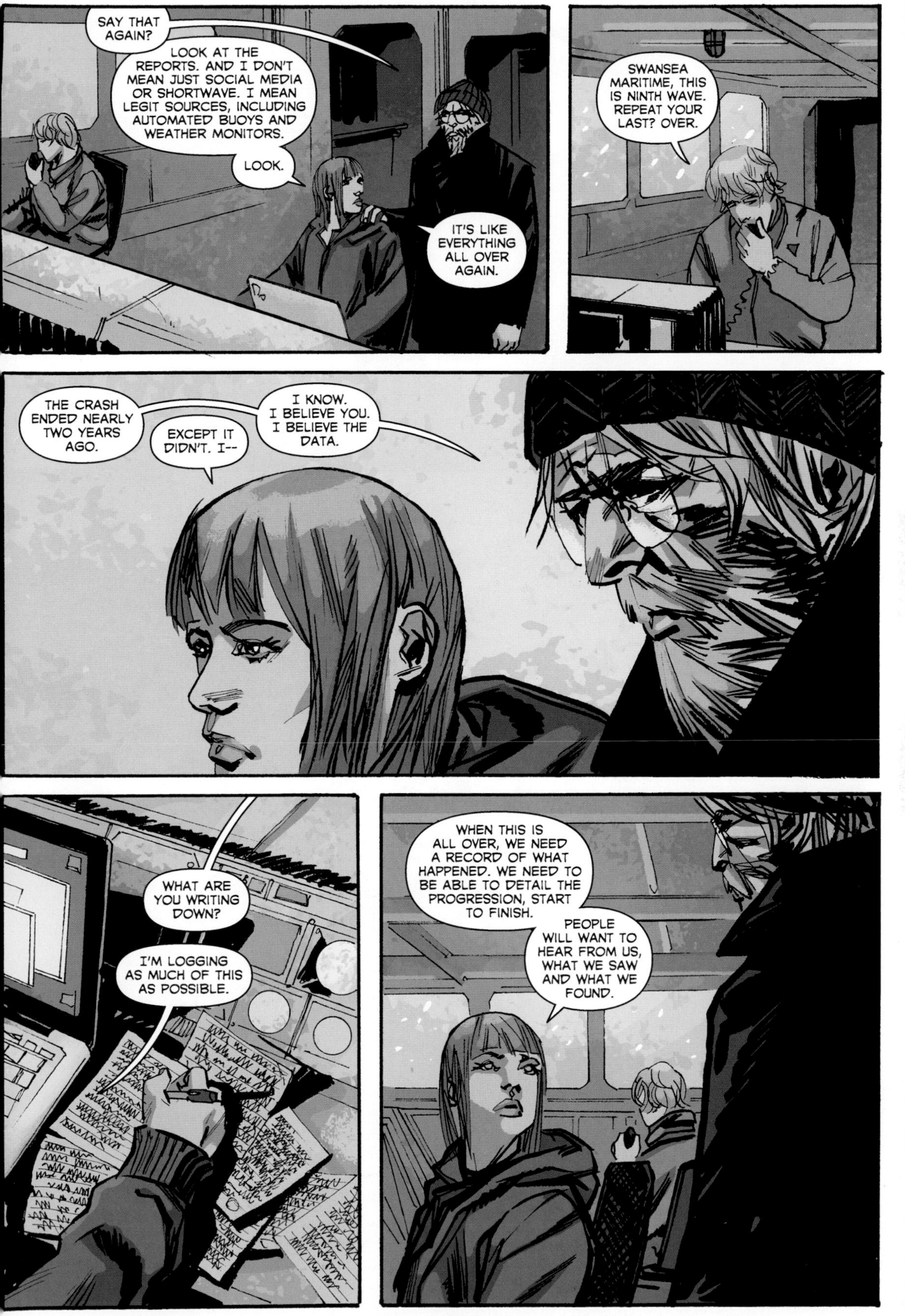
SAY THAT AGAIN?
LOOK AT THE REPORTS. AND I DON'T MEAN JUST SOCIAL MEDIA OR SHORTWAVE. I MEAN LEGIT SOURCES, INCLUDING AUTOMATED BUOYS AND WEATHER MONITORS.
LOOK.
IT'S LIKE EVERYTHING ALL OVER AGAIN.
SWANSEA MARITIME, THIS IS NINTH WAVE. REPEAT YOUR LAST? OVER.
THE CRASH ENDED NEARLY TWO YEARS AGO.
EXCEPT IT DIDN'T. I--
I KNOW. I BELIEVE YOU. I BELIEVE THE DATA.
WHAT ARE YOU WRITING DOWN?
I'M LOGGING AS MUCH OF THIS AS POSSIBLE.
WHEN THIS IS ALL OVER, WE NEED A RECORD OF WHAT HAPPENED. WE NEED TO BE ABLE TO DETAIL THE PROGRESSION, START TO FINISH.
PEOPLE WILL WANT TO HEAR FROM US, WHAT WE SAW AND WHAT WE FOUND.

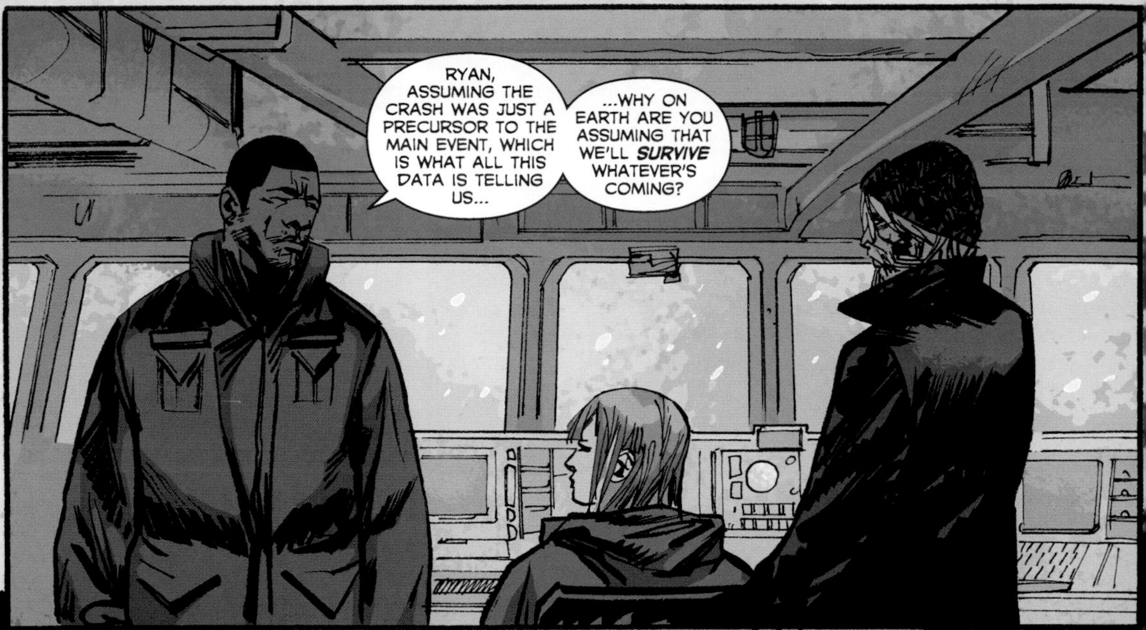
RYAN, ASSUMING THE CRASH WAS JUST A PRECURSOR TO THE MAIN EVENT, WHICH IS WHAT ALL THIS DATA IS TELLING US...
...WHY ON EARTH ARE YOU ASSUMING THAT WE'LL **SURVIVE** WHATEVER'S COMING?

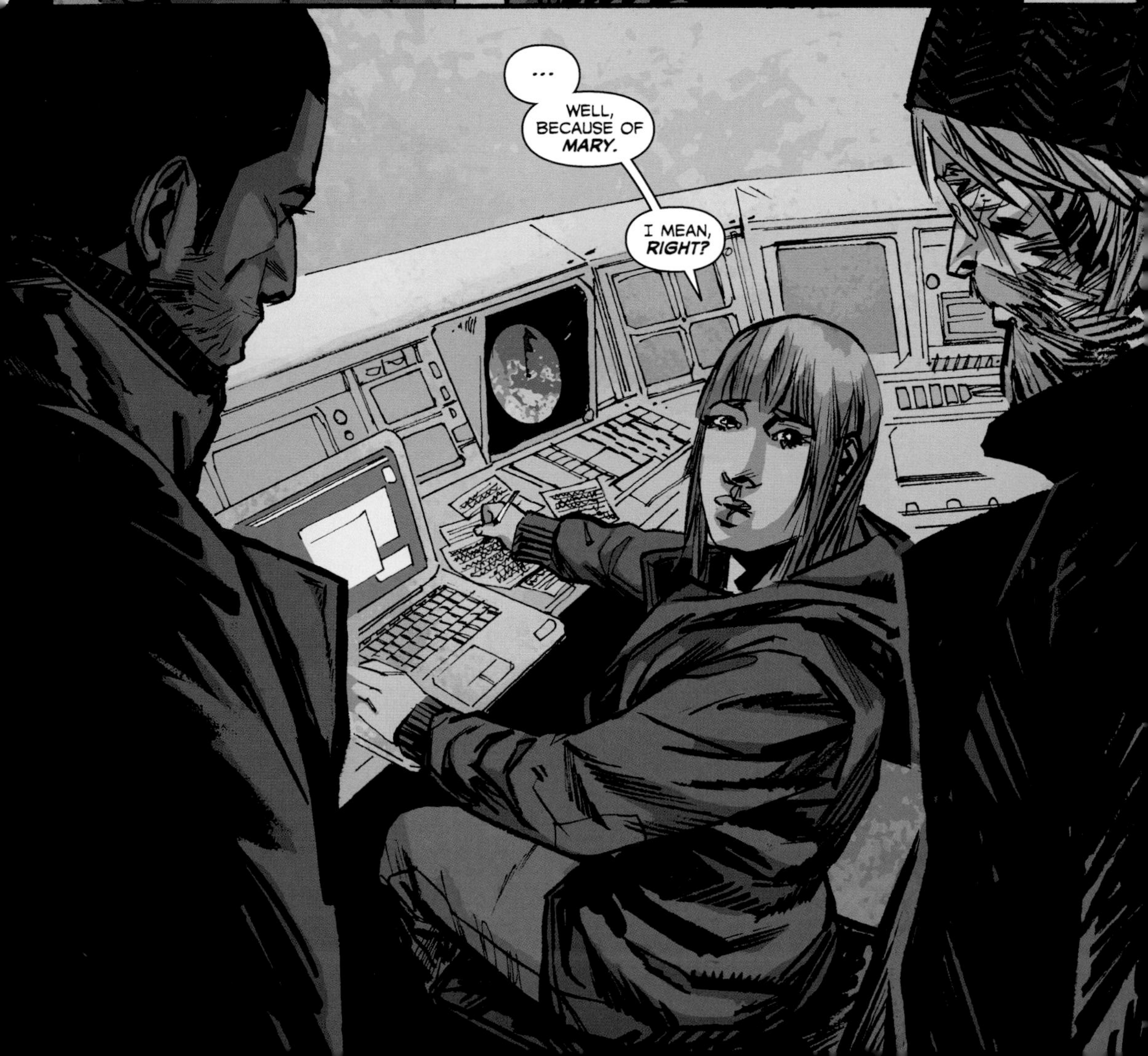
...
WELL, BECAUSE OF **MARY.**
I MEAN, **RIGHT?**

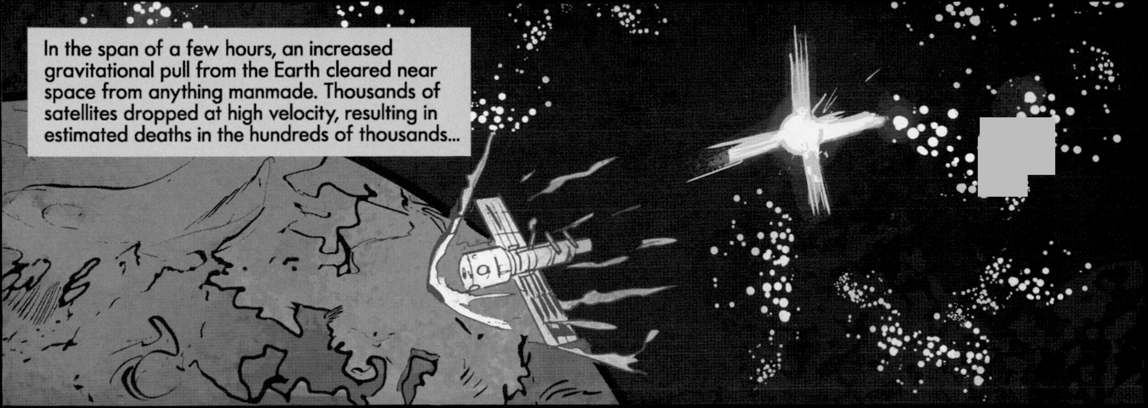
In the span of a few hours, an increased gravitational pull from the Earth cleared near space from anything manmade. Thousands of satellites dropped at high velocity, resulting in estimated deaths in the hundreds of thousands...

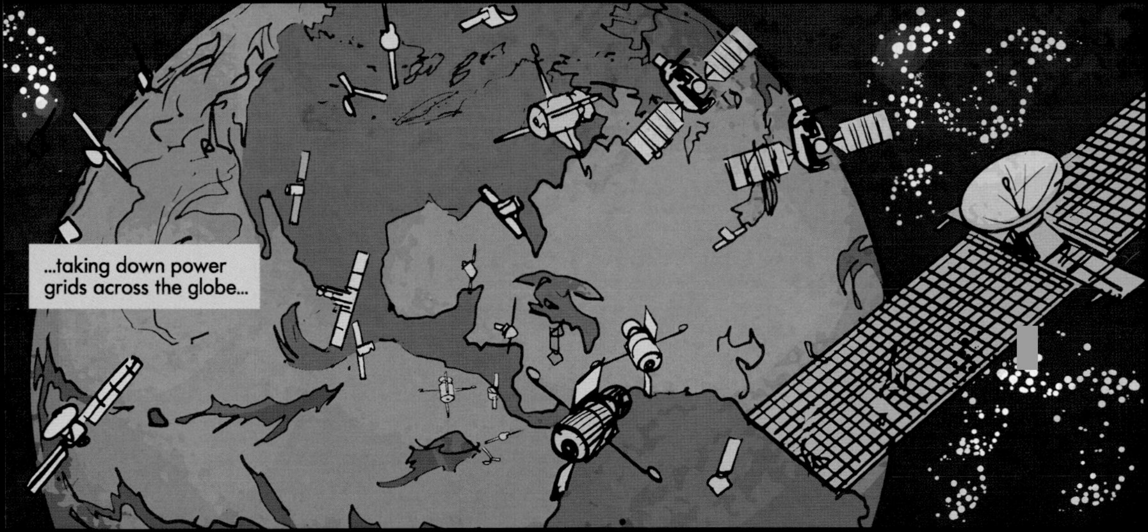
...taking down power grids across the globe...

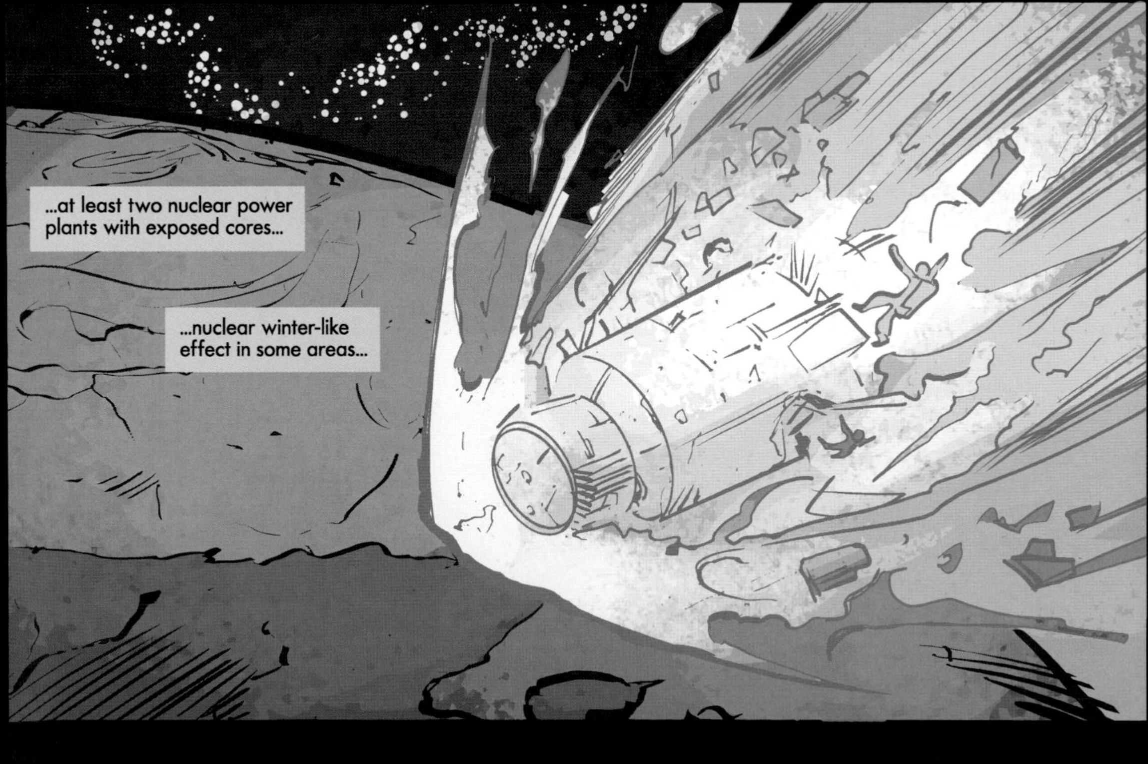
...at least two nuclear power plants with exposed cores...
...nuclear winter-like effect in some areas...

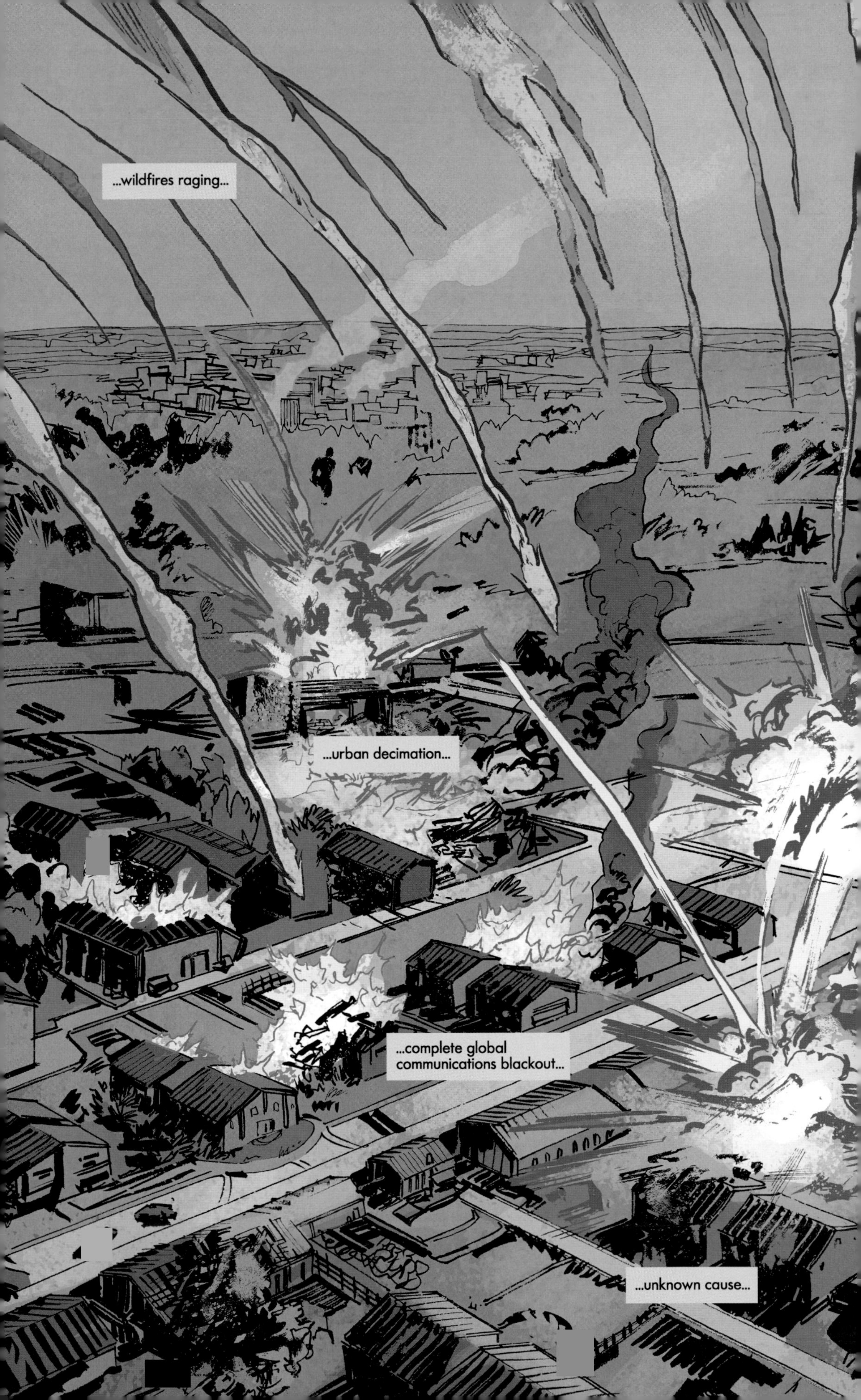
...wildfires raging...
...urban decimation...
...complete global communications blackout...
...unknown cause...

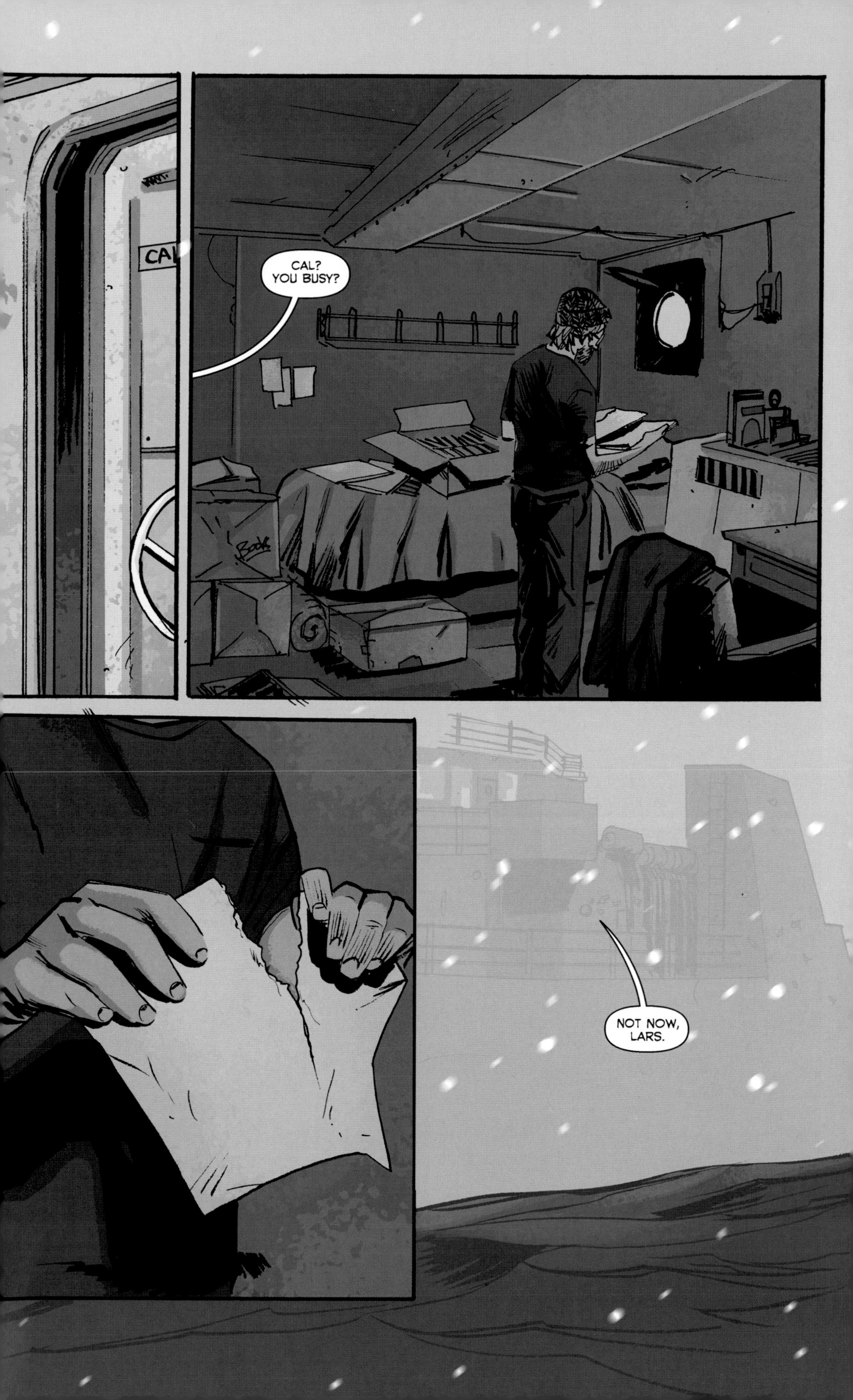
CAL? YOU BUSY?
NOT NOW, LARS.

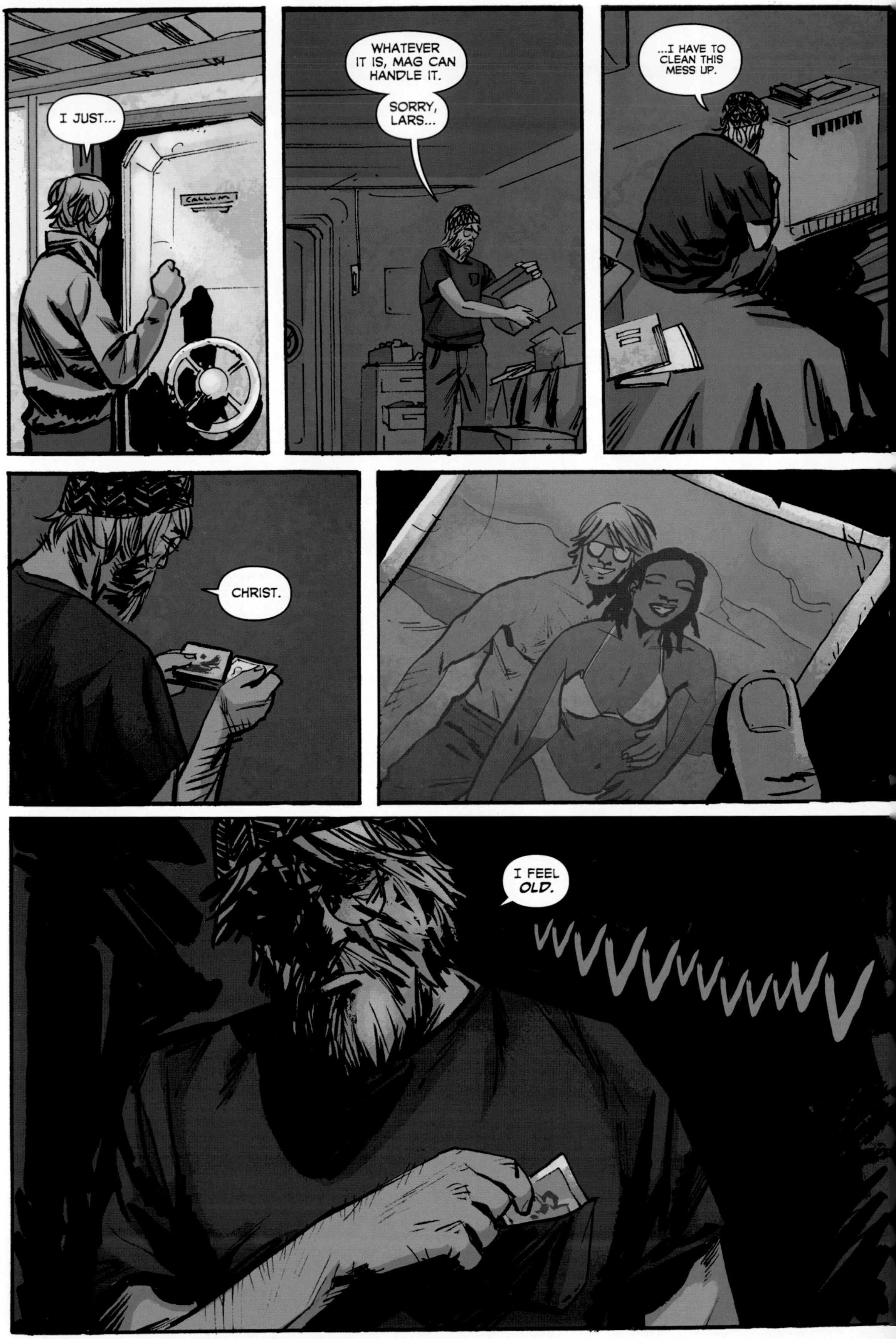
I JUST...
WHATEVER IT IS, MAG CAN HANDLE IT.
SORRY, LARS...
...I HAVE TO CLEAN THIS MESS UP.
CALLUM
CHRIST.
I FEEL OLD.
VVVVVVVVVVVVVV

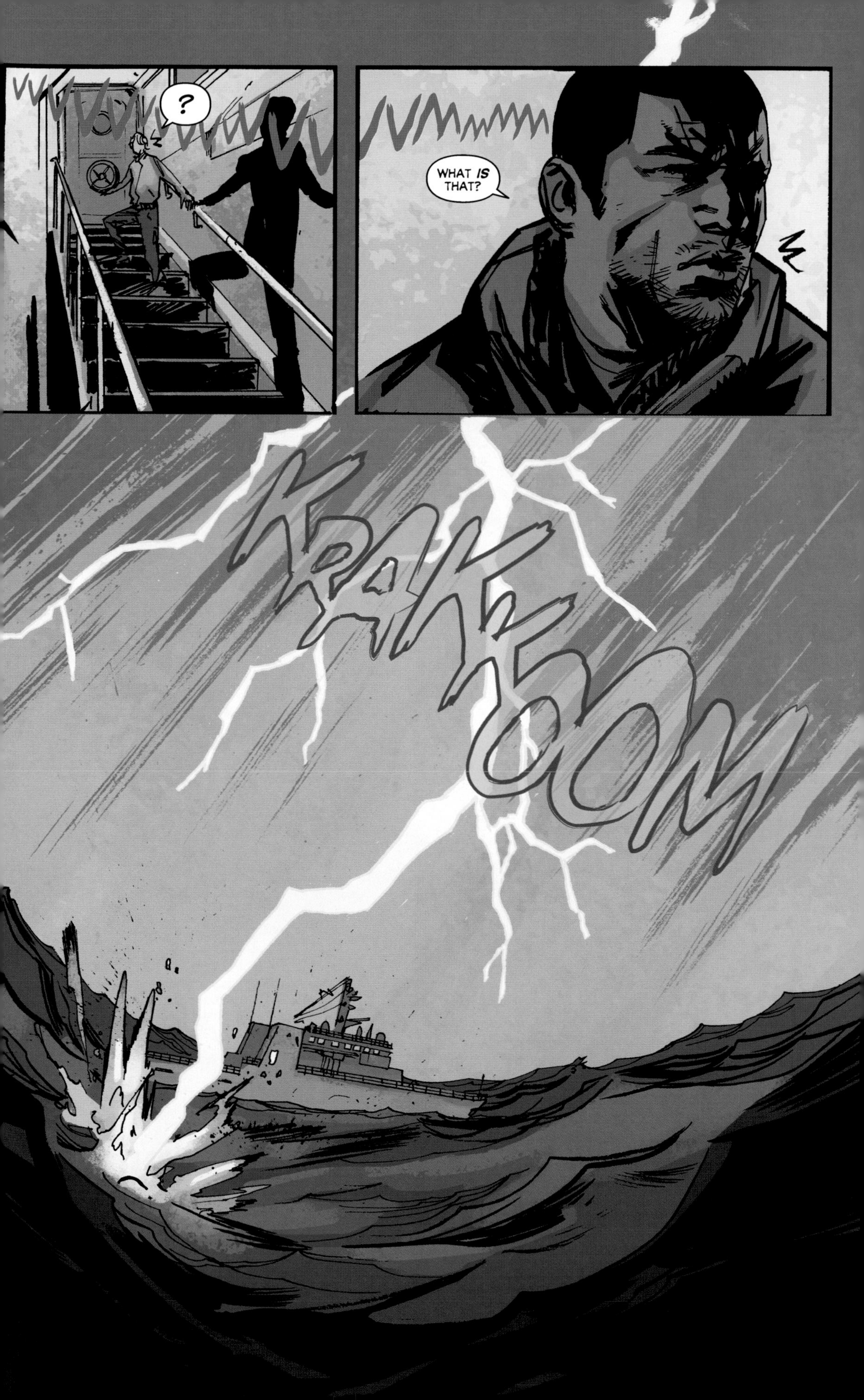
VVVVVVVVVVVUVMMMMMM
?
WHAT IS THAT?
KRAKABOOM

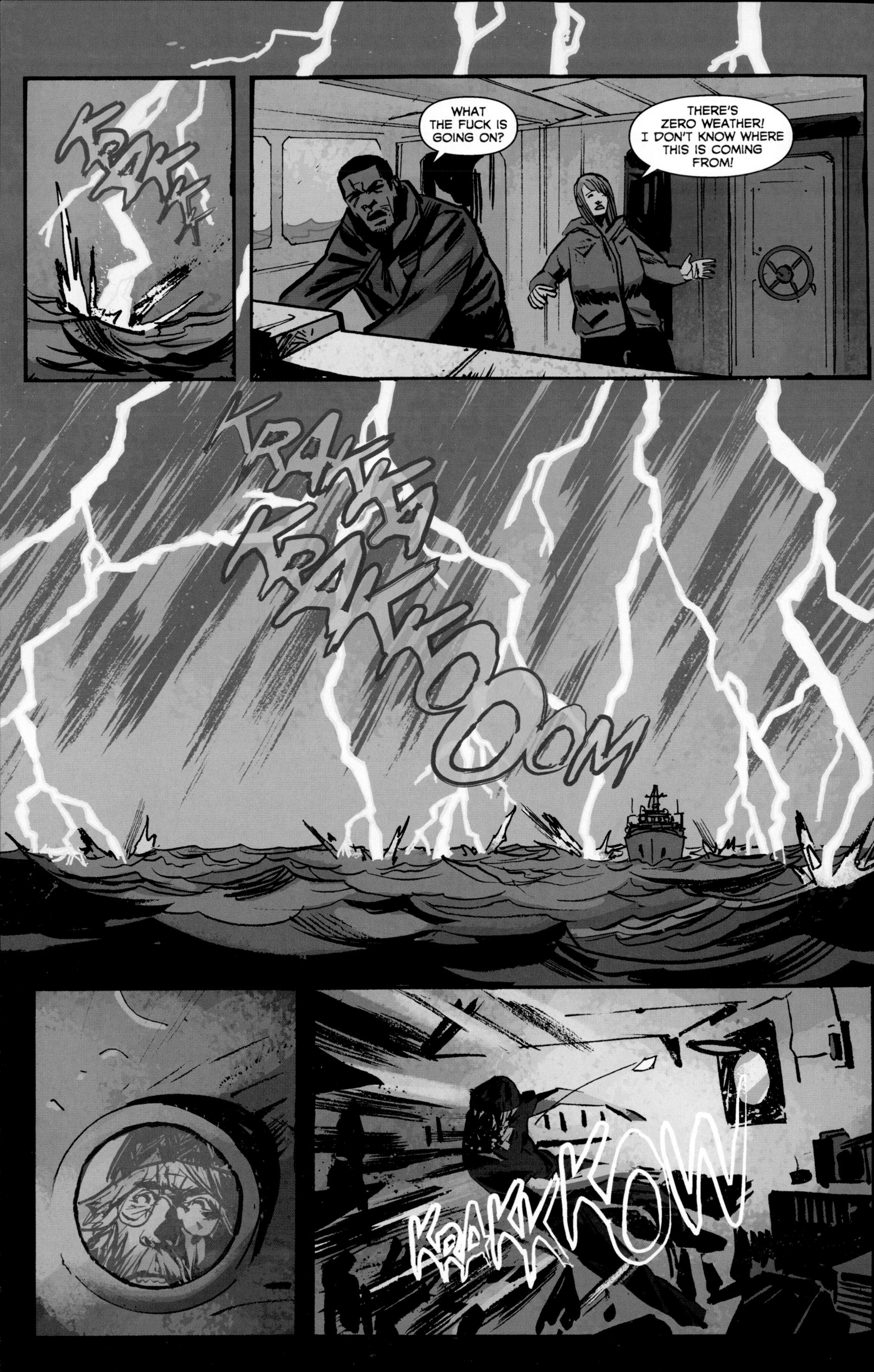
WHAT THE FUCK IS GOING ON?
THERE'S ZERO WEATHER! I DON'T KNOW WHERE THIS IS COMING FROM!

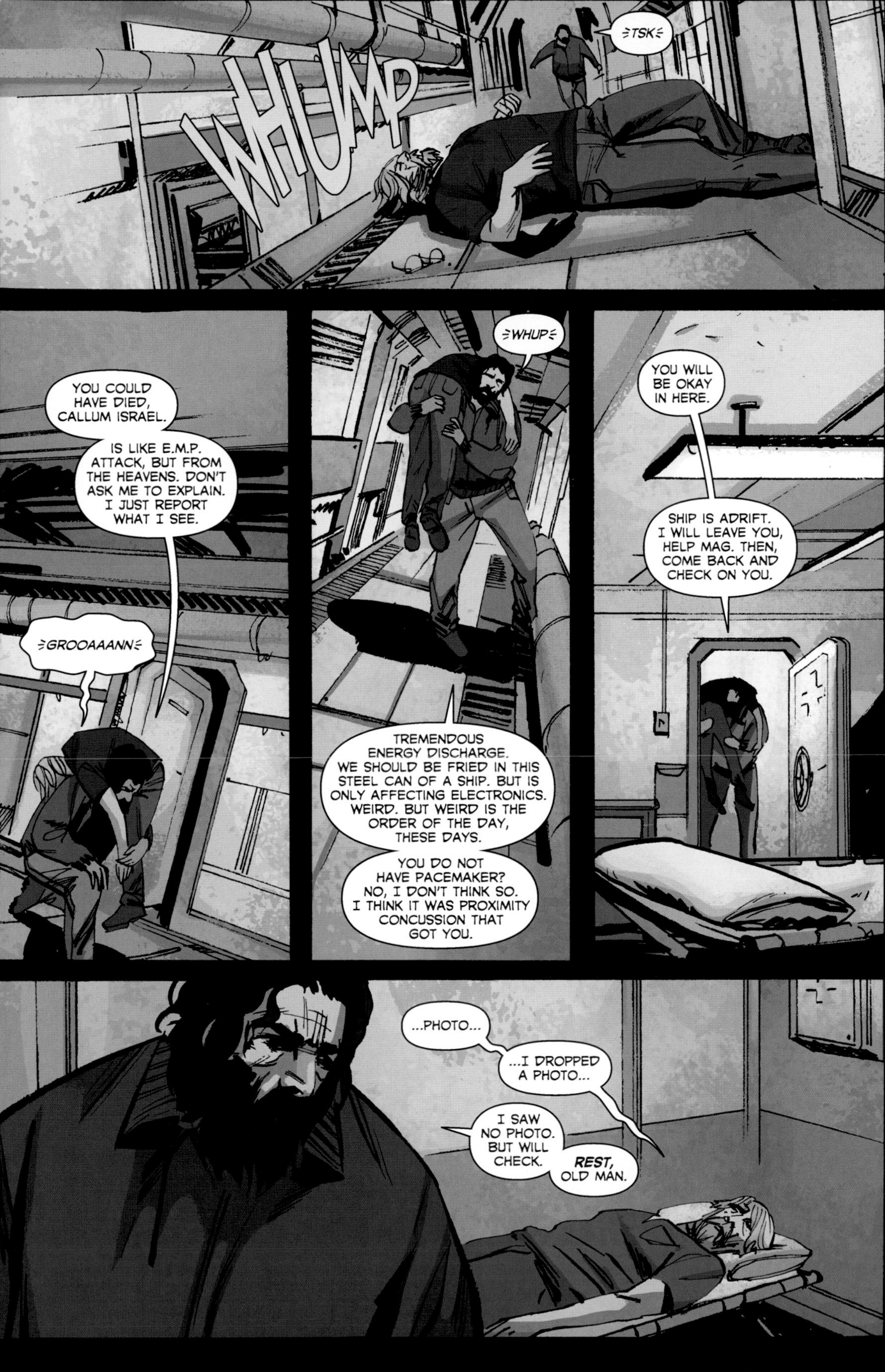
WHUMP
TSK
YOU COULD HAVE DIED, CALLUM ISRAEL.
IS LIKE E.M.P. ATTACK, BUT FROM THE HEAVENS. DON'T ASK ME TO EXPLAIN. I JUST REPORT WHAT I SEE.
GROOAAANN
WHUP
TREMENDOUS ENERGY DISCHARGE. WE SHOULD BE FRIED IN THIS STEEL CAN OF A SHIP. BUT IS ONLY AFFECTING ELECTRONICS. WEIRD. BUT WEIRD IS THE ORDER OF THE DAY, THESE DAYS.
YOU DO NOT HAVE PACEMAKER? NO, I DON'T THINK SO. I THINK IT WAS PROXIMITY CONCUSSION THAT GOT YOU.
YOU WILL BE OKAY IN HERE.
SHIP IS ADRIFT. I WILL LEAVE YOU, HELP MAG. THEN, COME BACK AND CHECK ON YOU.
...PHOTO...
...I DROPPED A PHOTO...
I SAW NO PHOTO. BUT WILL CHECK. **REST,** OLD MAN.

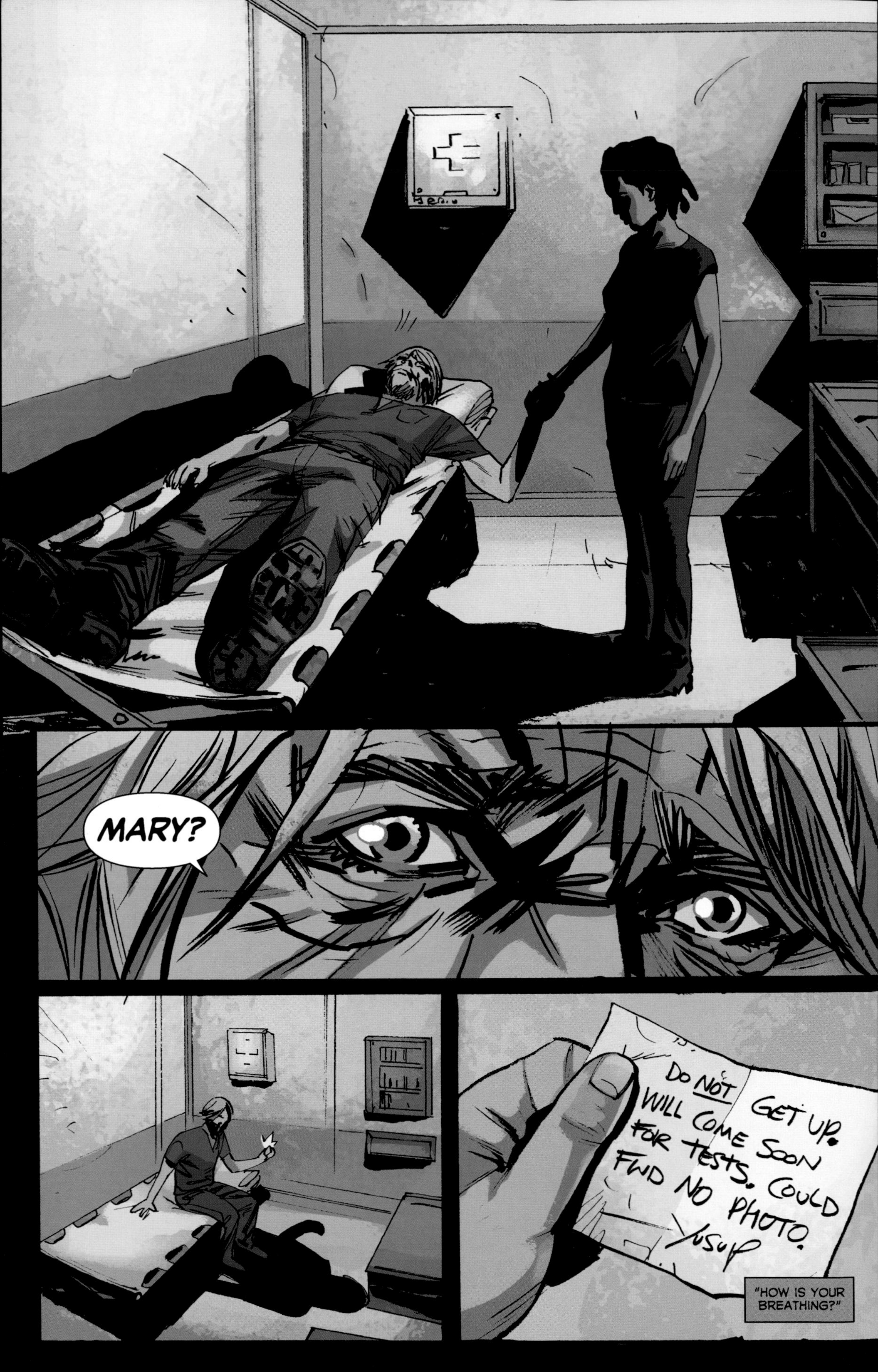
MARY?
DO NOT GET UP.
WILL COME SOON
FOR TESTS. COULD
FWD NO PHOTO.
YUSUF
"HOW IS YOUR BREATHING?"

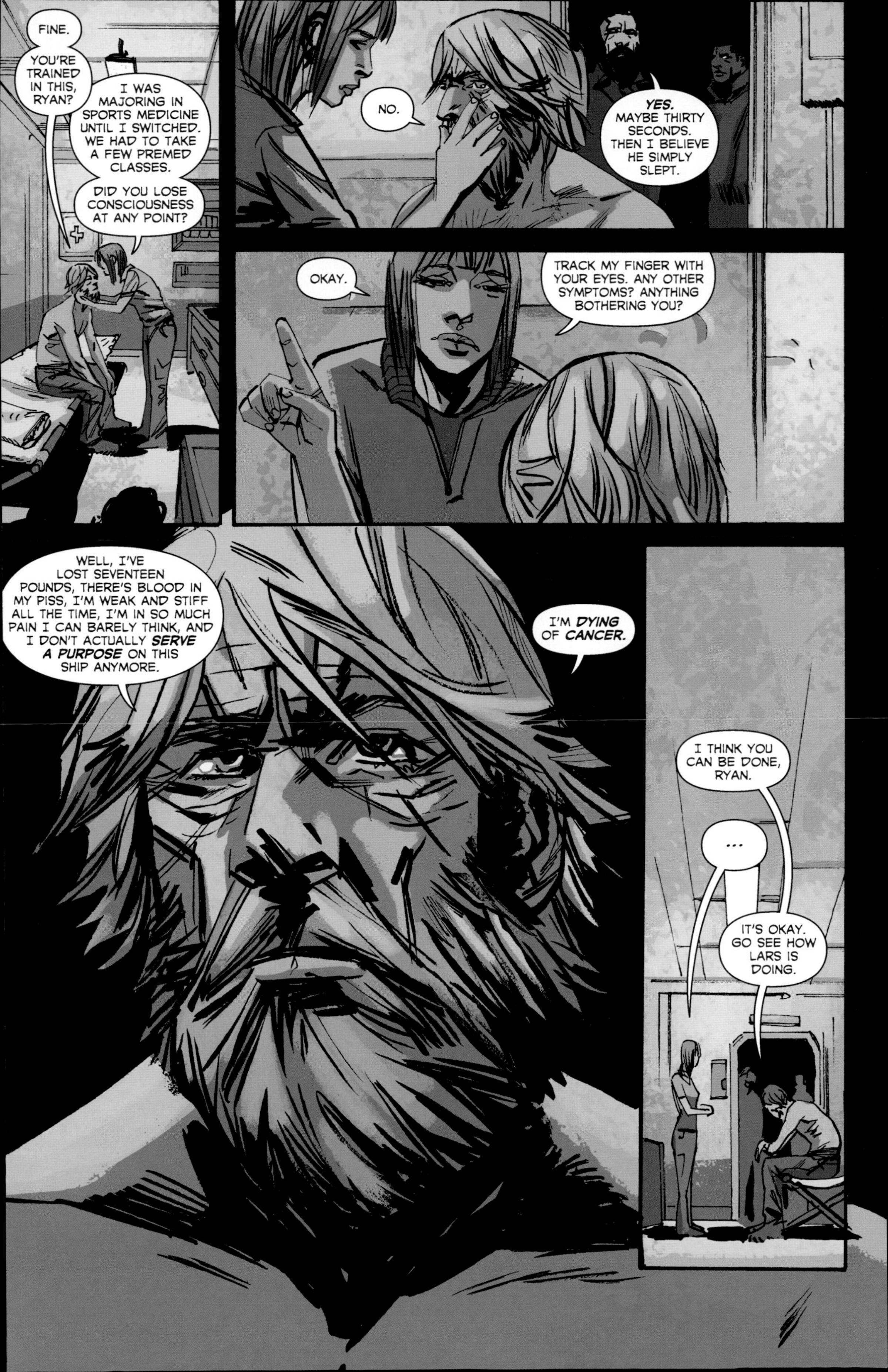
FINE.
YOU'RE TRAINED IN THIS, RYAN?
I WAS MAJORING IN SPORTS MEDICINE UNTIL I SWITCHED. WE HAD TO TAKE A FEW PREMED CLASSES.
DID YOU LOSE CONSCIOUSNESS AT ANY POINT?
NO.
YES. MAYBE THIRTY SECONDS. THEN I BELIEVE HE SIMPLY SLEPT.
OKAY.
TRACK MY FINGER WITH YOUR EYES. ANY OTHER SYMPTOMS? ANYTHING BOTHERING YOU?
WELL, I'VE LOST SEVENTEEN POUNDS, THERE'S BLOOD IN MY PISS, I'M WEAK AND STIFF ALL THE TIME, I'M IN SO MUCH PAIN I CAN BARELY THINK, AND I DON'T ACTUALLY SERVE A PURPOSE ON THIS SHIP ANYMORE.
I'M DYING OF CANCER.
I THINK YOU CAN BE DONE, RYAN.
...
IT'S OKAY. GO SEE HOW LARS IS DOING.

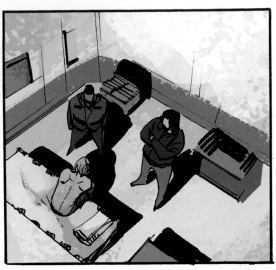

CAPTAIN.

THAT... ELECTRICAL STORM, WHATEVER IT WAS, IT KNOCKED OUT ALL POWER IN THIS SHIP.

LIKE E.M.P.

LIKE AN E.M.P. WEAPON. WE HAVE CREWS DOING REPAIRS.

WE'VE BEEN UNABLE TO ESTABLISH CONTACT WITH SWANSEA, SO THAT'S OUR RESUPPLY FUCKED. WHAT THAT LEAVES US IS SOMALIA.

NOT IDEAL, BUT WE DO HAVE A RELATIONSHIP THERE.

YOU DON'T NEED ME FOR THAT.

NO, BUT YOU NEED TO DO SOMETHING.

I WAS. I WAS CLEANING OUT MY CABIN. THAT'S ABOUT ALL I CAN DO.

I DISAGREE.

TELL ME.

AND DON'T CALL ME "CAPTAIN." IT'S A FUCKING JOKE.

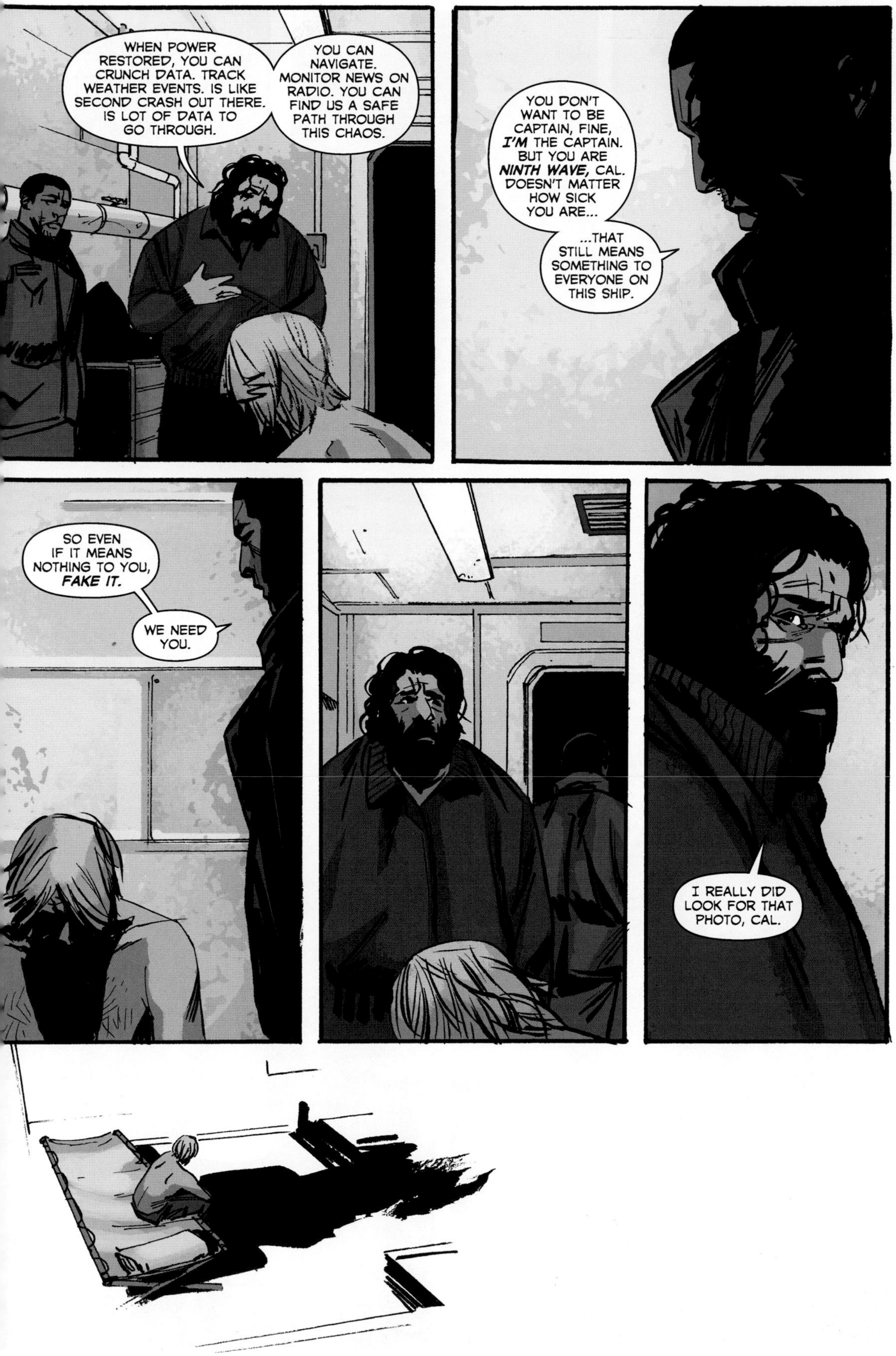
WHEN POWER RESTORED, YOU CAN CRUNCH DATA. TRACK WEATHER EVENTS. IS LIKE SECOND CRASH OUT THERE. IS LOT OF DATA TO GO THROUGH.
YOU CAN NAVIGATE. MONITOR NEWS ON RADIO. YOU CAN FIND US A SAFE PATH THROUGH THIS CHAOS.
YOU DON'T WANT TO BE CAPTAIN, FINE, *I'M* THE CAPTAIN. BUT YOU ARE *NINTH WAVE,* CAL. DOESN'T MATTER HOW SICK YOU ARE...
...THAT STILL MEANS SOMETHING TO EVERYONE ON THIS SHIP.
SO EVEN IF IT MEANS NOTHING TO YOU, *FAKE IT.*
WE NEED YOU.
I REALLY DID LOOK FOR THAT PHOTO, CAL.

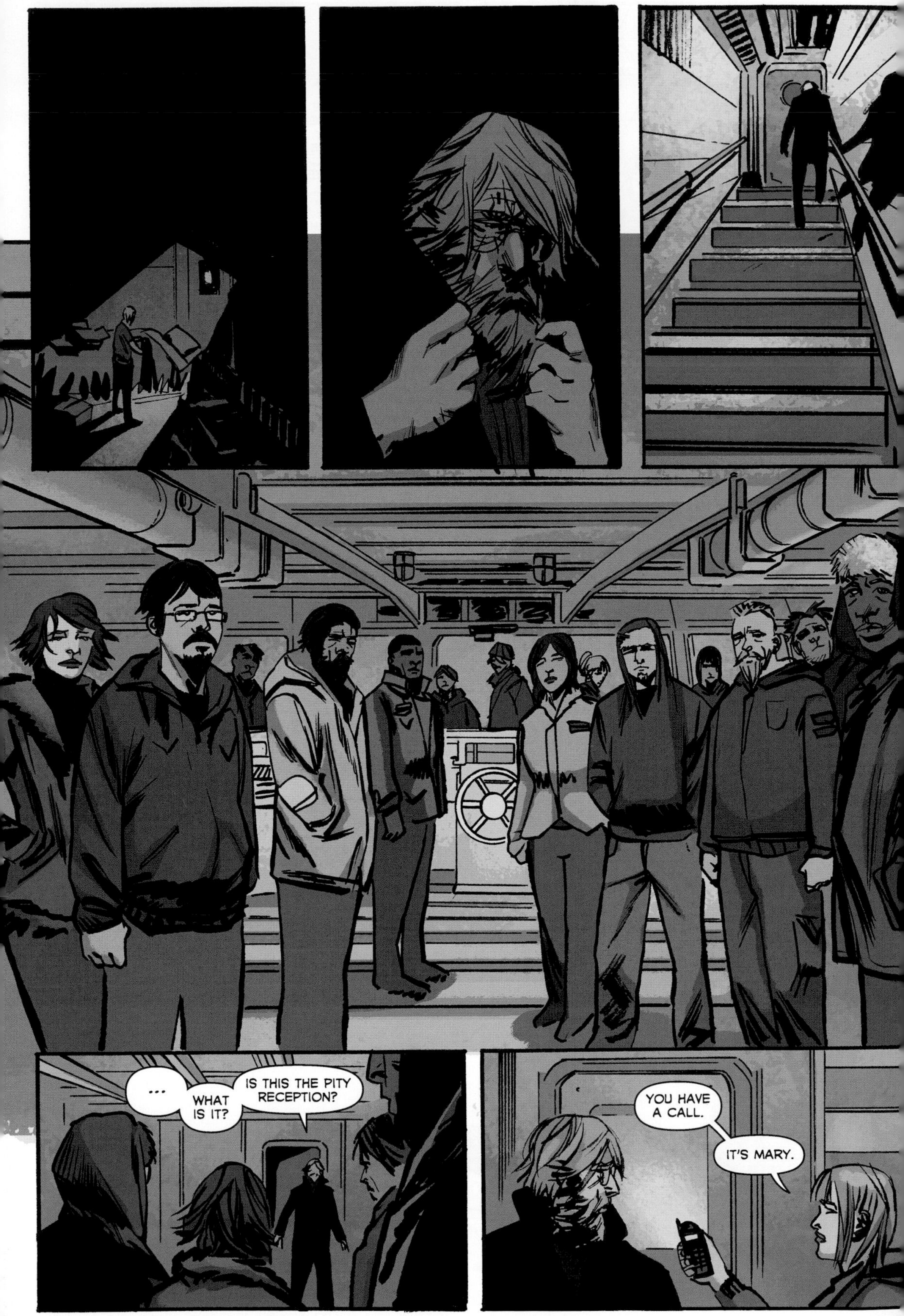
...
WHAT IS IT?
IS THIS THE PITY RECEPTION?
YOU HAVE A CALL.
IT'S MARY.

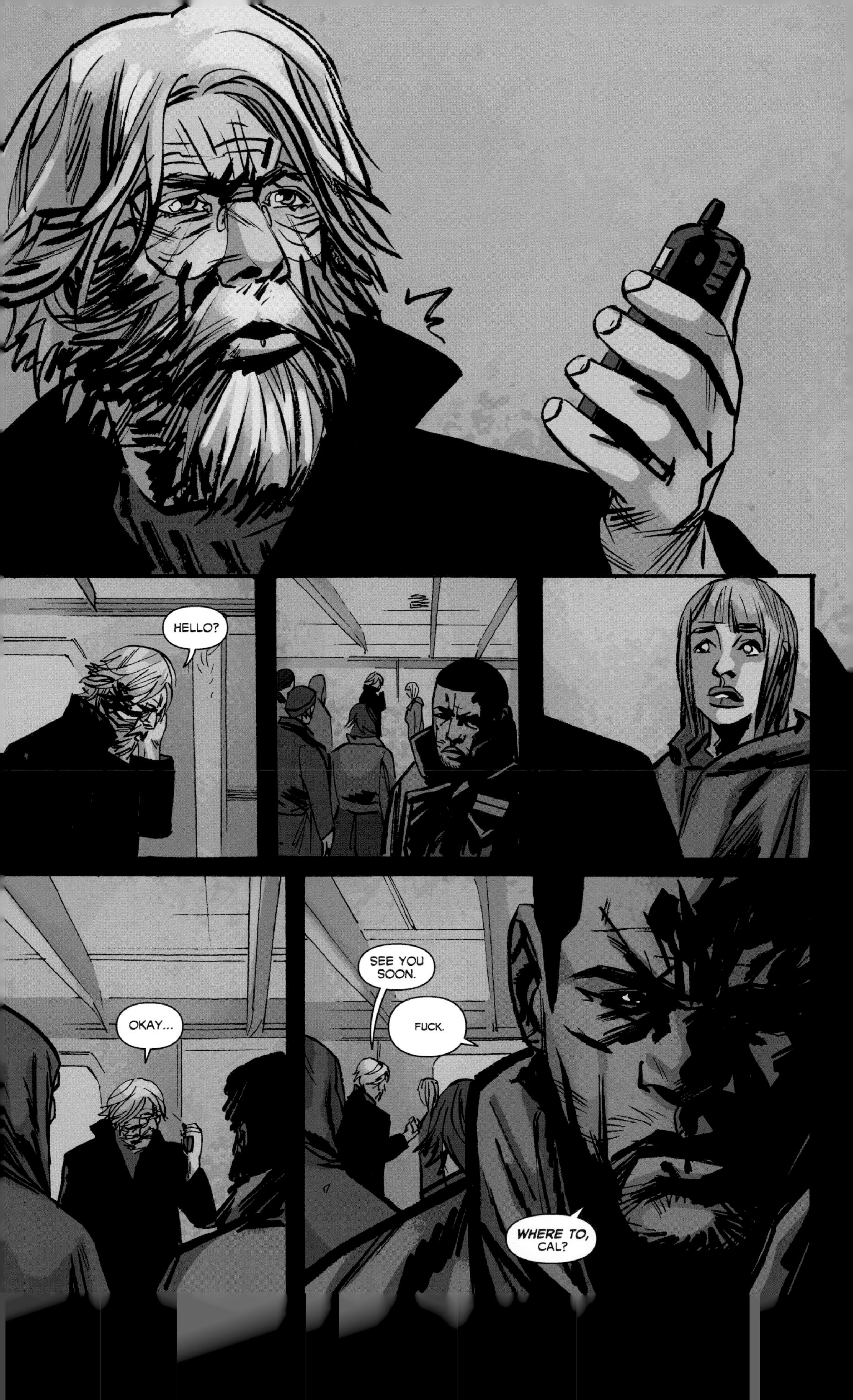
HELLO?
OKAY...
SEE YOU SOON.
FUCK.
WHERE TO, CAL?

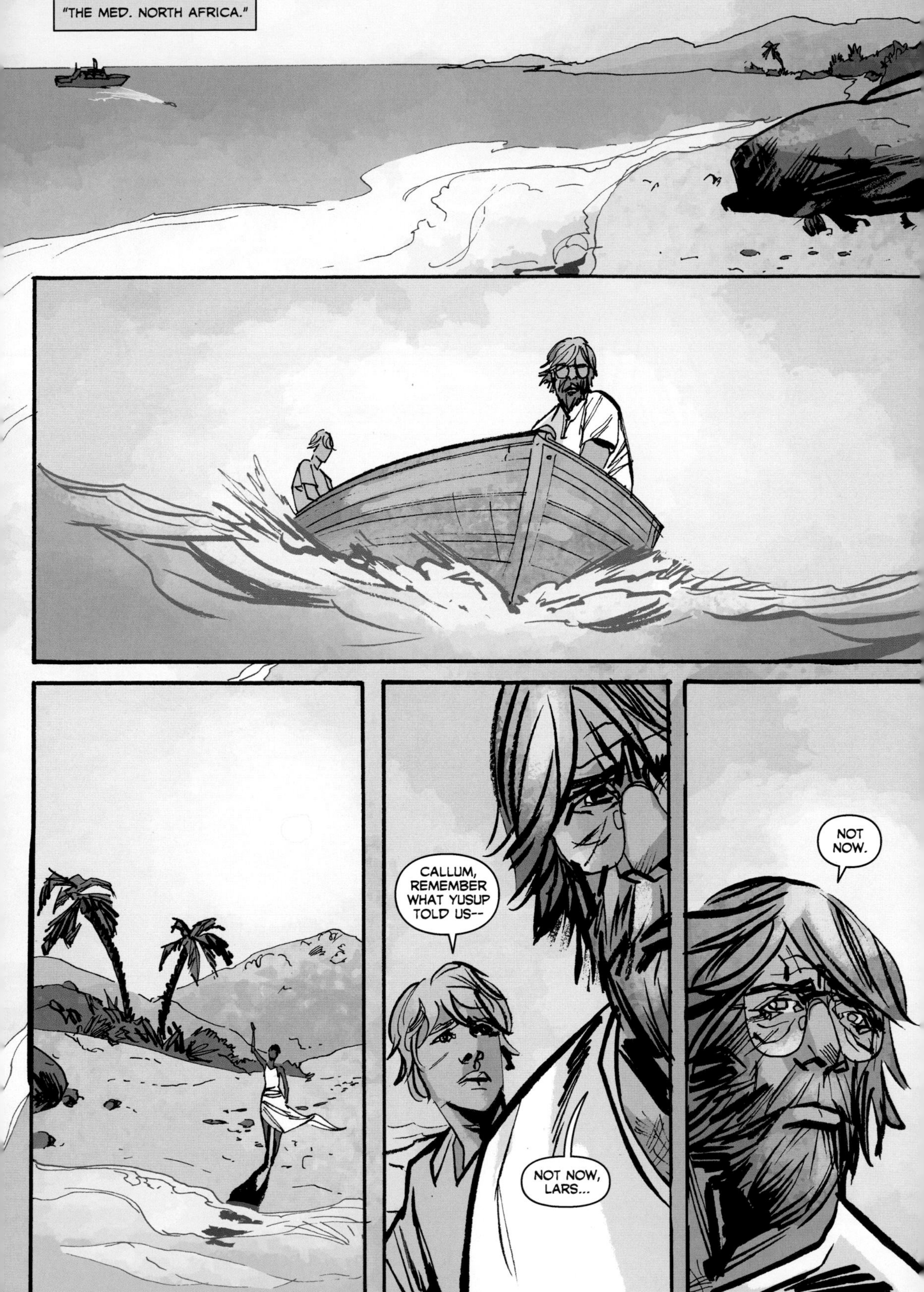
"THE MED. NORTH AFRICA."
CALLUM, REMEMBER WHAT YUSUP TOLD US--
NOT NOW, LARS...
NOT NOW.

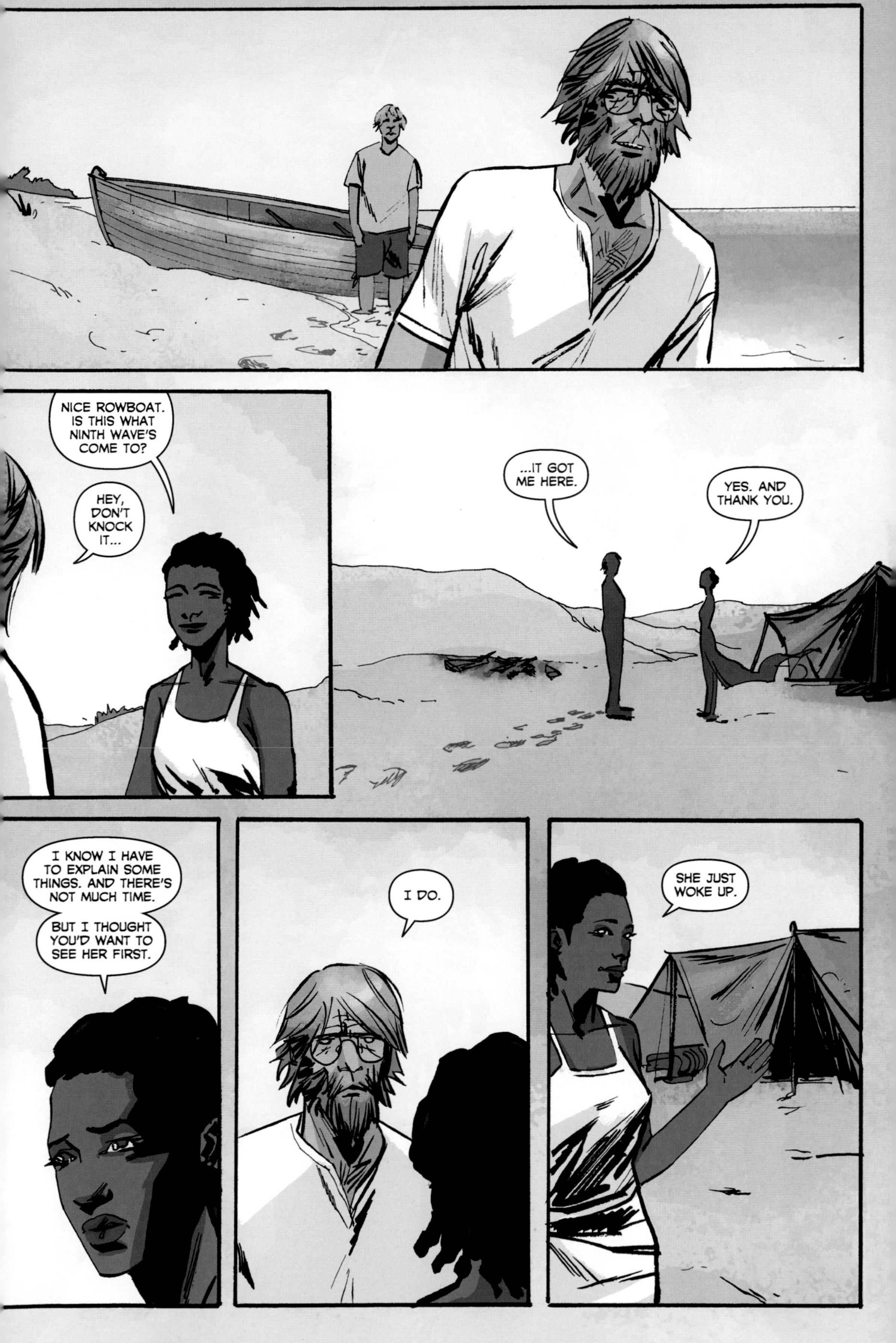

NICE ROWBOAT. IS THIS WHAT NINTH WAVE'S COME TO?
HEY, DON'T KNOCK IT...
...IT GOT ME HERE.
YES. AND THANK YOU.
I KNOW I HAVE TO EXPLAIN SOME THINGS. AND THERE'S NOT MUCH TIME.
BUT I THOUGHT YOU'D WANT TO SEE HER FIRST.
I DO.
SHE JUST WOKE UP.

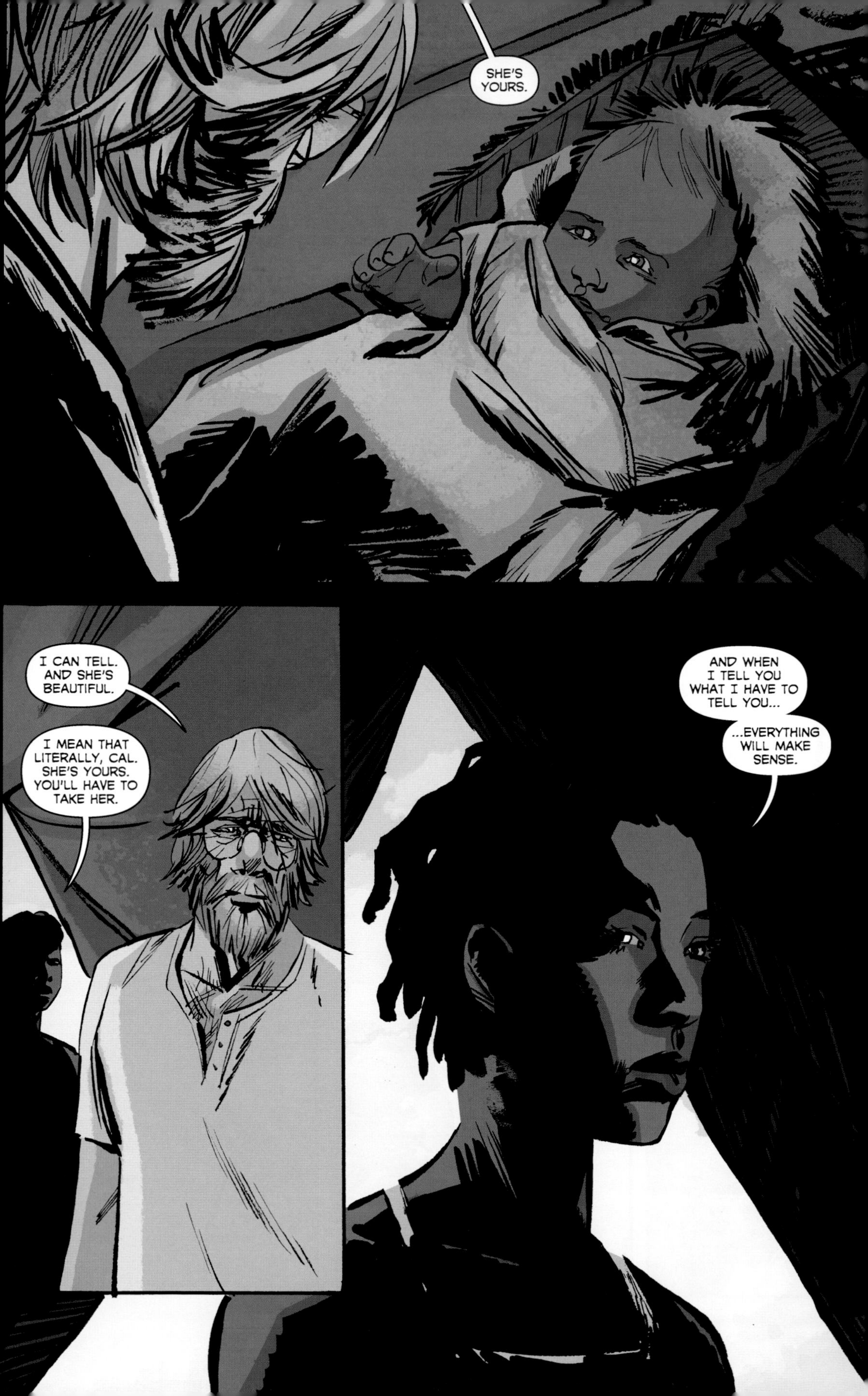
SHE'S YOURS.
I CAN TELL. AND SHE'S BEAUTIFUL.
I MEAN THAT LITERALLY, CAL. SHE'S YOURS. YOU'LL HAVE TO TAKE HER.
AND WHEN I TELL YOU WHAT I HAVE TO TELL YOU...
...EVERYTHING WILL MAKE SENSE.

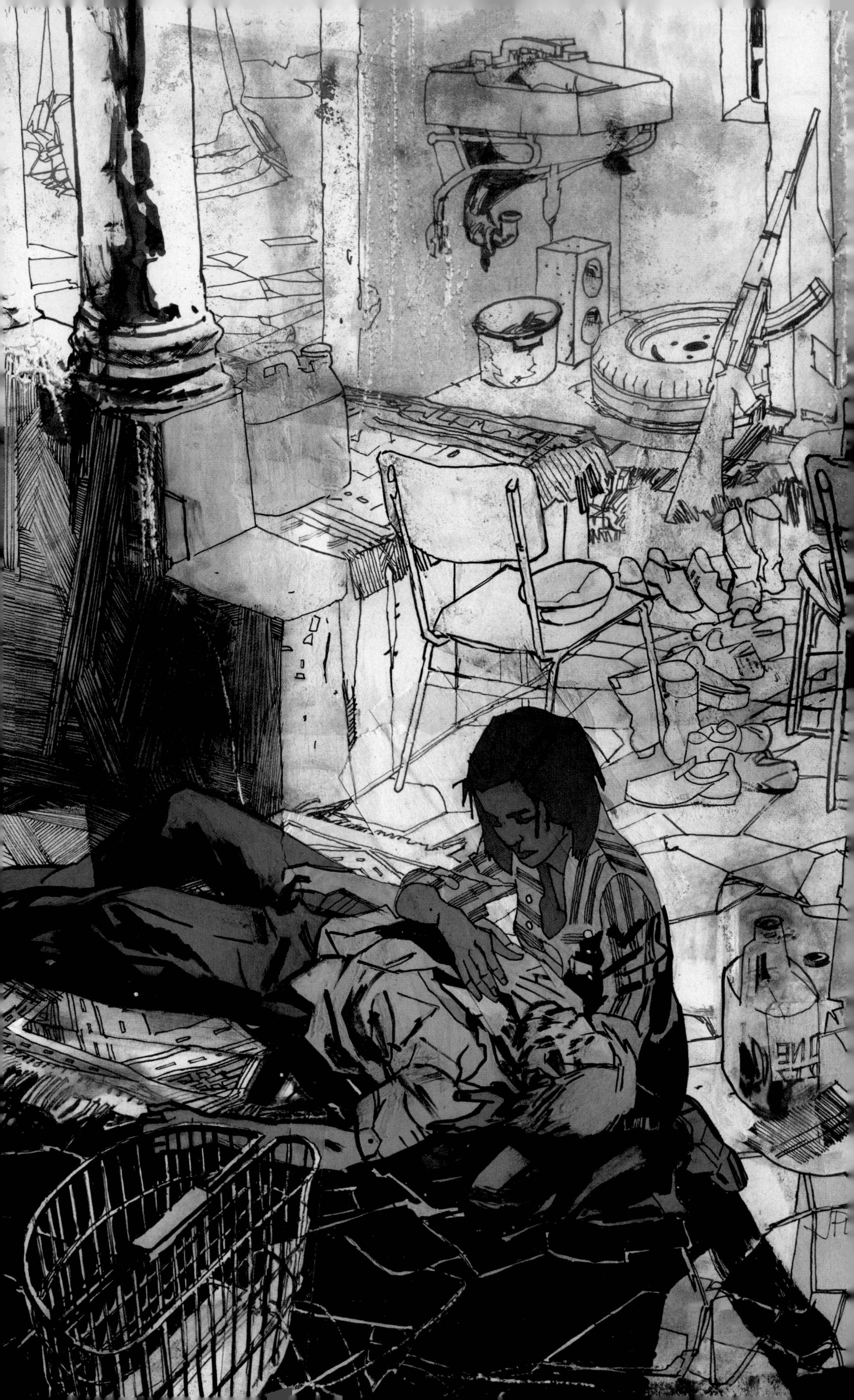

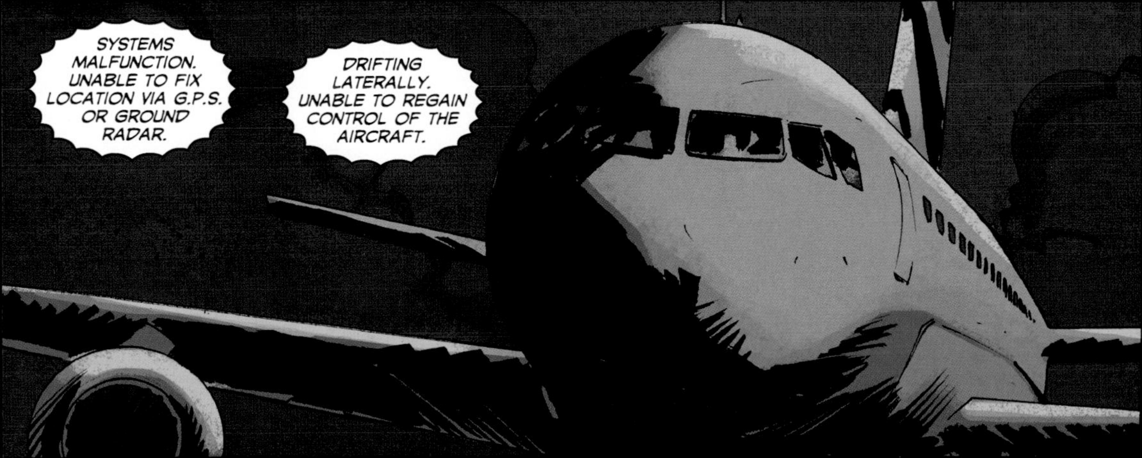
SYSTEMS MALFUNCTION. UNABLE TO FIX LOCATION VIA G.P.S. OR GROUND RADAR.
DRIFTING LATERALLY. UNABLE TO REGAIN CONTROL OF THE AIRCRAFT.

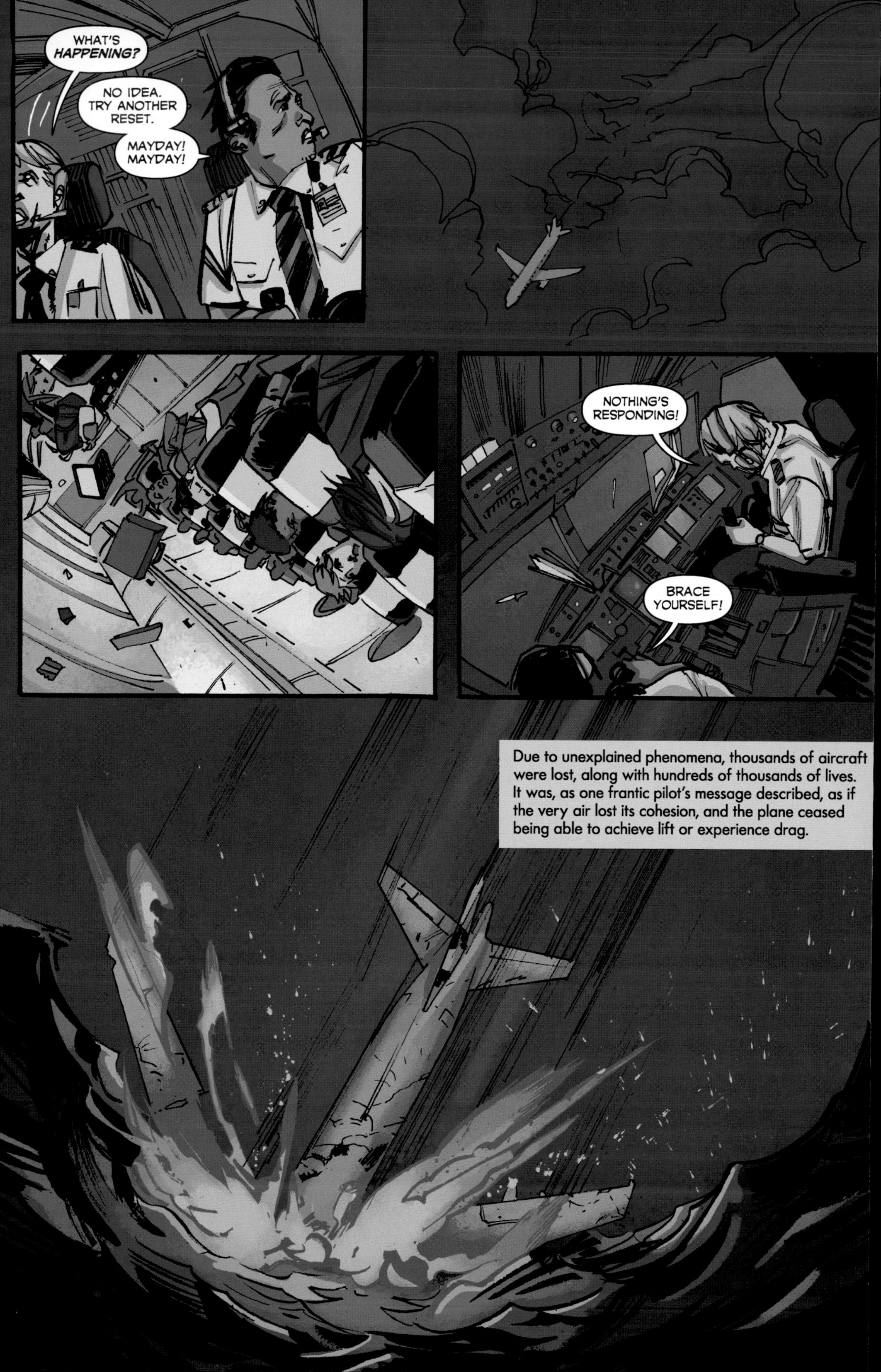
WHAT'S *HAPPENING?*
NO IDEA. TRY ANOTHER RESET.
MAYDAY! MAYDAY!
NOTHING'S RESPONDING!
BRACE YOURSELF!
Due to unexplained phenomena, thousands of aircraft were lost, along with hundreds of thousands of lives. It was, as one frantic pilot's message described, as if the very air lost its cohesion, and the plane ceased being able to achieve lift or experience drag.

On that date, designated "Crash One Plus Seven"...

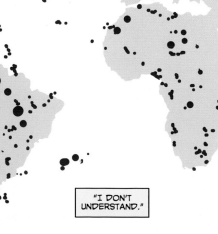

...the planet rid its atmosphere of all intruders.

"I DON'T UNDERSTAND."

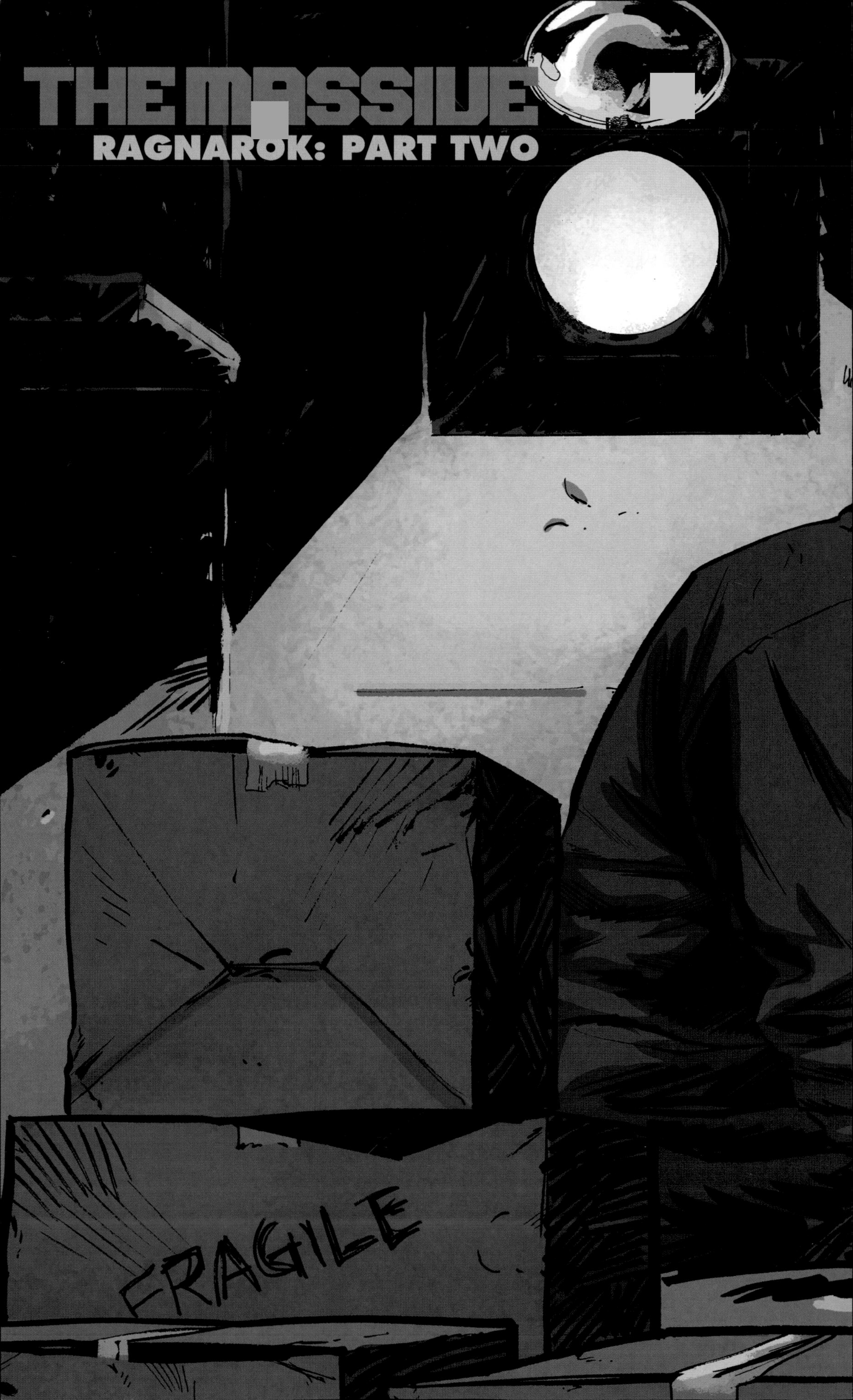
THE MASSIVE
RAGNAROK: PART TWO
FRAGILE

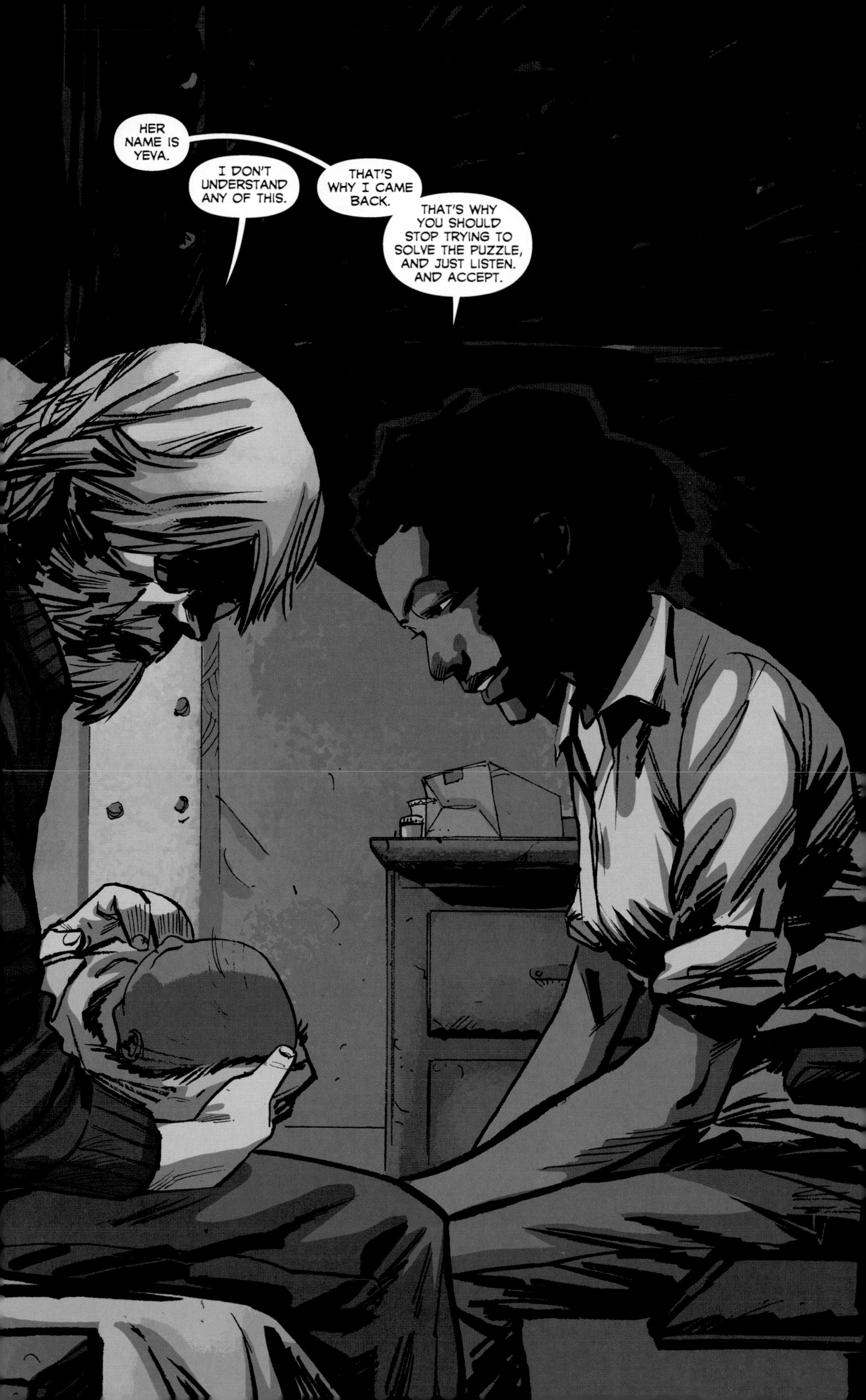
HER NAME IS YEVA.
I DON'T UNDERSTAND ANY OF THIS.
THAT'S WHY I CAME BACK.
THAT'S WHY YOU SHOULD STOP TRYING TO SOLVE THE PUZZLE, AND JUST LISTEN. AND ACCEPT.

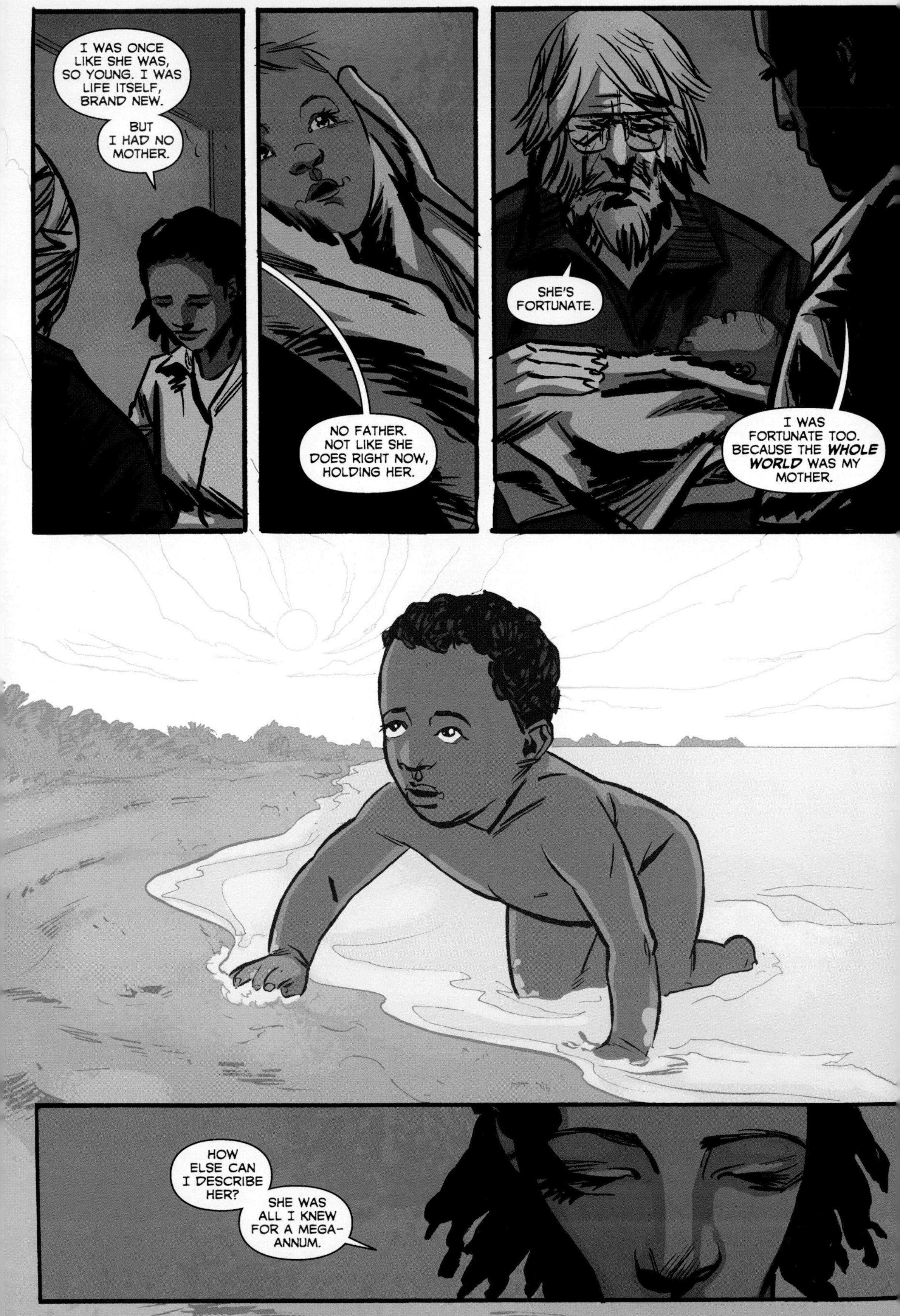
I WAS ONCE LIKE SHE WAS, SO YOUNG. I WAS LIFE ITSELF, BRAND NEW.
BUT I HAD NO MOTHER.
NO FATHER. NOT LIKE SHE DOES RIGHT NOW, HOLDING HER.
SHE'S FORTUNATE.
I WAS FORTUNATE TOO. BECAUSE THE ***WHOLE WORLD*** WAS MY MOTHER.
HOW ELSE CAN I DESCRIBE HER?
SHE WAS ALL I KNEW FOR A MEGA-ANNUM.

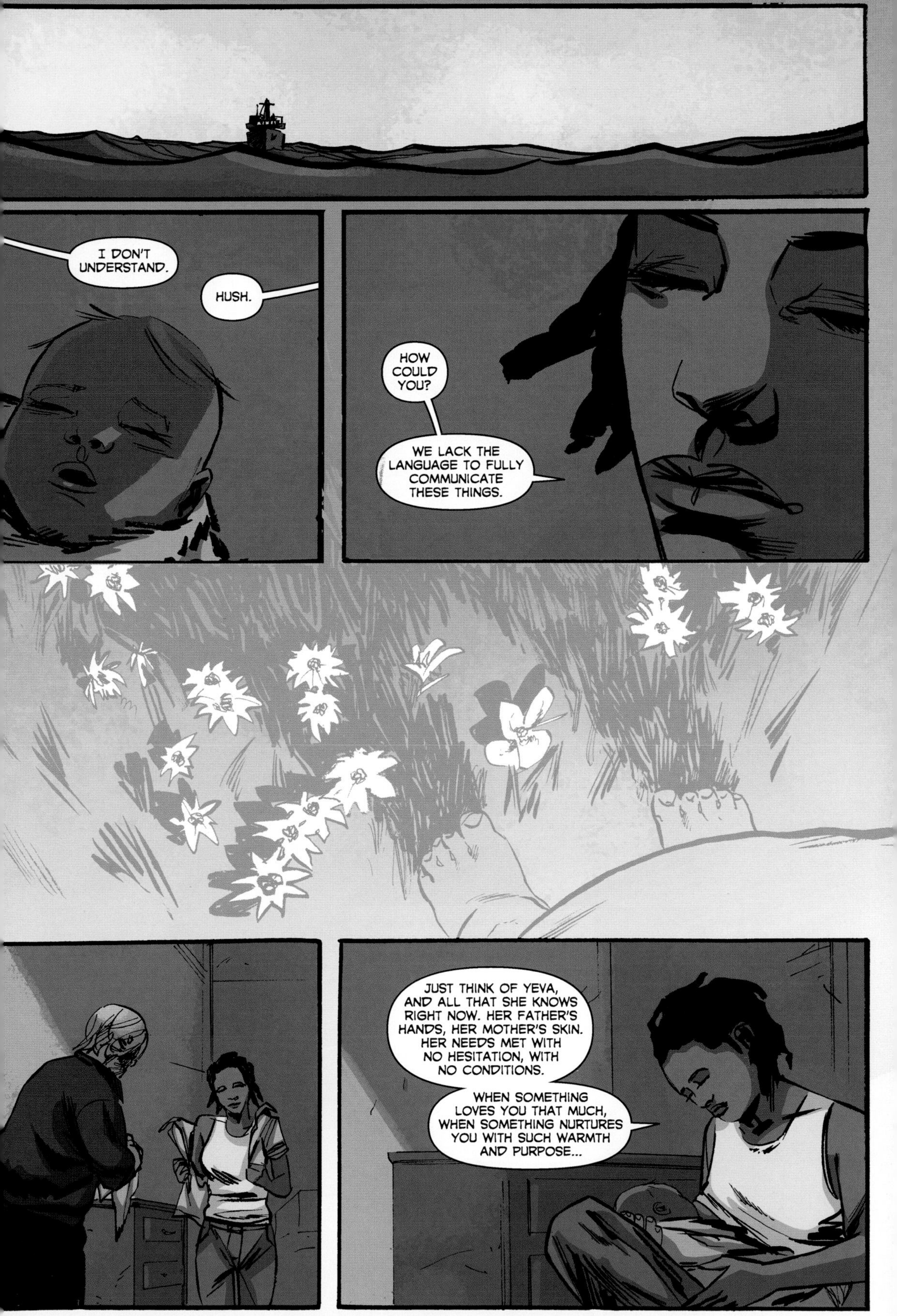
I DON'T UNDERSTAND.
HUSH.
HOW COULD YOU?
WE LACK THE LANGUAGE TO FULLY COMMUNICATE THESE THINGS.
JUST THINK OF YEVA, AND ALL THAT SHE KNOWS RIGHT NOW. HER FATHER'S HANDS, HER MOTHER'S SKIN. HER NEEDS MET WITH NO HESITATION, WITH NO CONDITIONS.
WHEN SOMETHING LOVES YOU THAT MUCH, WHEN SOMETHING NURTURES YOU WITH SUCH WARMTH AND PURPOSE...

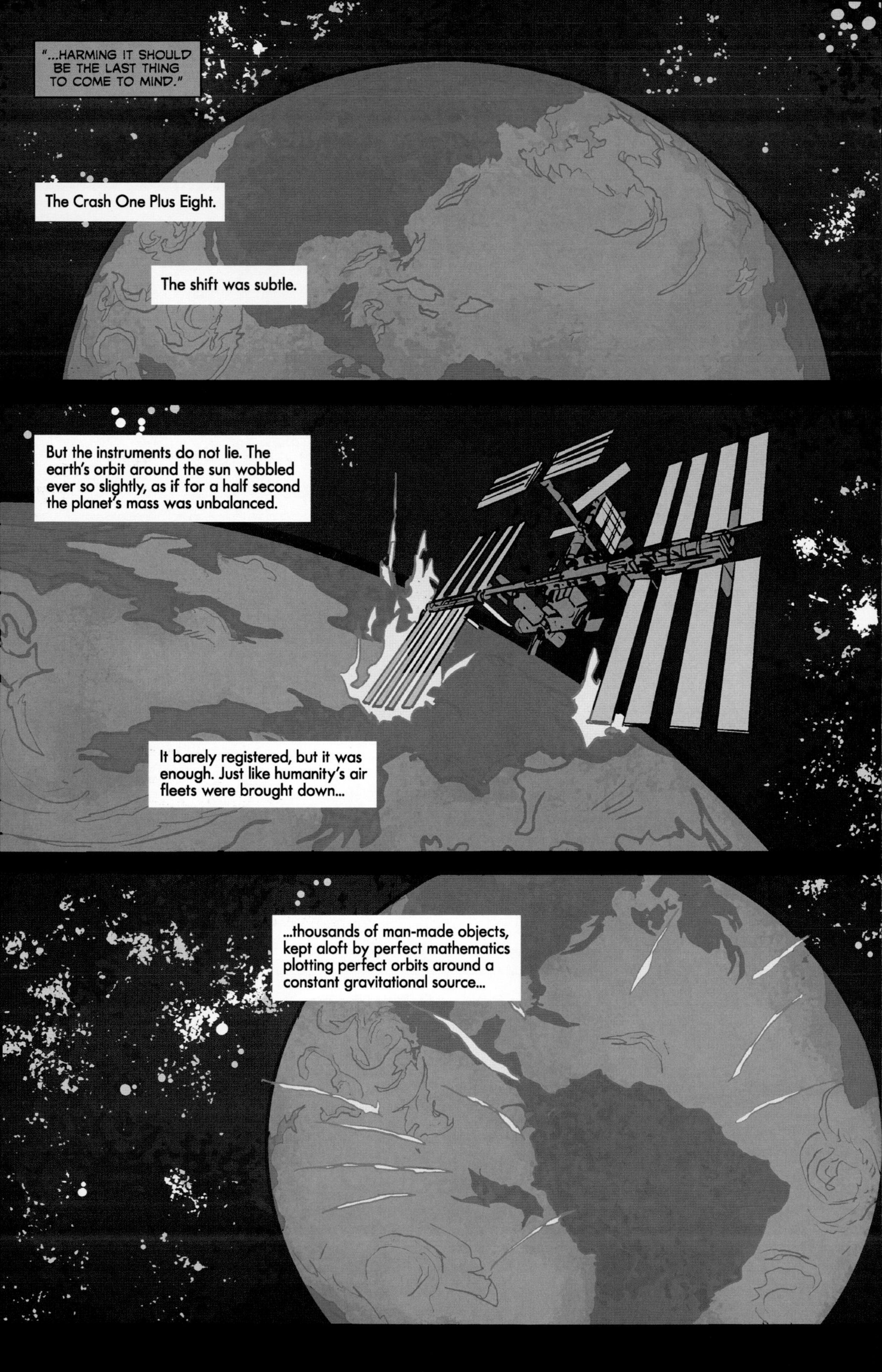
"...HARMING IT SHOULD BE THE LAST THING TO COME TO MIND."
The Crash One Plus Eight.
The shift was subtle.
But the instruments do not lie. The earth's orbit around the sun wobbled ever so slightly, as if for a half second the planet's mass was unbalanced.
It barely registered, but it was enough. Just like humanity's air fleets were brought down...
...thousands of man-made objects, kept aloft by perfect mathematics plotting perfect orbits around a constant gravitational source...

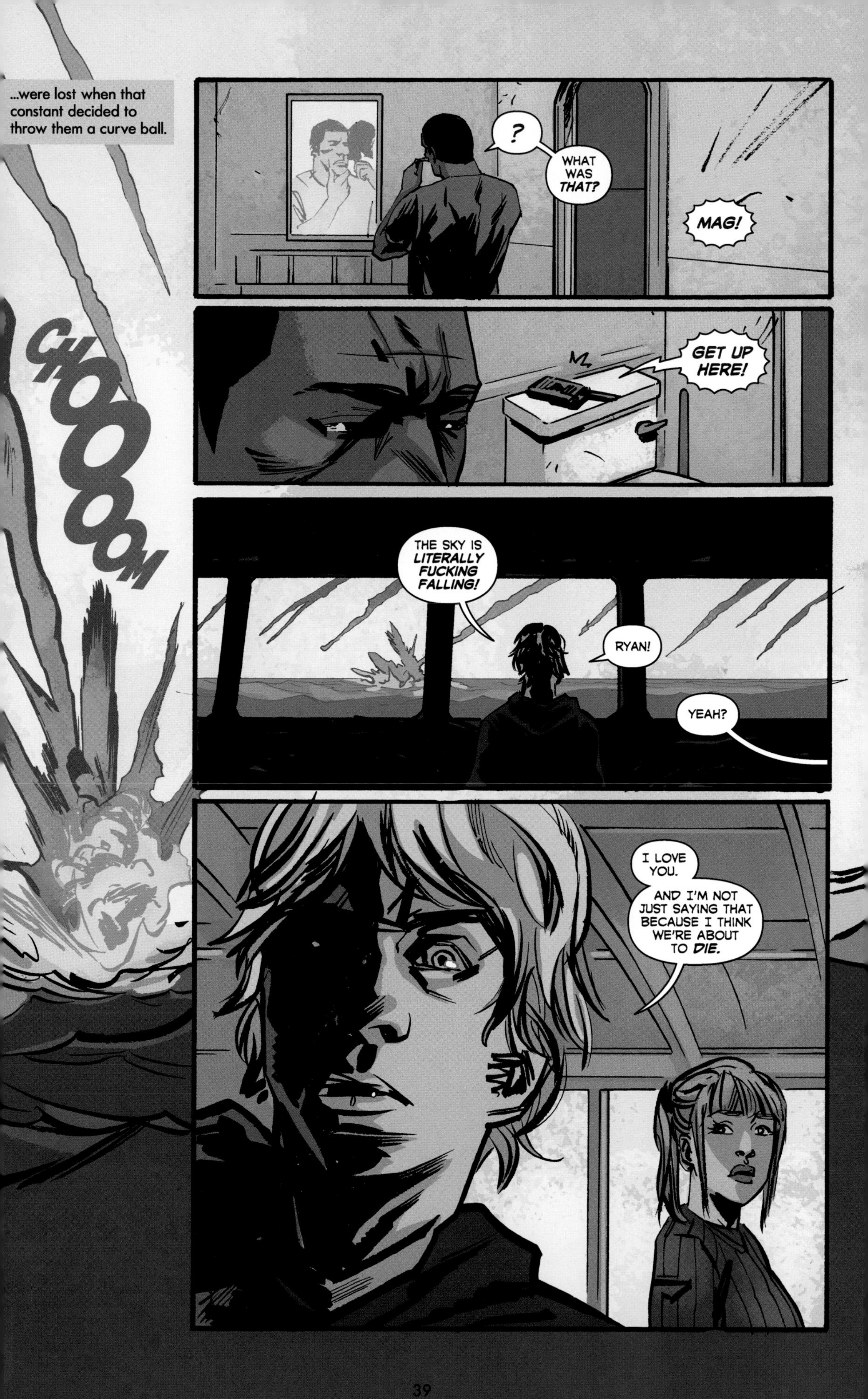
...were lost when that constant decided to throw them a curve ball.
?
WHAT WAS THAT?
MAG!
CHOOOOOM
GET UP HERE!
THE SKY IS LITERALLY FUCKING FALLING!
RYAN!
YEAH?
I LOVE YOU.
AND I'M NOT JUST SAYING THAT BECAUSE I THINK WE'RE ABOUT TO DIE.

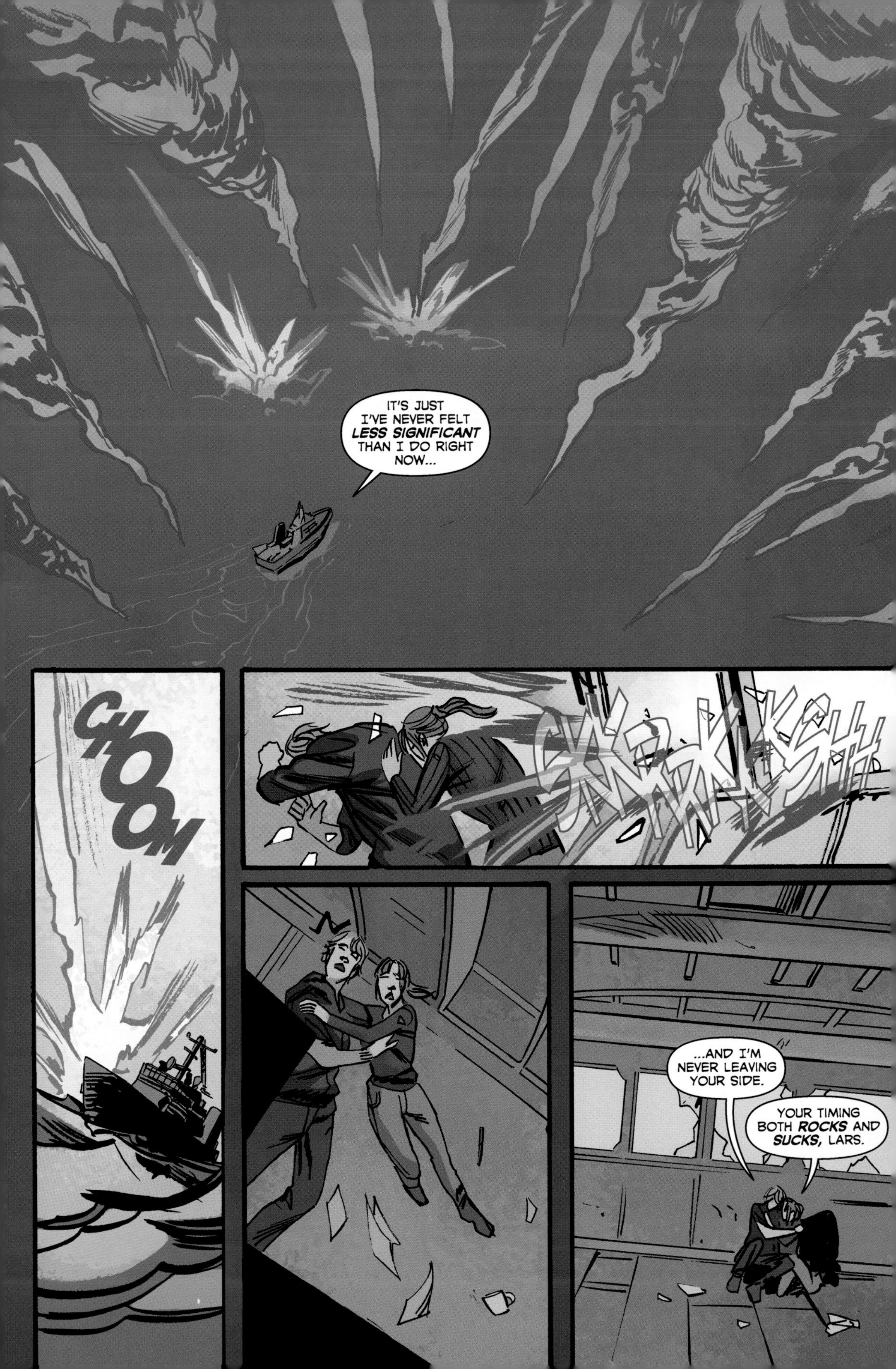
IT'S JUST I'VE NEVER FELT **LESS SIGNIFICANT** THAN I DO RIGHT NOW...
CHOOM
...AND I'M NEVER LEAVING YOUR SIDE.
YOUR TIMING BOTH **ROCKS** AND **SUCKS,** LARS.

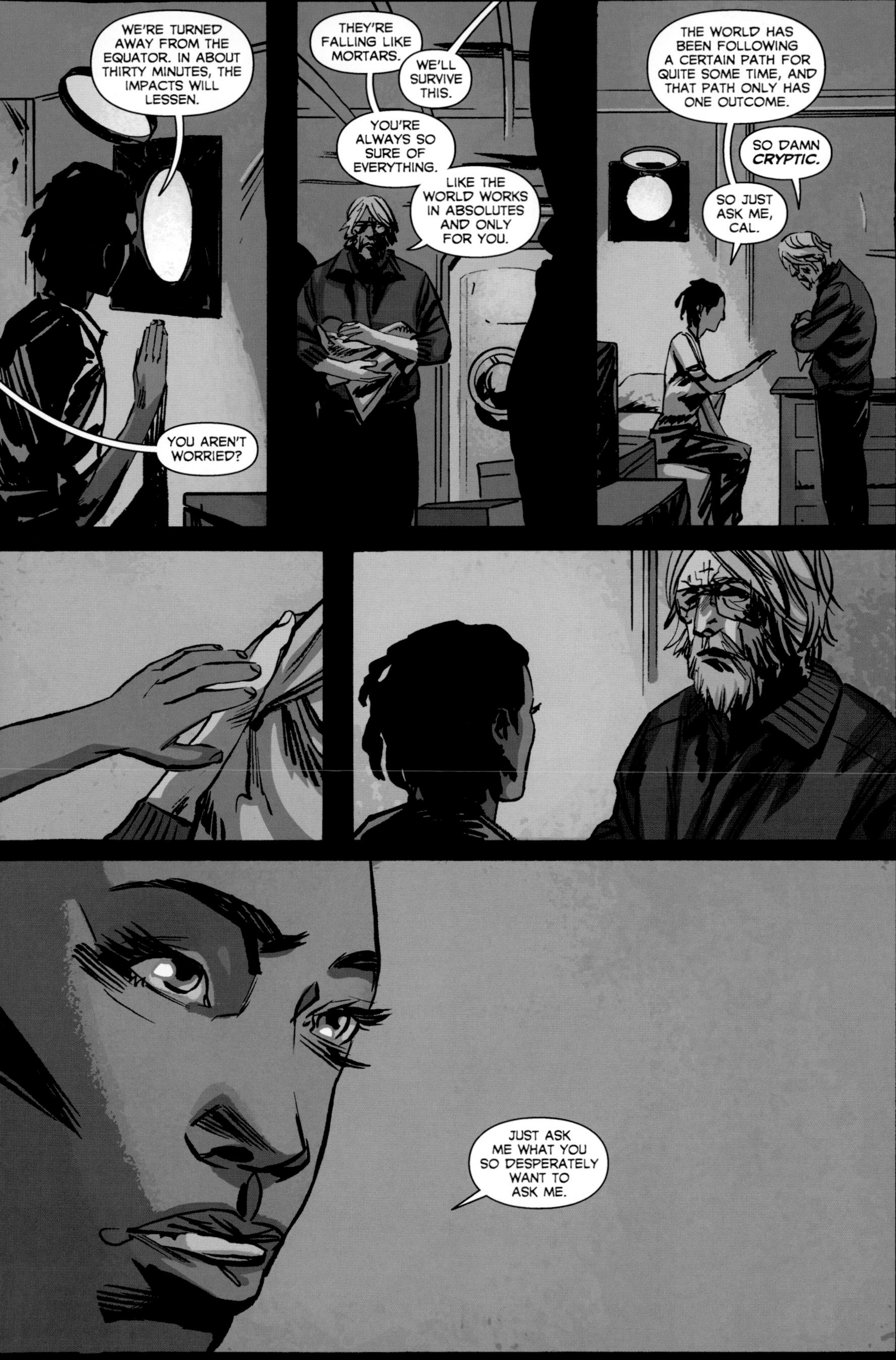
WE'RE TURNED AWAY FROM THE EQUATOR. IN ABOUT THIRTY MINUTES, THE IMPACTS WILL LESSEN.
YOU AREN'T WORRIED?
THEY'RE FALLING LIKE MORTARS.
WE'LL SURVIVE THIS.
YOU'RE ALWAYS SO SURE OF EVERYTHING.
LIKE THE WORLD WORKS IN ABSOLUTES AND ONLY FOR YOU.
THE WORLD HAS BEEN FOLLOWING A CERTAIN PATH FOR QUITE SOME TIME, AND THAT PATH ONLY HAS ONE OUTCOME.
SO DAMN ***CRYPTIC.***
SO JUST ASK ME, CAL.
JUST ASK ME WHAT YOU SO DESPERATELY WANT TO ASK ME.

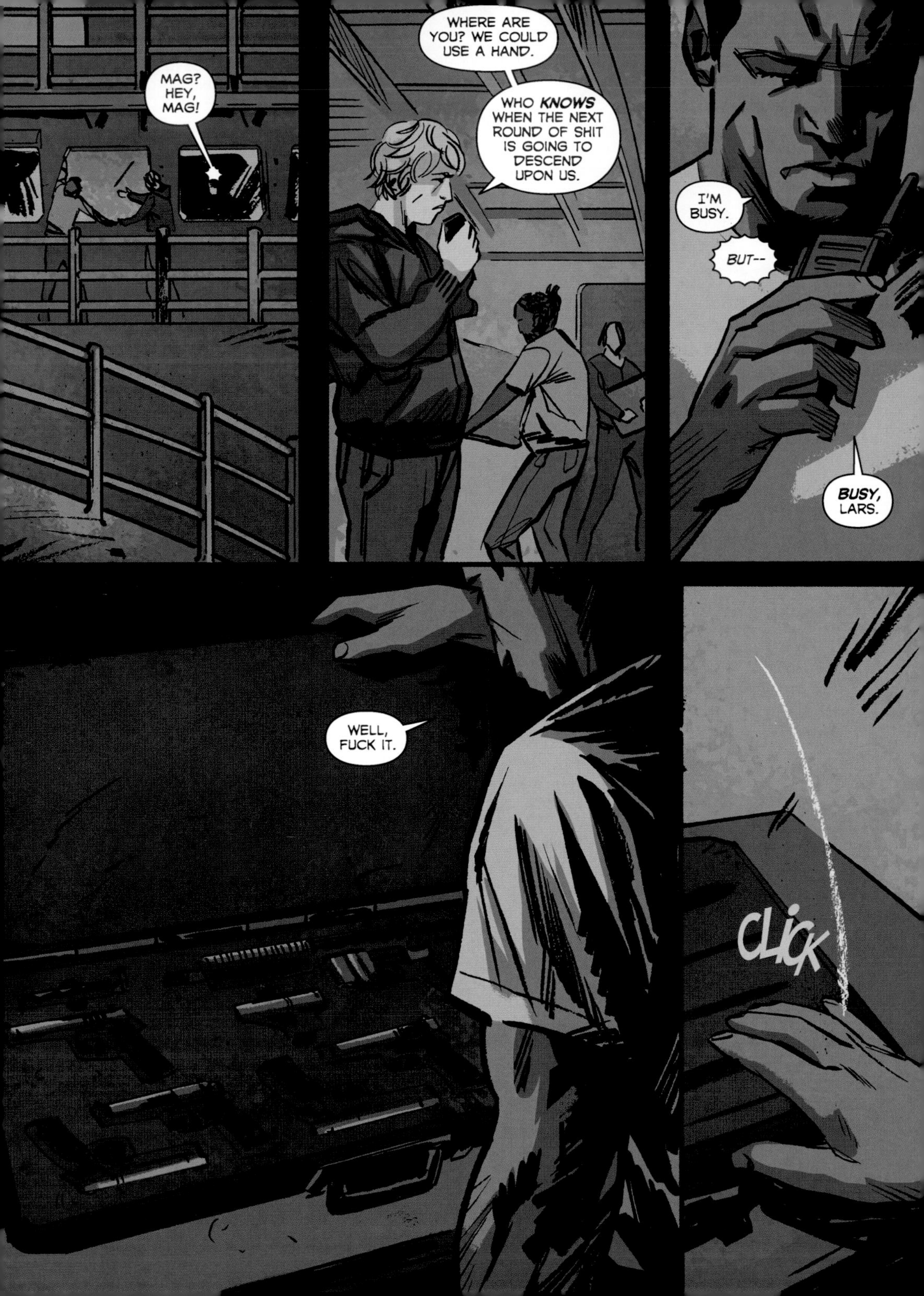
MAG? HEY, MAG!
WHERE ARE YOU? WE COULD USE A HAND.
WHO *KNOWS* WHEN THE NEXT ROUND OF SHIT IS GOING TO DESCEND UPON US.
I'M BUSY.
BUT--
BUSY, LARS.
WELL, FUCK IT.
CLICK

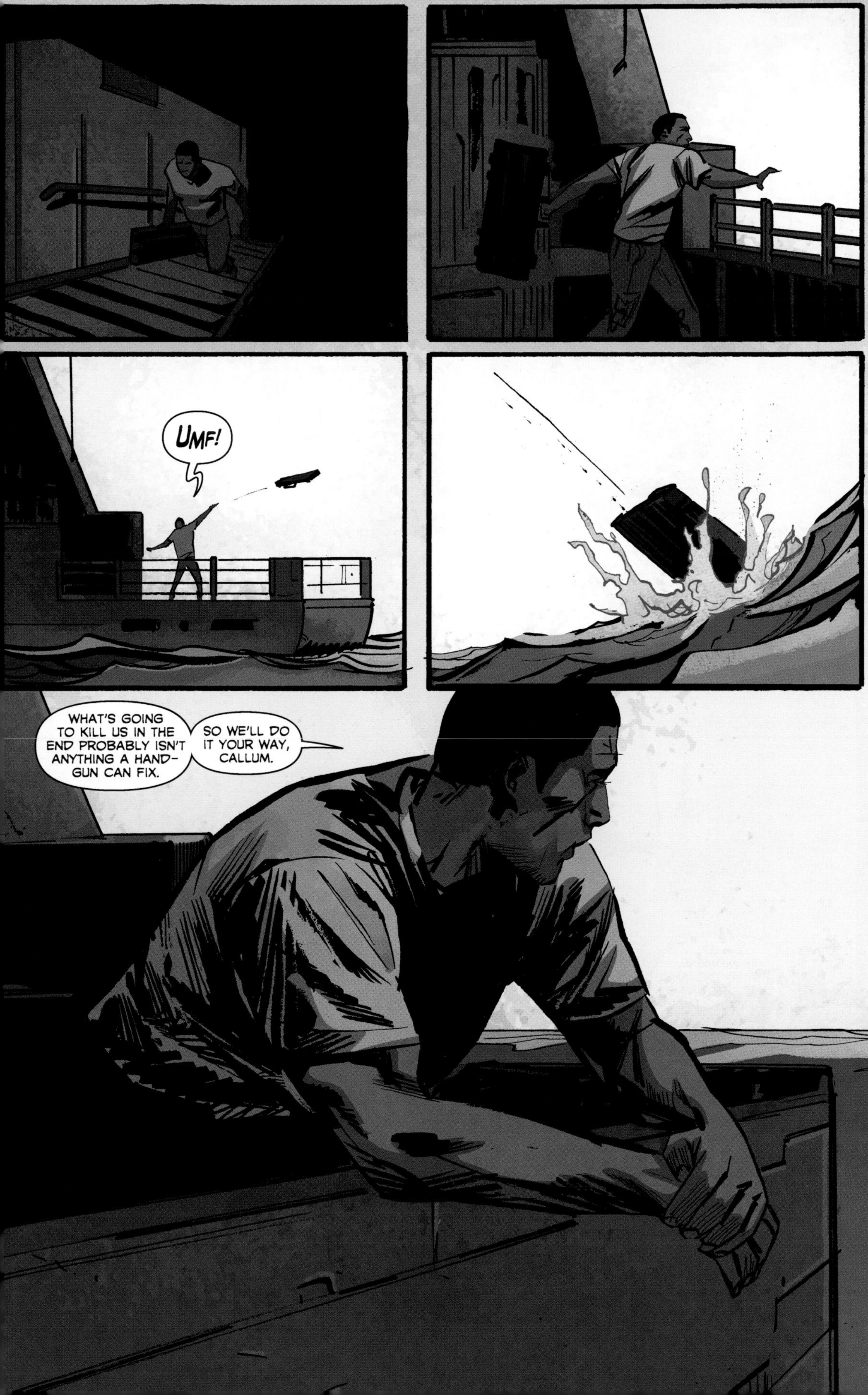
UMF!
WHAT'S GOING TO KILL US IN THE END PROBABLY ISN'T ANYTHING A HAND-GUN CAN FIX.
SO WE'LL DO IT YOUR WAY, CALLUM.

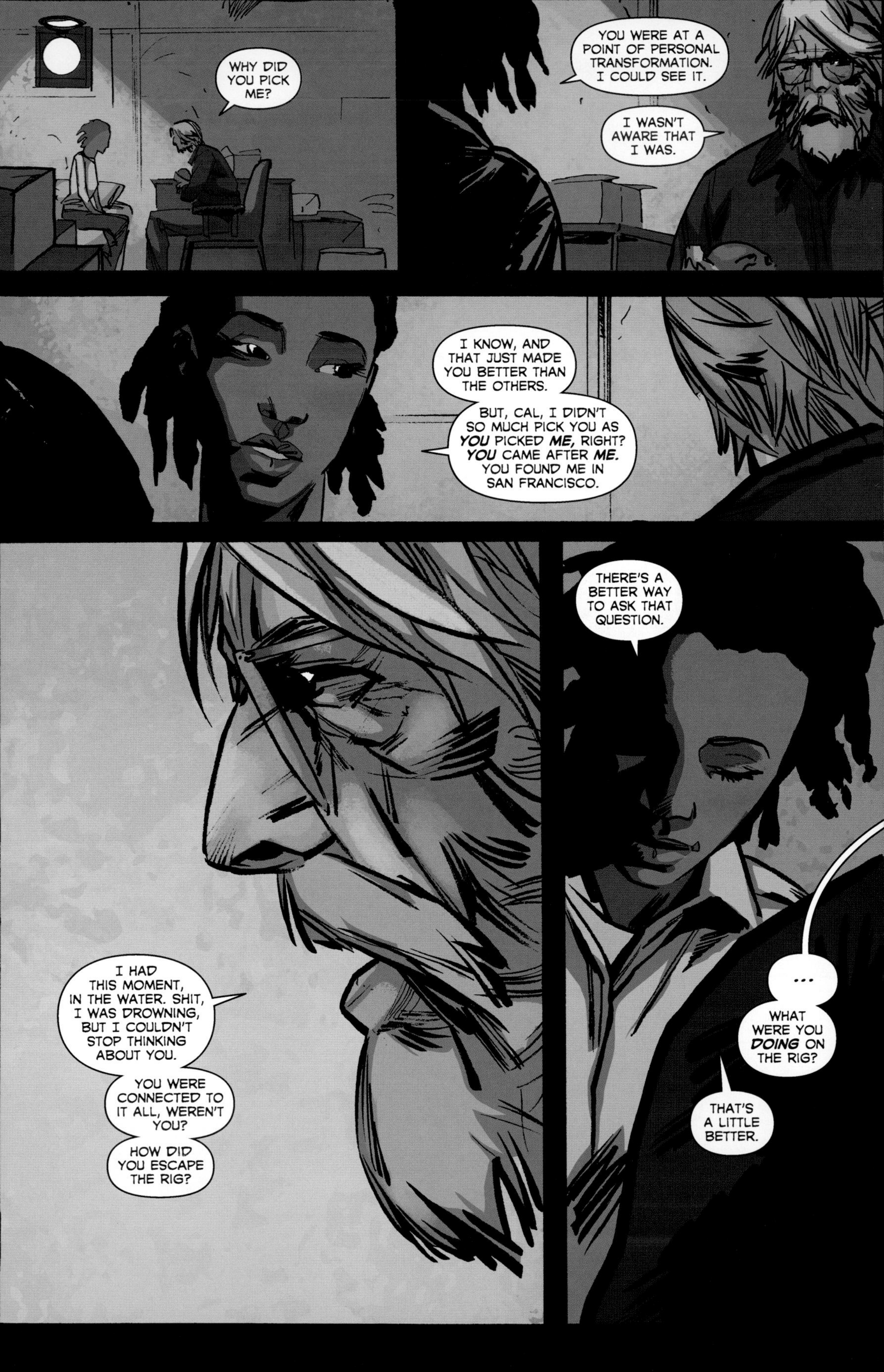
WHY DID YOU PICK ME?
YOU WERE AT A POINT OF PERSONAL TRANSFORMATION. I COULD SEE IT.
I WASN'T AWARE THAT I WAS.
I KNOW, AND THAT JUST MADE YOU BETTER THAN THE OTHERS.
BUT, CAL, I DIDN'T SO MUCH PICK YOU AS *YOU* PICKED *ME,* RIGHT? *YOU* CAME AFTER *ME.* YOU FOUND ME IN SAN FRANCISCO.
I HAD THIS MOMENT, IN THE WATER. SHIT, I WAS DROWNING, BUT I COULDN'T STOP THINKING ABOUT YOU.
YOU WERE CONNECTED TO IT ALL, WEREN'T YOU?
HOW DID YOU ESCAPE THE RIG?
THERE'S A BETTER WAY TO ASK THAT QUESTION.
...
WHAT WERE YOU *DOING* ON THE RIG?
THAT'S A LITTLE BETTER.

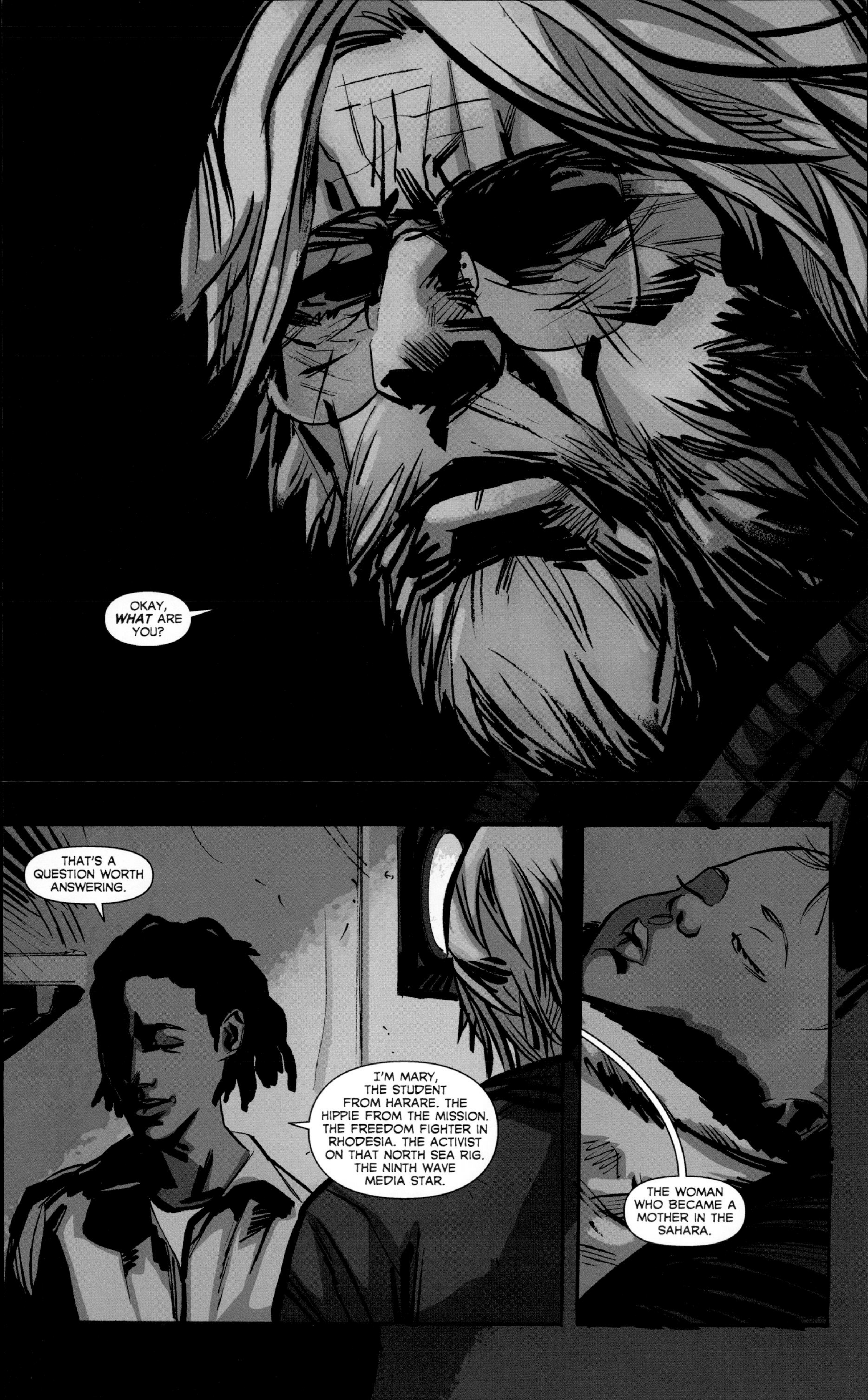
OKAY, *WHAT* ARE YOU?
THAT'S A QUESTION WORTH ANSWERING.
I'M MARY, THE STUDENT FROM HARARE. THE HIPPIE FROM THE MISSION. THE FREEDOM FIGHTER IN RHODESIA. THE ACTIVIST ON THAT NORTH SEA RIG. THE NINTH WAVE MEDIA STAR.
THE WOMAN WHO BECAME A MOTHER IN THE SAHARA.

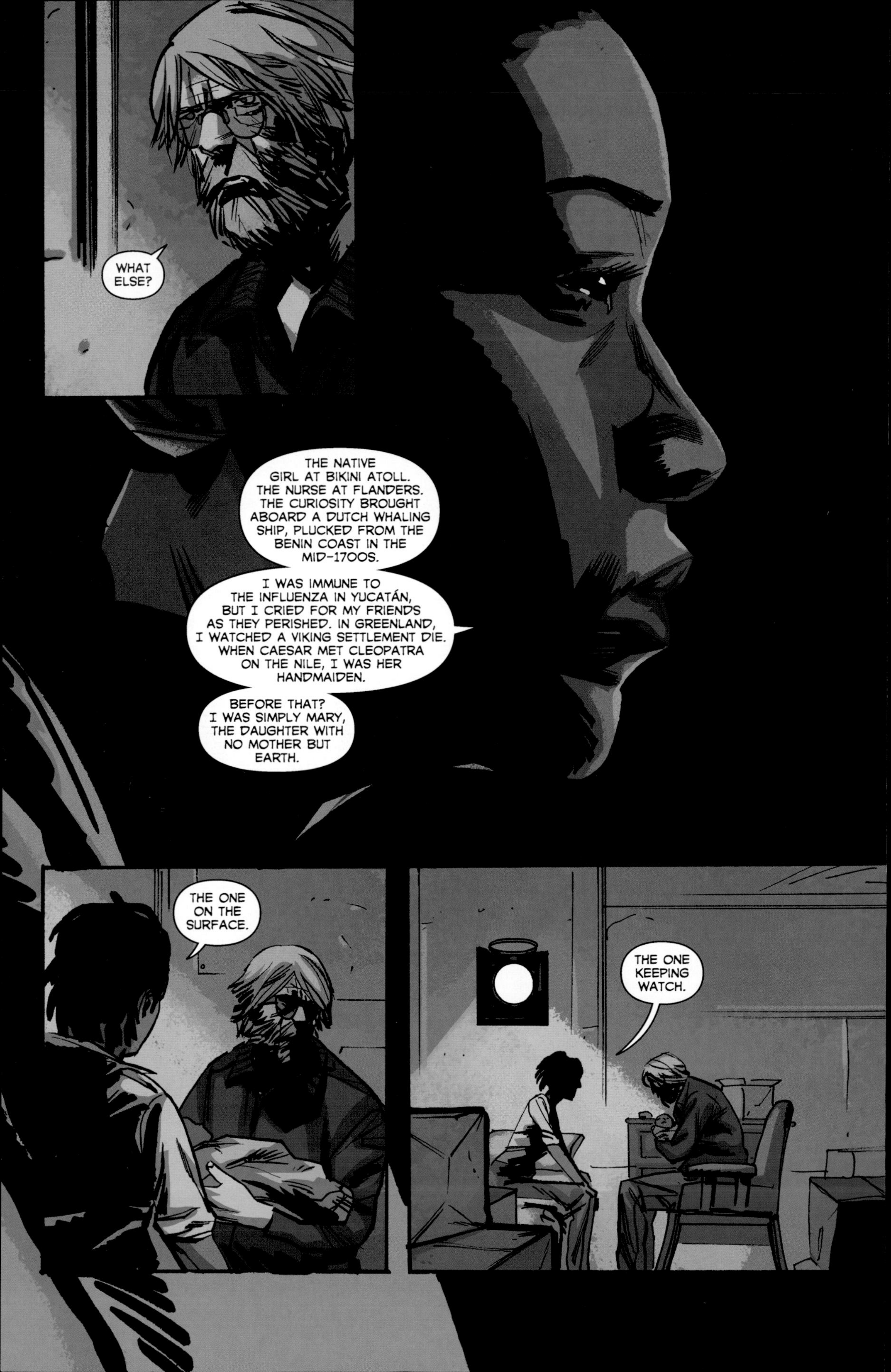
WHAT ELSE?
THE NATIVE GIRL AT BIKINI ATOLL. THE NURSE AT FLANDERS. THE CURIOSITY BROUGHT ABOARD A DUTCH WHALING SHIP, PLUCKED FROM THE BENIN COAST IN THE MID-1700S.
I WAS IMMUNE TO THE INFLUENZA IN YUCATÁN, BUT I CRIED FOR MY FRIENDS AS THEY PERISHED. IN GREENLAND, I WATCHED A VIKING SETTLEMENT DIE. WHEN CAESAR MET CLEOPATRA ON THE NILE, I WAS HER HANDMAIDEN.
BEFORE THAT? I WAS SIMPLY MARY, THE DAUGHTER WITH NO MOTHER BUT EARTH.
THE ONE ON THE SURFACE.
THE ONE KEEPING WATCH.

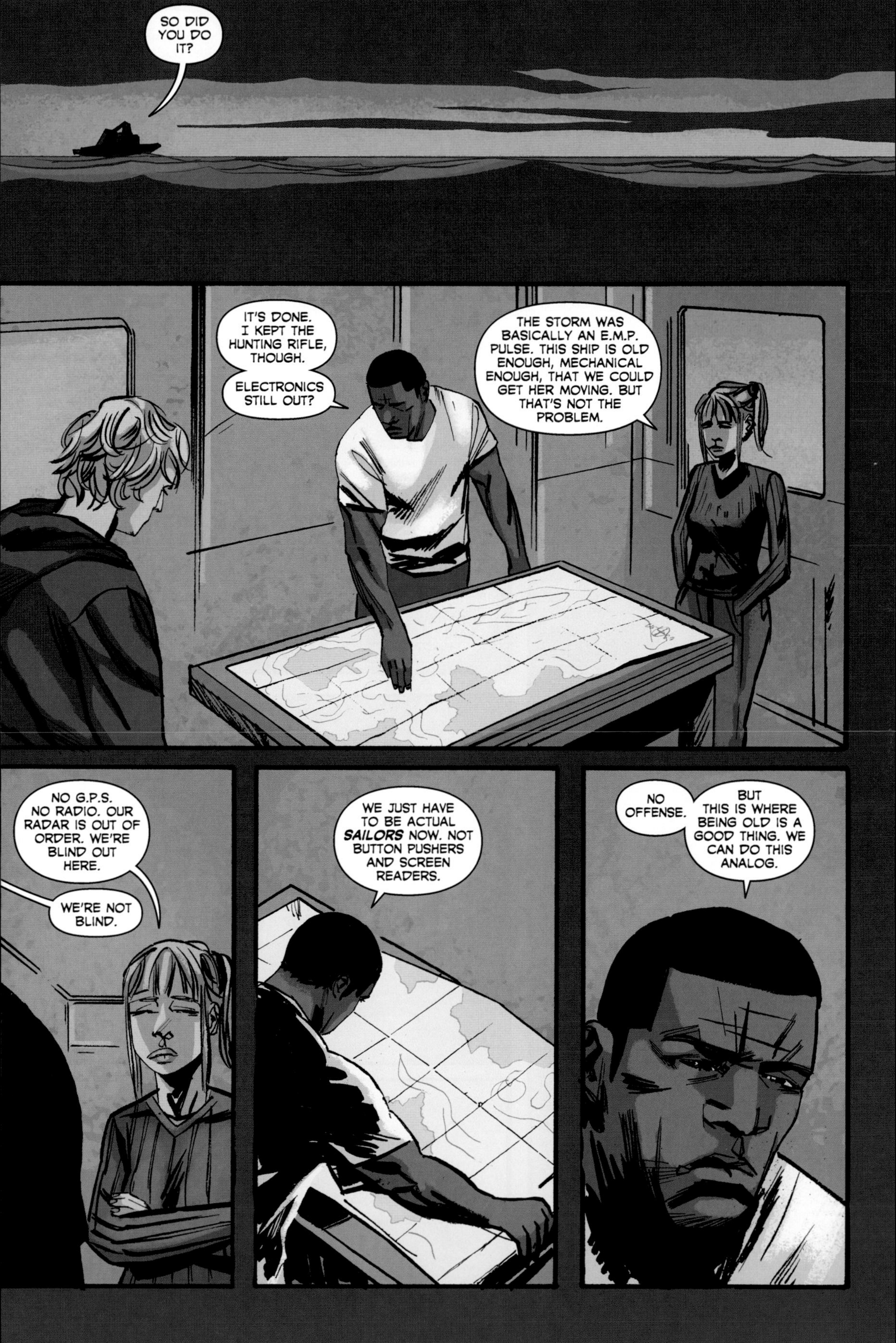
SO DID YOU DO IT?
IT'S DONE. I KEPT THE HUNTING RIFLE, THOUGH.
ELECTRONICS STILL OUT?
THE STORM WAS BASICALLY AN E.M.P. PULSE. THIS SHIP IS OLD ENOUGH, MECHANICAL ENOUGH, THAT WE COULD GET HER MOVING. BUT THAT'S NOT THE PROBLEM.
NO G.P.S. NO RADIO. OUR RADAR IS OUT OF ORDER. WE'RE BLIND OUT HERE.
WE'RE NOT BLIND.
WE JUST HAVE TO BE ACTUAL ***SAILORS*** NOW. NOT BUTTON PUSHERS AND SCREEN READERS.
NO OFFENSE.
BUT THIS IS WHERE BEING OLD IS A GOOD THING. WE CAN DO THIS ANALOG.

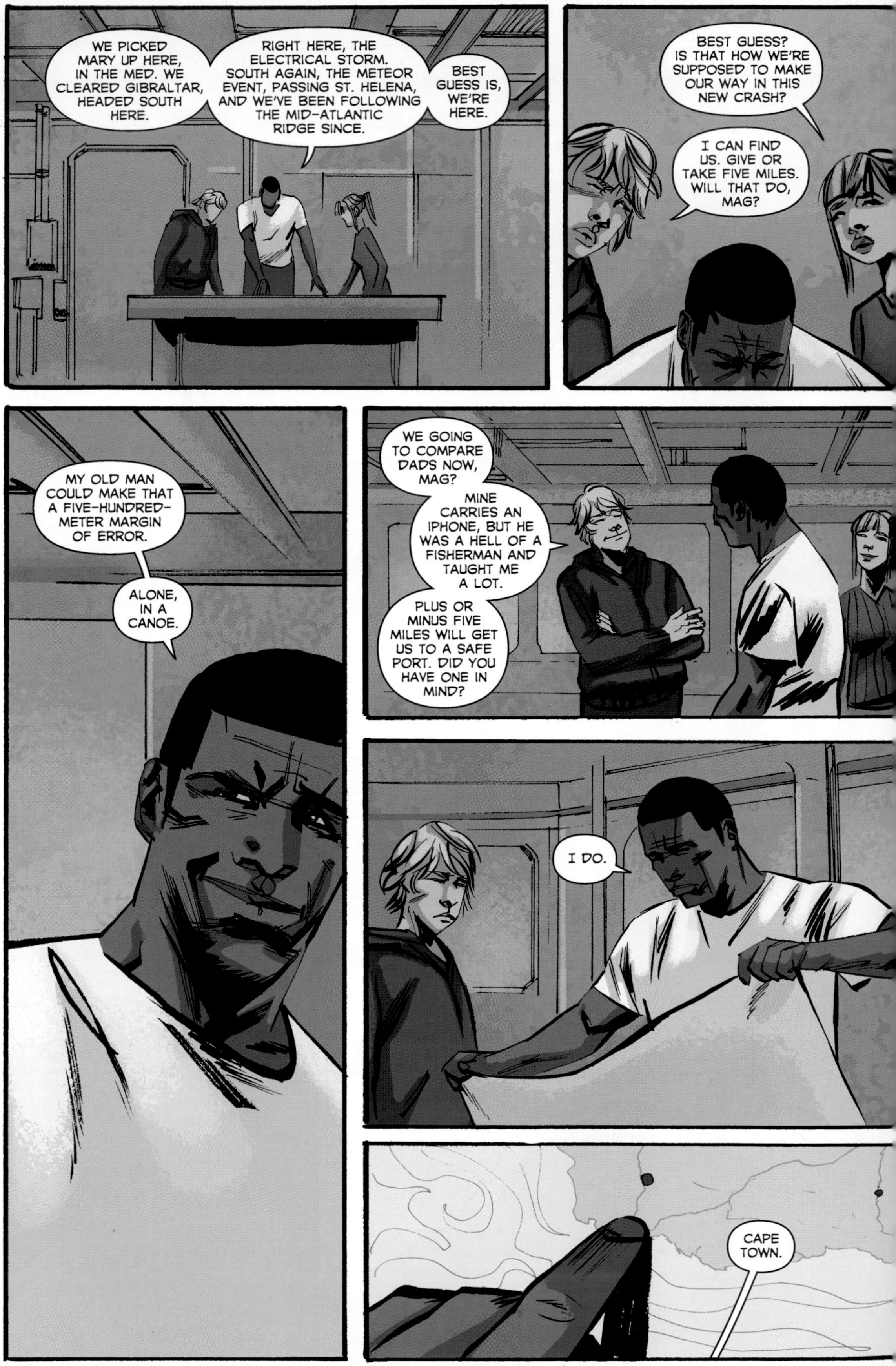
WE PICKED MARY UP HERE, IN THE MED. WE CLEARED GIBRALTAR, HEADED SOUTH HERE.
RIGHT HERE, THE ELECTRICAL STORM. SOUTH AGAIN, THE METEOR EVENT, PASSING ST. HELENA, AND WE'VE BEEN FOLLOWING THE MID-ATLANTIC RIDGE SINCE.
BEST GUESS IS, WE'RE HERE.
BEST GUESS? IS THAT HOW WE'RE SUPPOSED TO MAKE OUR WAY IN THIS NEW CRASH?
I CAN FIND US. GIVE OR TAKE FIVE MILES. WILL THAT DO, MAG?
MY OLD MAN COULD MAKE THAT A FIVE-HUNDRED-METER MARGIN OF ERROR.
ALONE, IN A CANOE.
WE GOING TO COMPARE DADS NOW, MAG?
MINE CARRIES AN IPHONE, BUT HE WAS A HELL OF A FISHERMAN AND TAUGHT ME A LOT.
PLUS OR MINUS FIVE MILES WILL GET US TO A SAFE PORT. DID YOU HAVE ONE IN MIND?
I DO.
CAPE TOWN.

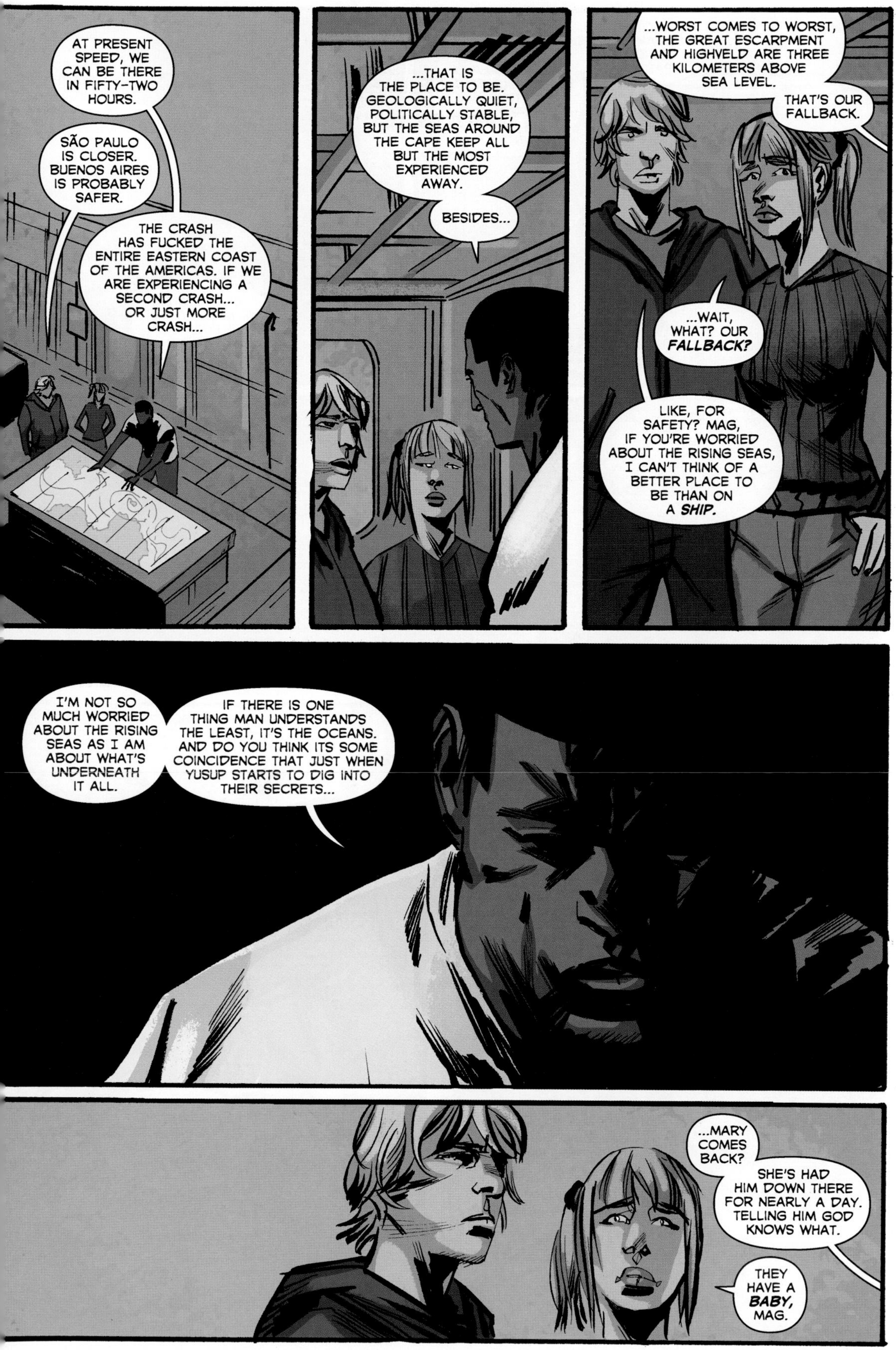
AT PRESENT SPEED, WE CAN BE THERE IN FIFTY-TWO HOURS.
SÃO PAULO IS CLOSER. BUENOS AIRES IS PROBABLY SAFER.
THE CRASH HAS FUCKED THE ENTIRE EASTERN COAST OF THE AMERICAS. IF WE ARE EXPERIENCING A SECOND CRASH... OR JUST MORE CRASH...
...THAT IS THE PLACE TO BE. GEOLOGICALLY QUIET, POLITICALLY STABLE, BUT THE SEAS AROUND THE CAPE KEEP ALL BUT THE MOST EXPERIENCED AWAY.
BESIDES...
...WORST COMES TO WORST, THE GREAT ESCARPMENT AND HIGHVELD ARE THREE KILOMETERS ABOVE SEA LEVEL.
THAT'S OUR FALLBACK.
...WAIT, WHAT? OUR *FALLBACK?*
LIKE, FOR SAFETY? MAG, IF YOU'RE WORRIED ABOUT THE RISING SEAS, I CAN'T THINK OF A BETTER PLACE TO BE THAN ON A *SHIP.*
I'M NOT SO MUCH WORRIED ABOUT THE RISING SEAS AS I AM ABOUT WHAT'S UNDERNEATH IT ALL.
IF THERE IS ONE THING MAN UNDERSTANDS THE LEAST, IT'S THE OCEANS. AND DO YOU THINK ITS SOME COINCIDENCE THAT JUST WHEN YUSUP STARTS TO DIG INTO THEIR SECRETS...
...MARY COMES BACK?
SHE'S HAD HIM DOWN THERE FOR NEARLY A DAY. TELLING HIM GOD KNOWS WHAT.
THEY HAVE A *BABY,* MAG.

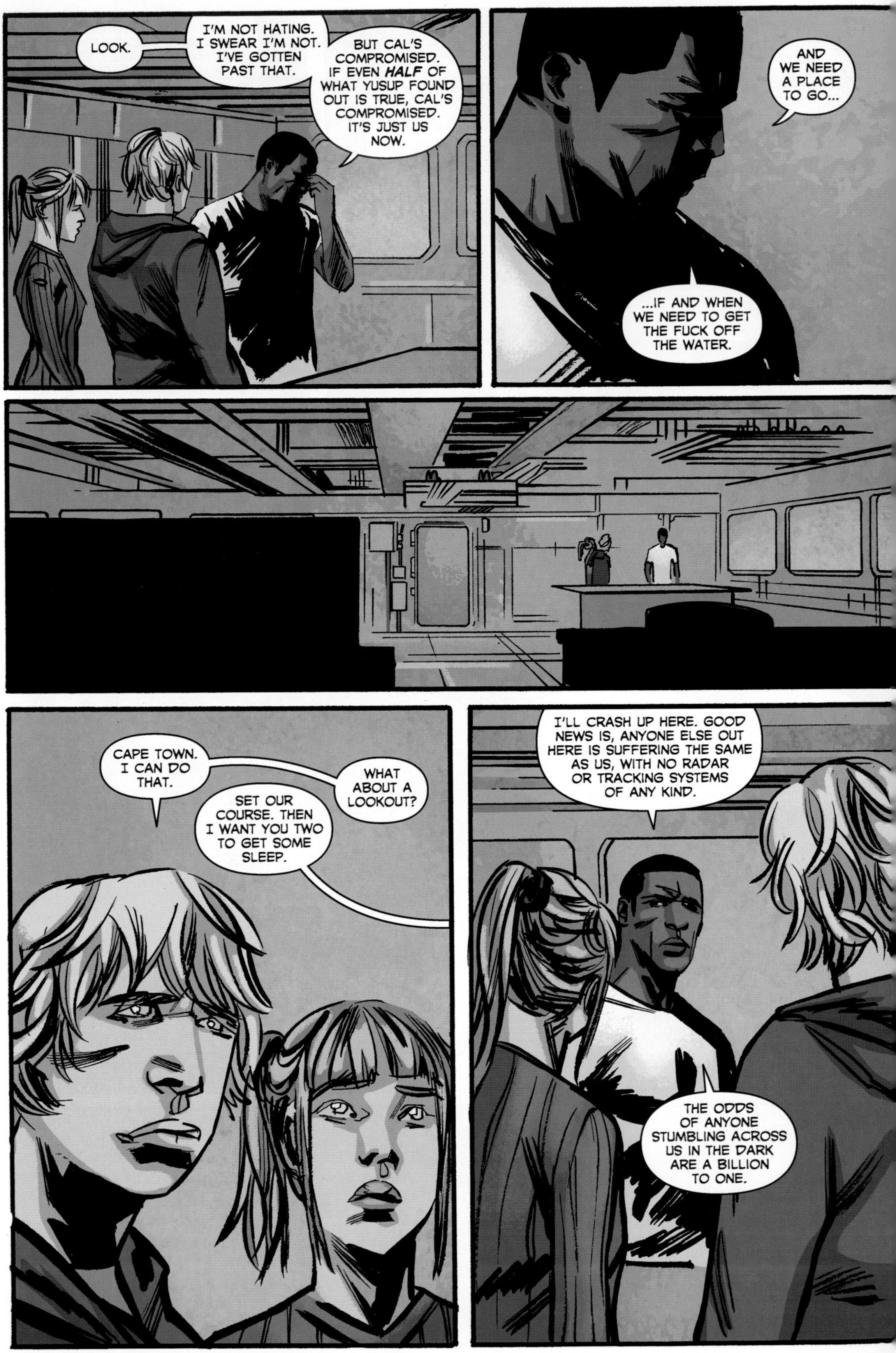
LOOK.
I'M NOT HATING. I SWEAR I'M NOT. I'VE GOTTEN PAST THAT.
BUT CAL'S COMPROMISED. IF EVEN HALF OF WHAT YUSUP FOUND OUT IS TRUE, CAL'S COMPROMISED. IT'S JUST US NOW.
AND WE NEED A PLACE TO GO...
...IF AND WHEN WE NEED TO GET THE FUCK OFF THE WATER.
CAPE TOWN. I CAN DO THAT.
SET OUR COURSE. THEN I WANT YOU TWO TO GET SOME SLEEP.
WHAT ABOUT A LOOKOUT?
I'LL CRASH UP HERE. GOOD NEWS IS, ANYONE ELSE OUT HERE IS SUFFERING THE SAME AS US, WITH NO RADAR OR TRACKING SYSTEMS OF ANY KIND.
THE ODDS OF ANYONE STUMBLING ACROSS US IN THE DARK ARE A BILLION TO ONE.

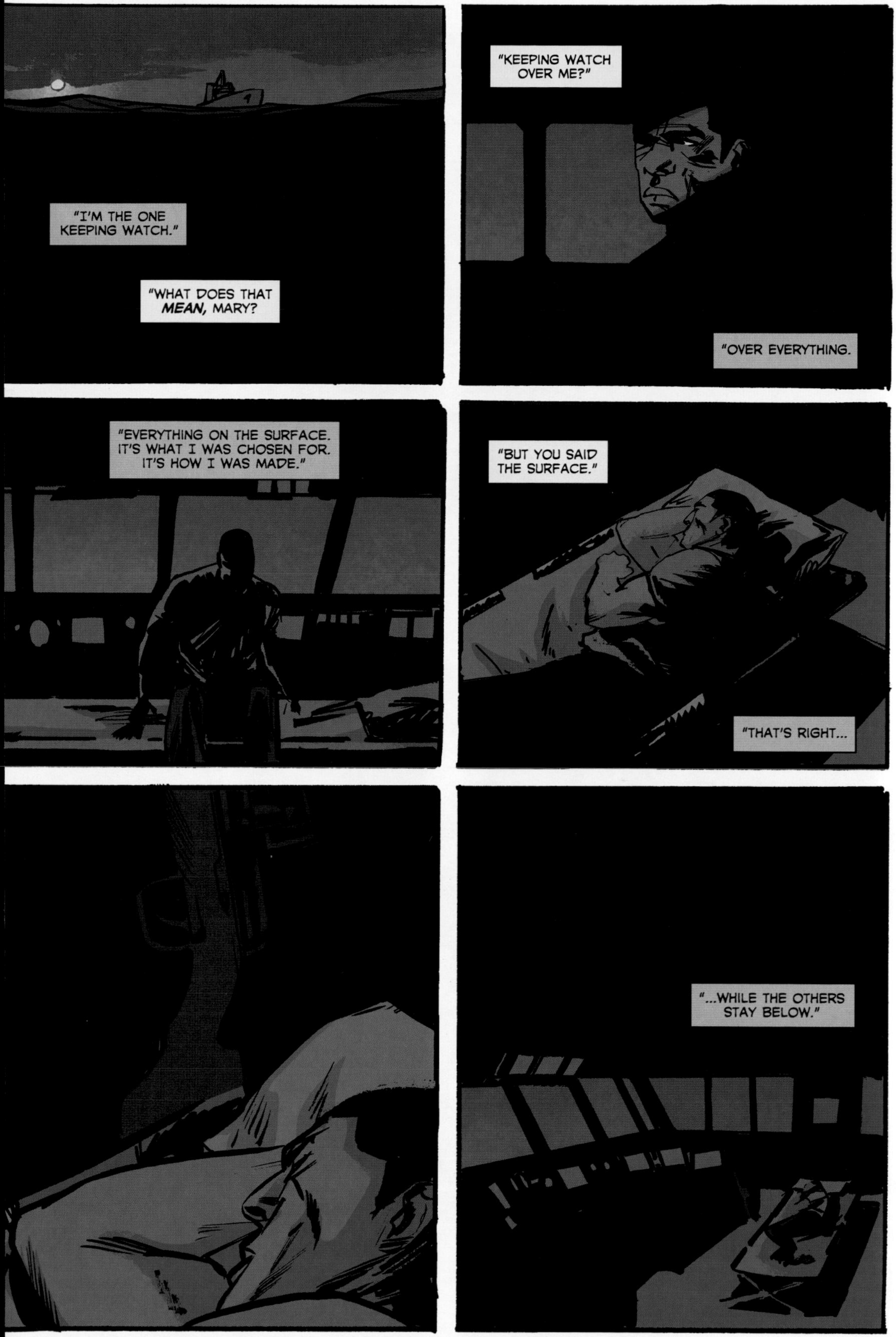
"I'M THE ONE KEEPING WATCH."
"WHAT DOES THAT *MEAN,* MARY?
"KEEPING WATCH OVER ME?"
"OVER EVERYTHING.
"EVERYTHING ON THE SURFACE. IT'S WHAT I WAS CHOSEN FOR. IT'S HOW I WAS MADE."
"BUT YOU SAID THE SURFACE."
"THAT'S RIGHT...
"...WHILE THE OTHERS STAY BELOW."

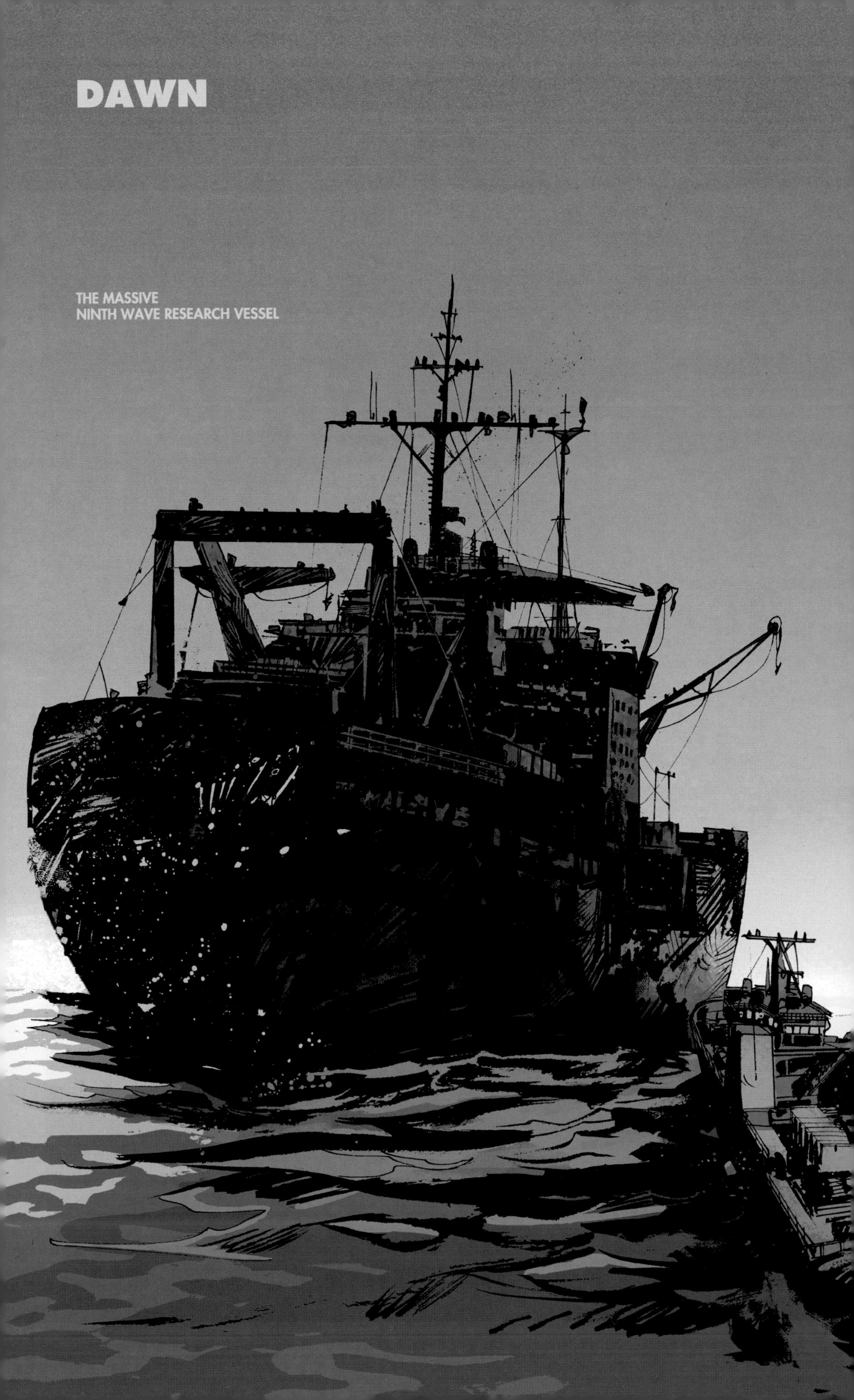
DAWN
THE MASSIVE
NINTH WAVE RESEARCH VESSEL

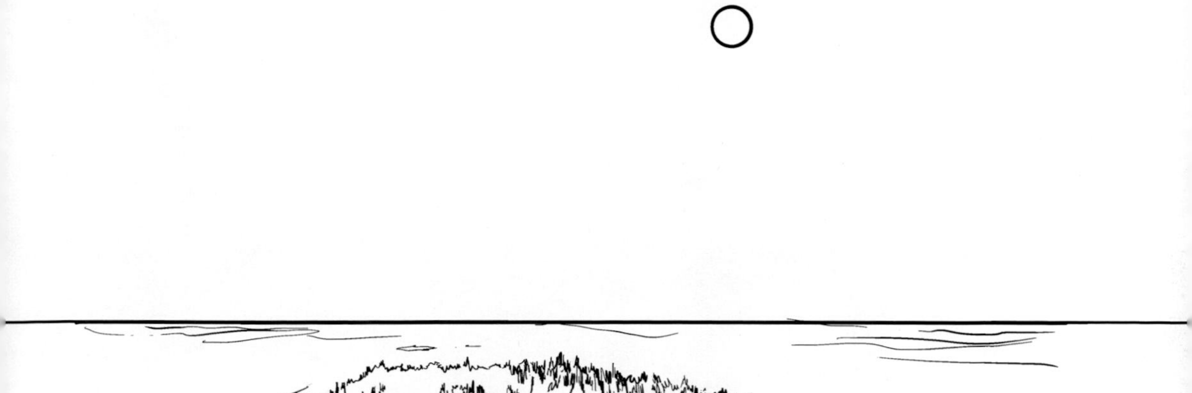

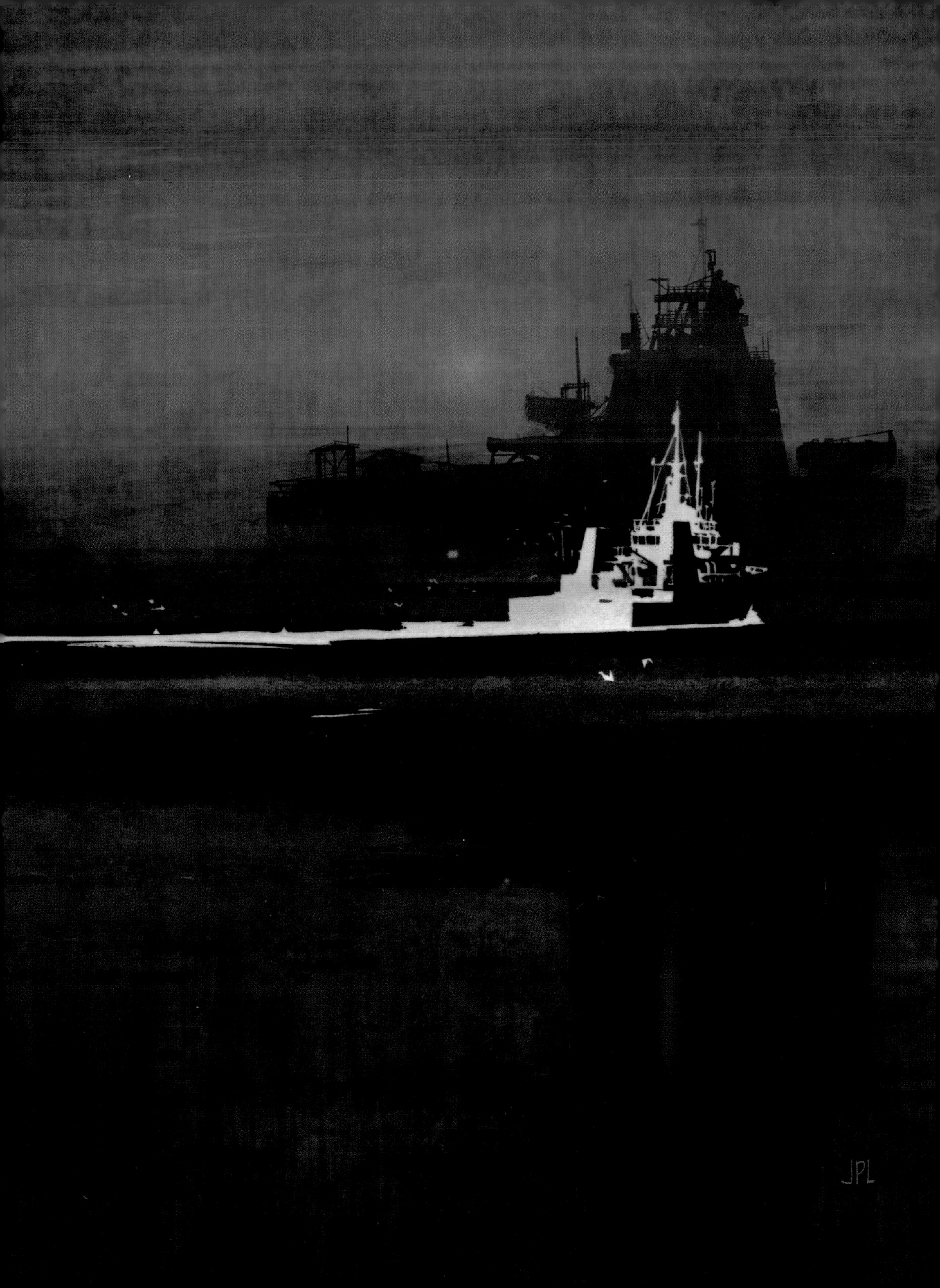
JPL

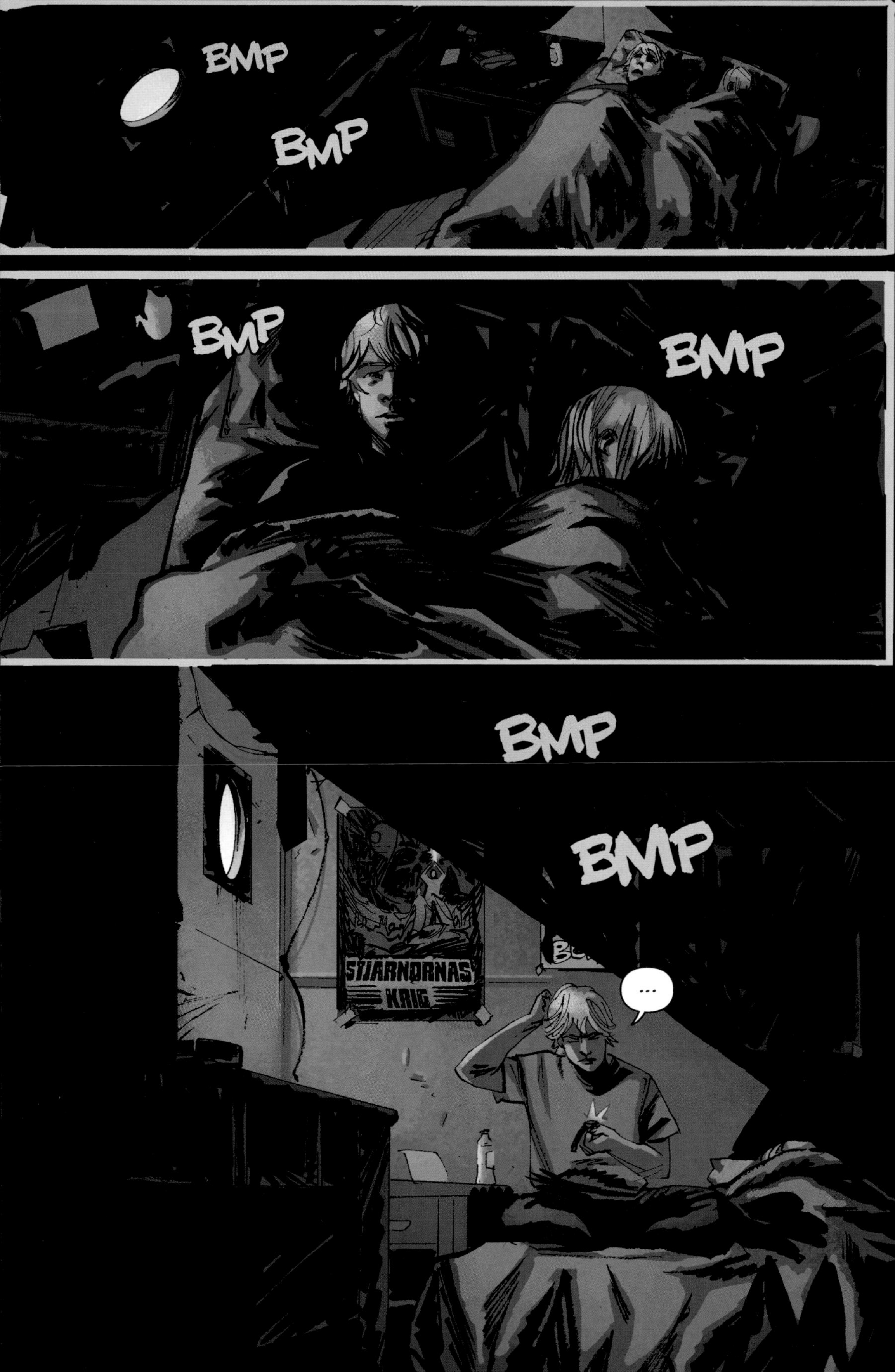
BMP
BMP
BMP
BMP
BMP
BMP
STJÄRNORNAS KRIG
...

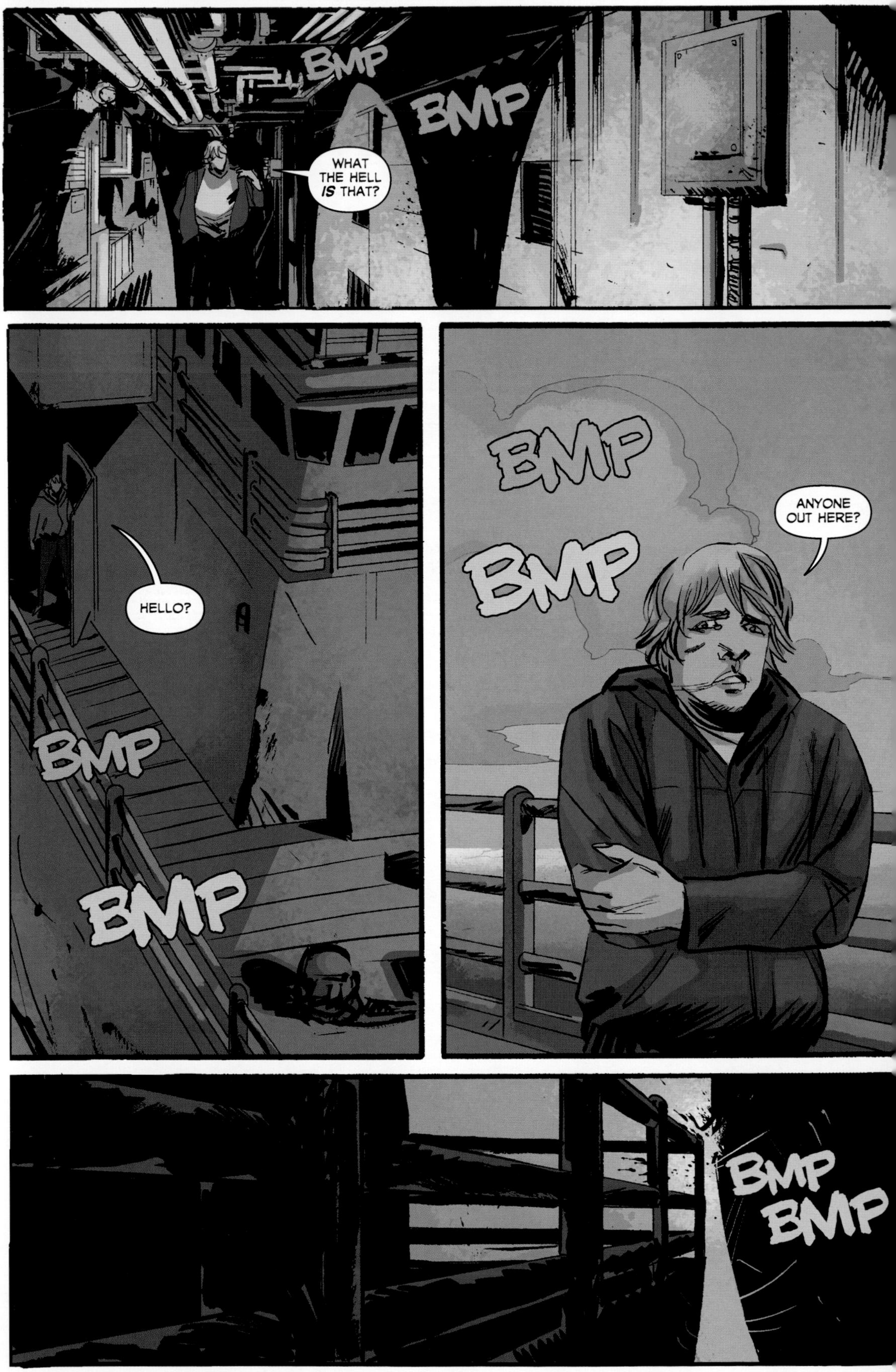
BMP
BMP
WHAT THE HELL *IS* THAT?
HELLO?
BMP
BMP
BMP
BMP
ANYONE OUT HERE?
BMP
BMP

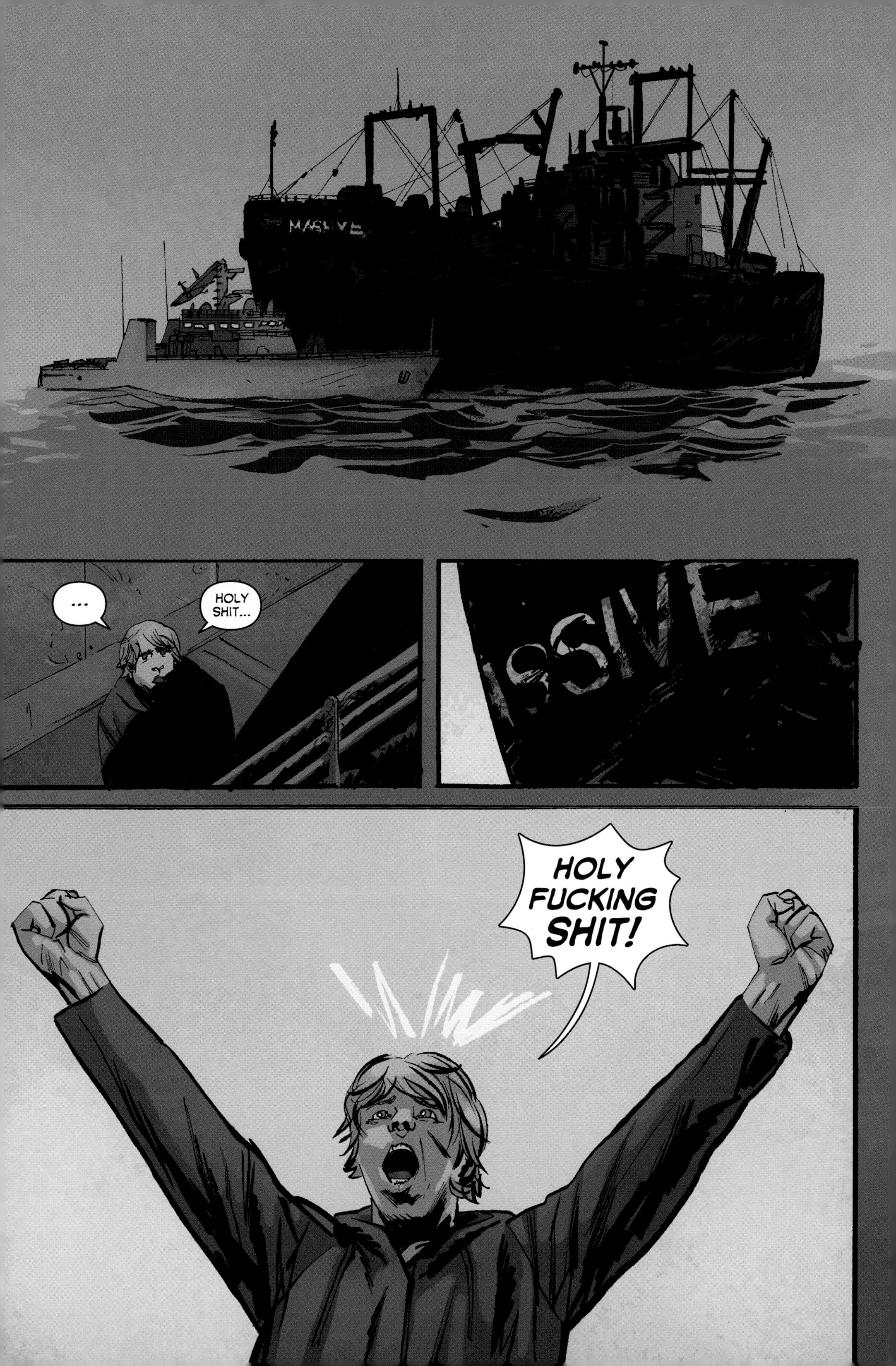
...
HOLY SHIT...
SSIVE
HOLY FUCKING SHIT!

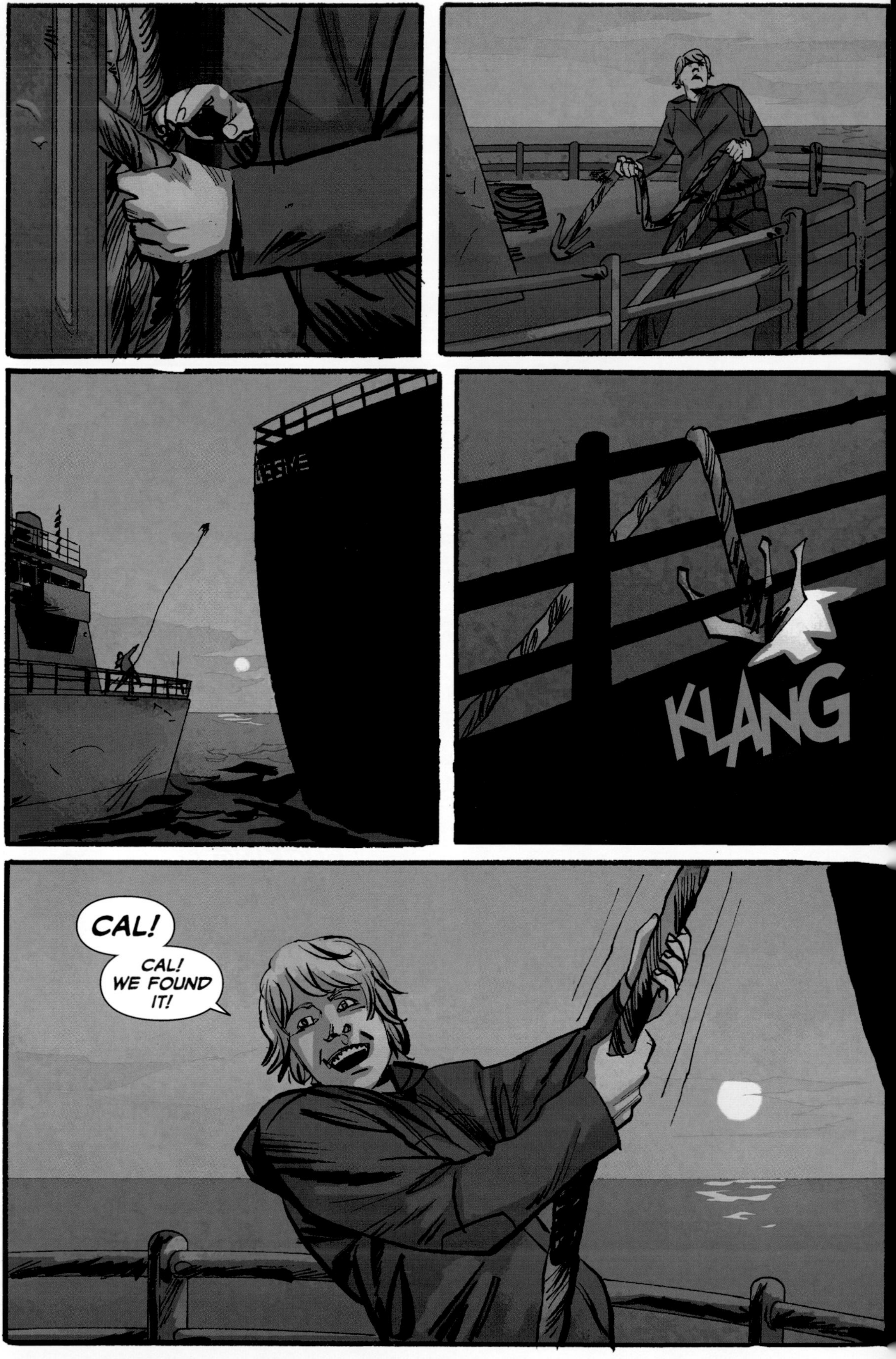
KLANG
CAL!
CAL! WE FOUND IT!

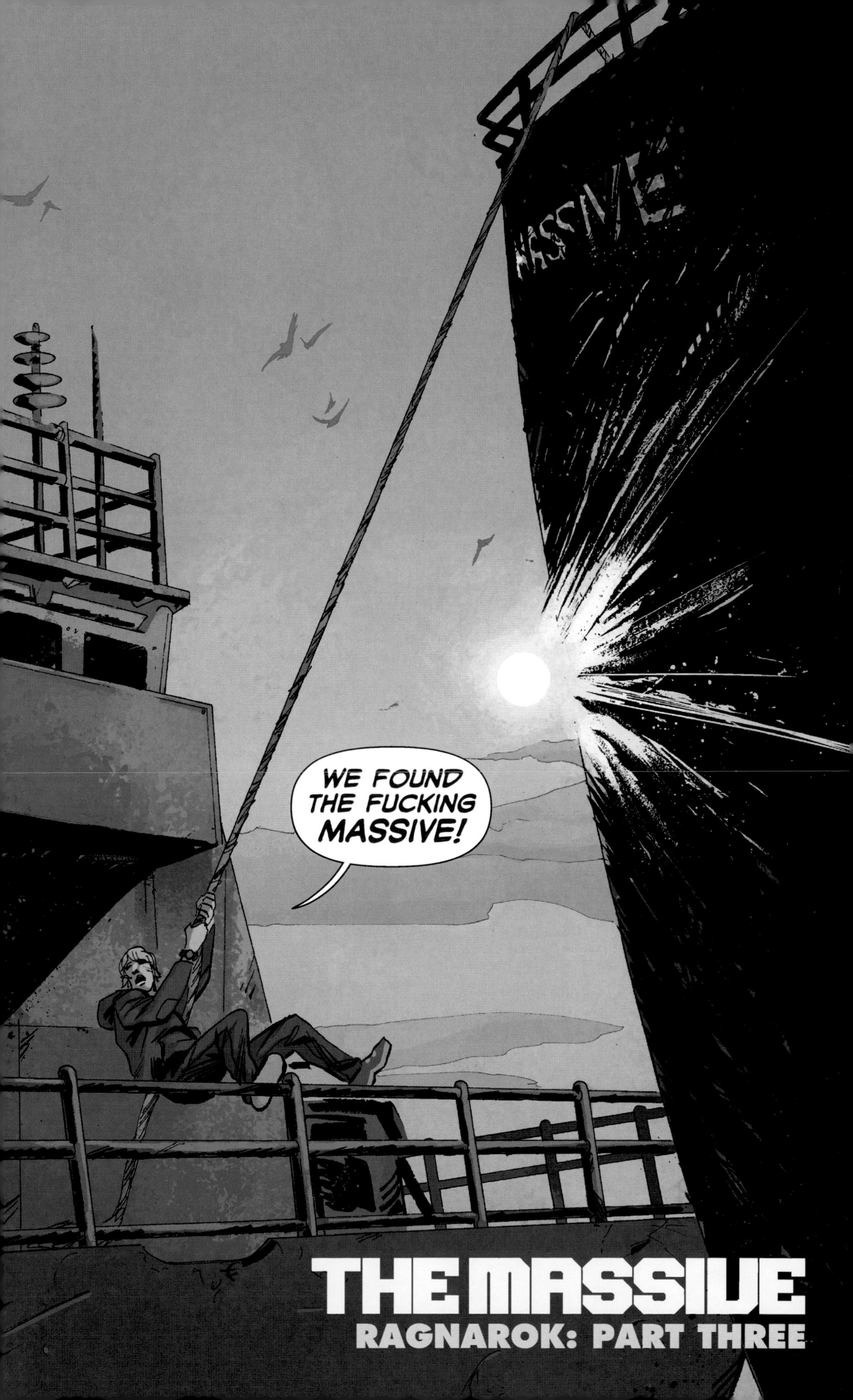
MASSIVE
WE FOUND THE FUCKING MASSIVE!
THE MASSIVE
RAGNAROK: PART THREE

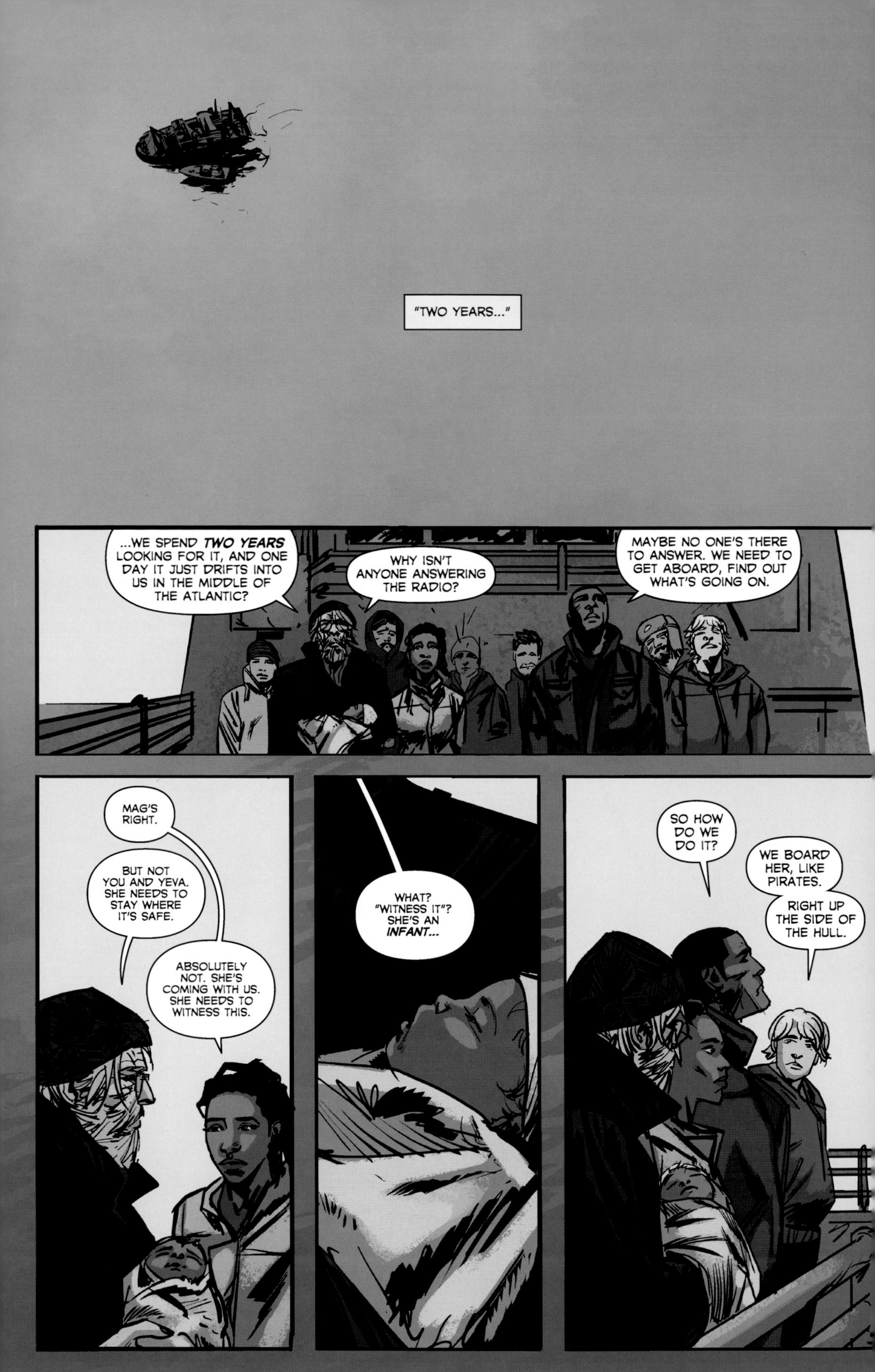
"TWO YEARS..."
...WE SPEND ***TWO YEARS*** LOOKING FOR IT, AND ONE DAY IT JUST DRIFTS INTO US IN THE MIDDLE OF THE ATLANTIC?
WHY ISN'T ANYONE ANSWERING THE RADIO?
MAYBE NO ONE'S THERE TO ANSWER. WE NEED TO GET ABOARD, FIND OUT WHAT'S GOING ON.
MAG'S RIGHT.
BUT NOT YOU AND YEVA. SHE NEEDS TO STAY WHERE IT'S SAFE.
ABSOLUTELY NOT. SHE'S COMING WITH US. SHE NEEDS TO WITNESS THIS.
WHAT? "WITNESS IT"? SHE'S AN ***INFANT...***
SO HOW DO WE DO IT?
WE BOARD HER, LIKE PIRATES.
RIGHT UP THE SIDE OF THE HULL.

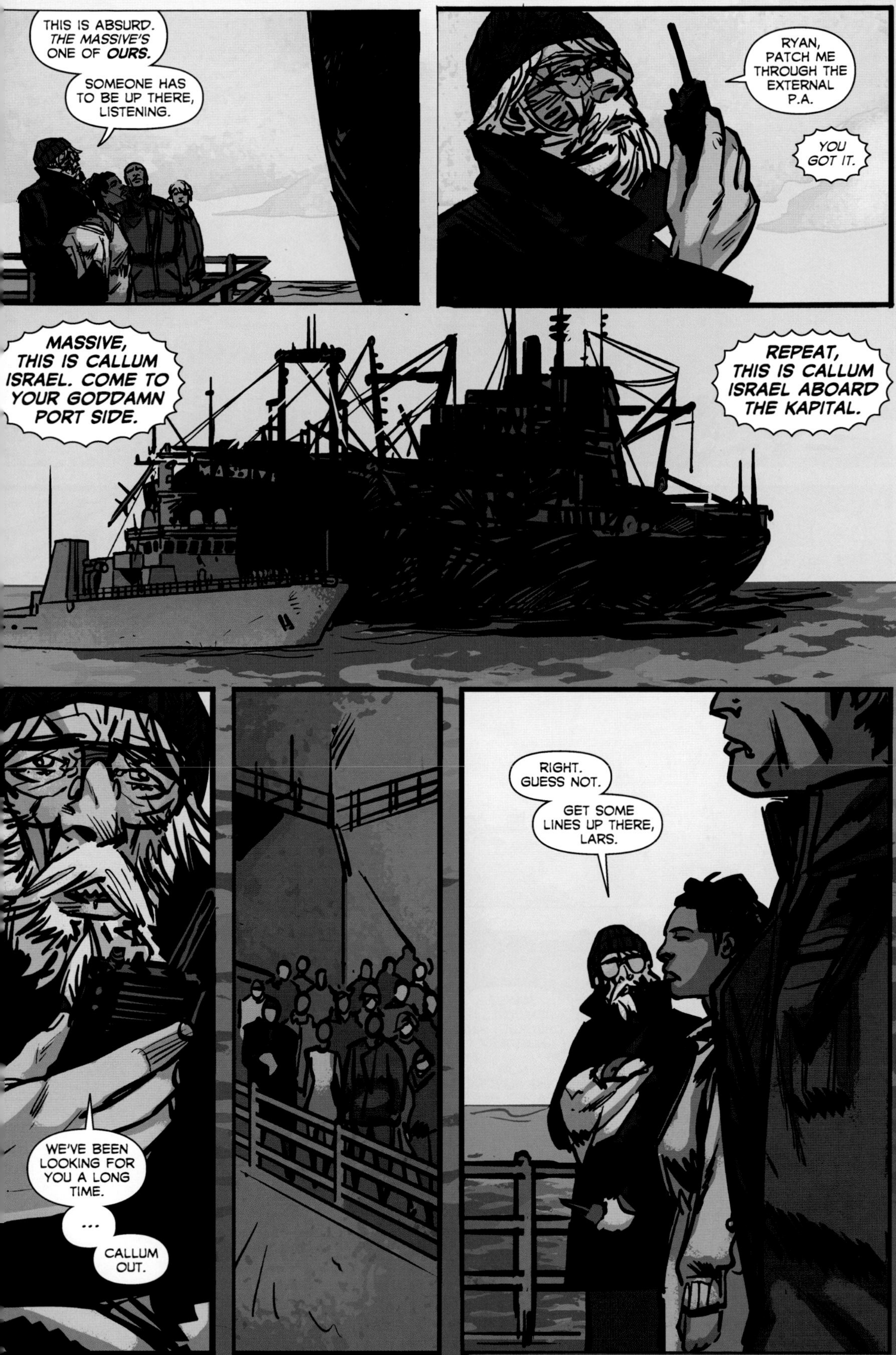
THIS IS ABSURD. *THE MASSIVE'S* ONE OF ***OURS.***
SOMEONE HAS TO BE UP THERE, LISTENING.
RYAN, PATCH ME THROUGH THE EXTERNAL P.A.
YOU GOT IT.
MASSIVE, THIS IS CALLUM ISRAEL. COME TO YOUR GODDAMN PORT SIDE.
REPEAT, THIS IS CALLUM ISRAEL ABOARD THE KAPITAL.
WE'VE BEEN LOOKING FOR YOU A LONG TIME.
...
CALLUM OUT.
RIGHT. GUESS NOT.
GET SOME LINES UP THERE, LARS.

SO WHAT DO YOU THINK, YUSUP?

I THINK I AM TOO FAT TO GO UP THOSE ROPES, AND I THINK THAT IS A GOOD THING. I'LL STAY HERE WITH YOU.

FUCKING GHOST SHIP.

...

THAT'S MORBID.

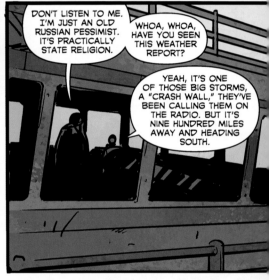

DON'T LISTEN TO ME. I'M JUST AN OLD RUSSIAN PESSIMIST. IT'S PRACTICALLY STATE RELIGION.

WHOA, WHOA, HAVE YOU SEEN THIS WEATHER REPORT?

YEAH, IT'S ONE OF THOSE BIG STORMS, A "CRASH WALL," THEY'VE BEEN CALLING THEM ON THE RADIO. BUT IT'S NINE HUNDRED MILES AWAY AND HEADING SOUTH.

MAYBE WHEN YOU LAST CHECKED, NINE HUNDRED. NOW, *FOUR HUNDRED.* HEADED *HERE.*

WHAT?

SHIT!

"CRASH WALL," WHAT DOES THAT MEAN?

TO *US?*

IT MEANS WE DON'T SURVIVE IT...

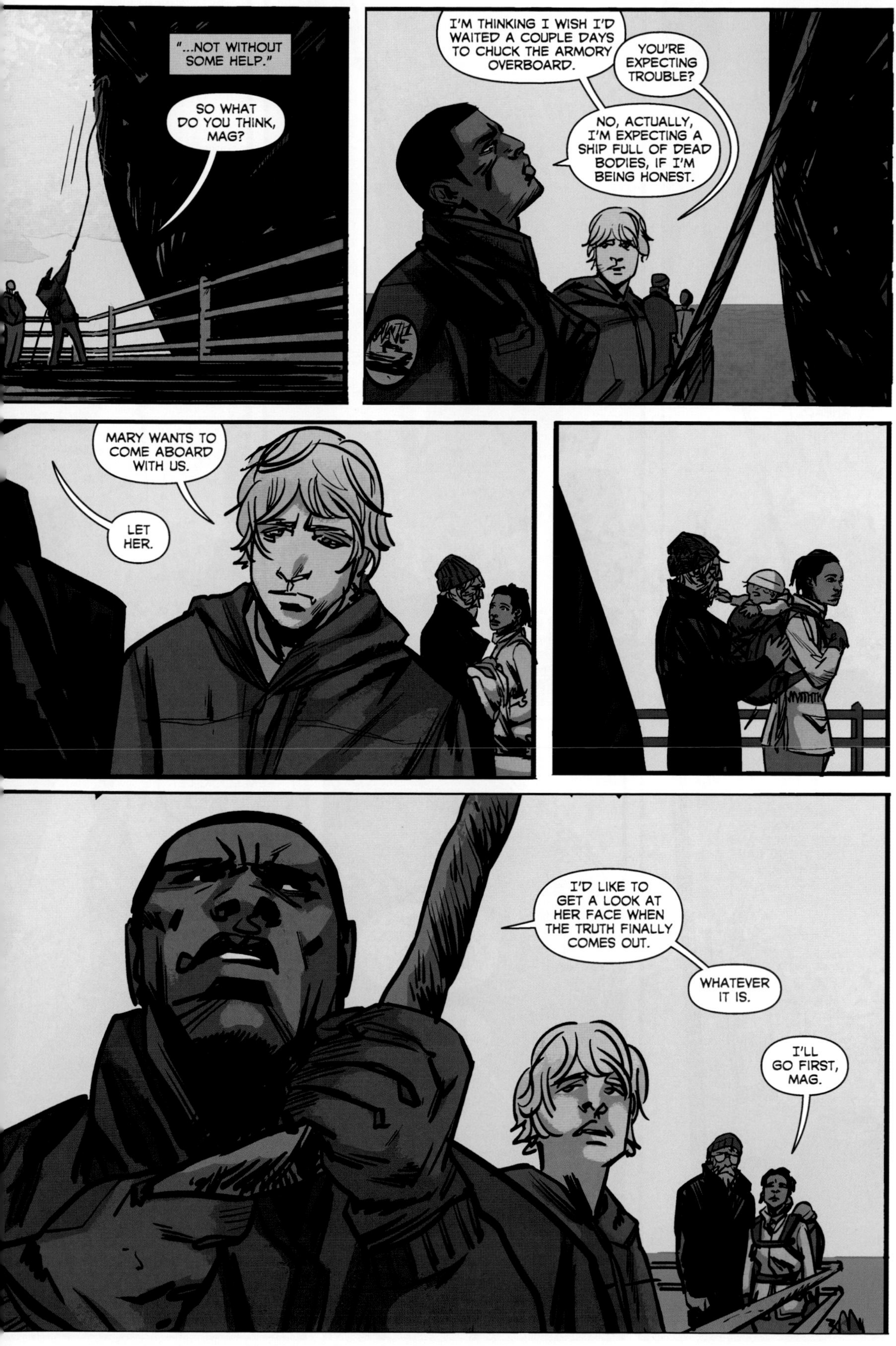
"...NOT WITHOUT SOME HELP."
SO WHAT DO YOU THINK, MAG?
I'M THINKING I WISH I'D WAITED A COUPLE DAYS TO CHUCK THE ARMORY OVERBOARD.
YOU'RE EXPECTING TROUBLE?
NO, ACTUALLY, I'M EXPECTING A SHIP FULL OF DEAD BODIES, IF I'M BEING HONEST.
MARY WANTS TO COME ABOARD WITH US.
LET HER.
I'D LIKE TO GET A LOOK AT HER FACE WHEN THE TRUTH FINALLY COMES OUT.
WHATEVER IT IS.
I'LL GO FIRST, MAG.

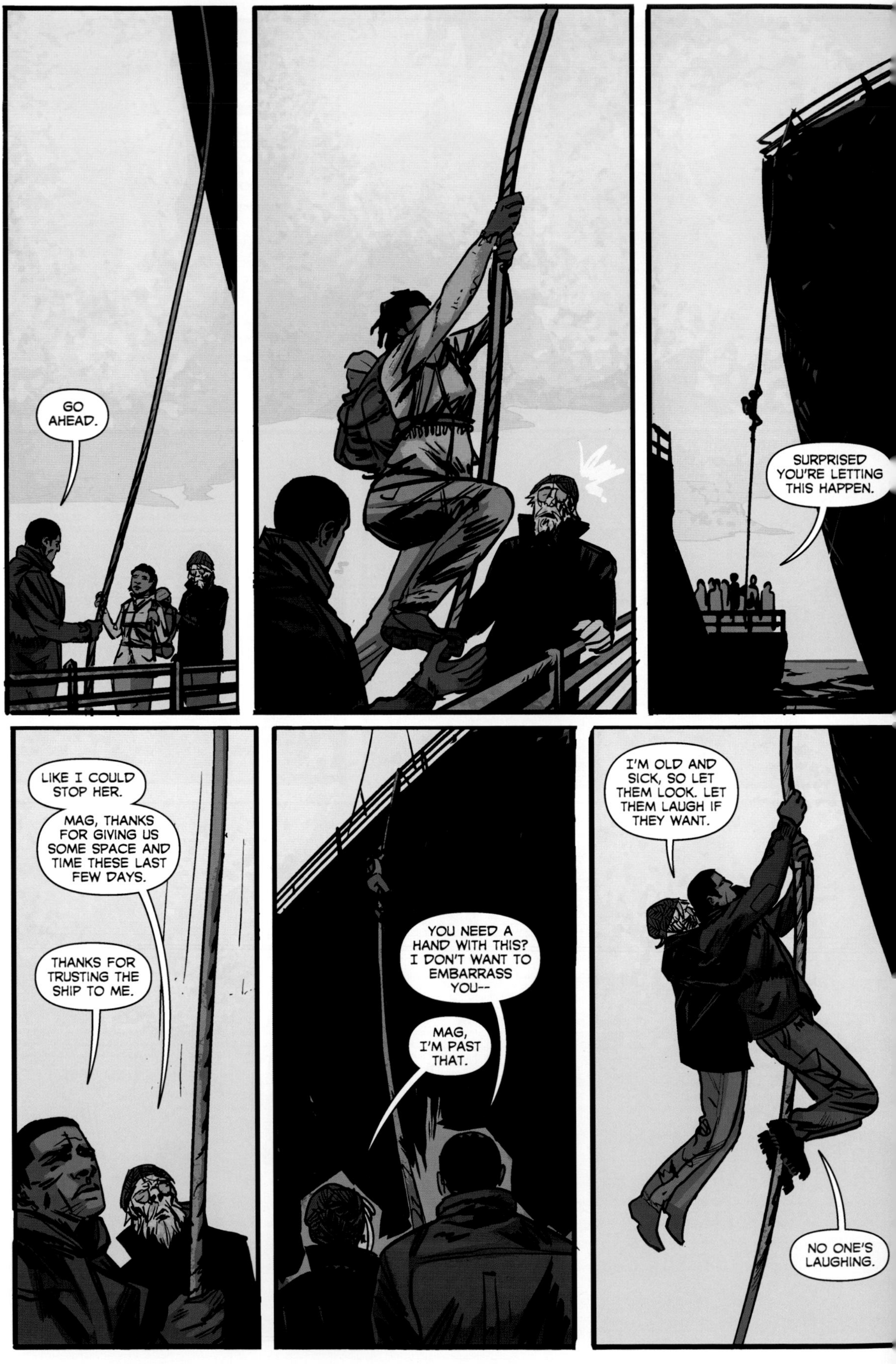
GO AHEAD.
SURPRISED YOU'RE LETTING THIS HAPPEN.
LIKE I COULD STOP HER.
MAG, THANKS FOR GIVING US SOME SPACE AND TIME THESE LAST FEW DAYS.
THANKS FOR TRUSTING THE SHIP TO ME.
YOU NEED A HAND WITH THIS? I DON'T WANT TO EMBARRASS YOU--
MAG, I'M PAST THAT.
I'M OLD AND SICK, SO LET THEM LOOK. LET THEM LAUGH IF THEY WANT.
NO ONE'S LAUGHING.

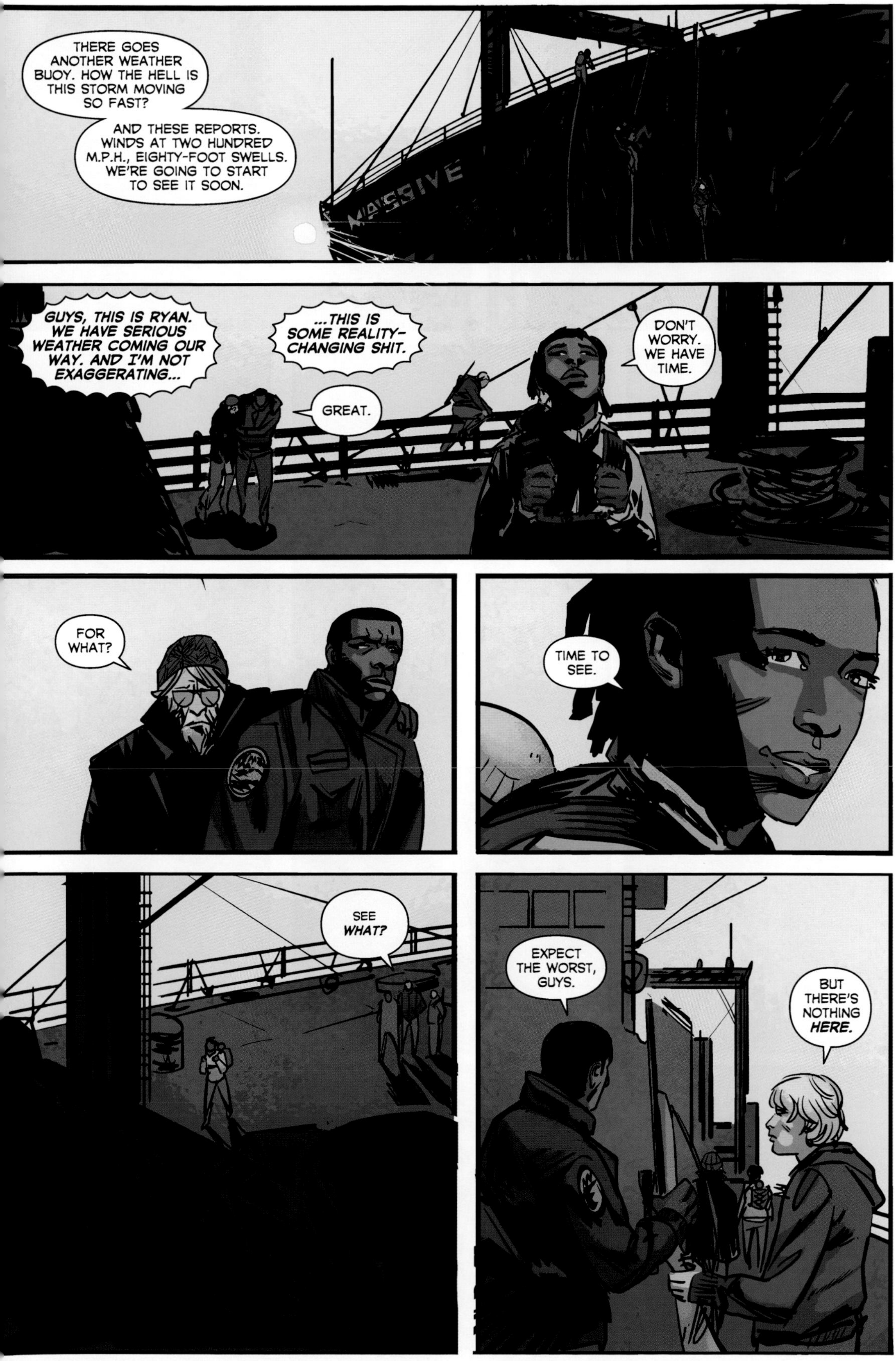
THERE GOES ANOTHER WEATHER BUOY. HOW THE HELL IS THIS STORM MOVING SO FAST?
AND THESE REPORTS. WINDS AT TWO HUNDRED M.P.H., EIGHTY-FOOT SWELLS. WE'RE GOING TO START TO SEE IT SOON.
MASSIVE
GUYS, THIS IS RYAN. WE HAVE SERIOUS WEATHER COMING OUR WAY. AND I'M NOT EXAGGERATING...
...THIS IS SOME REALITY-CHANGING SHIT.
GREAT.
DON'T WORRY. WE HAVE TIME.
FOR WHAT?
TIME TO SEE.
SEE *WHAT?*
EXPECT THE WORST, GUYS.
BUT THERE'S NOTHING *HERE.*

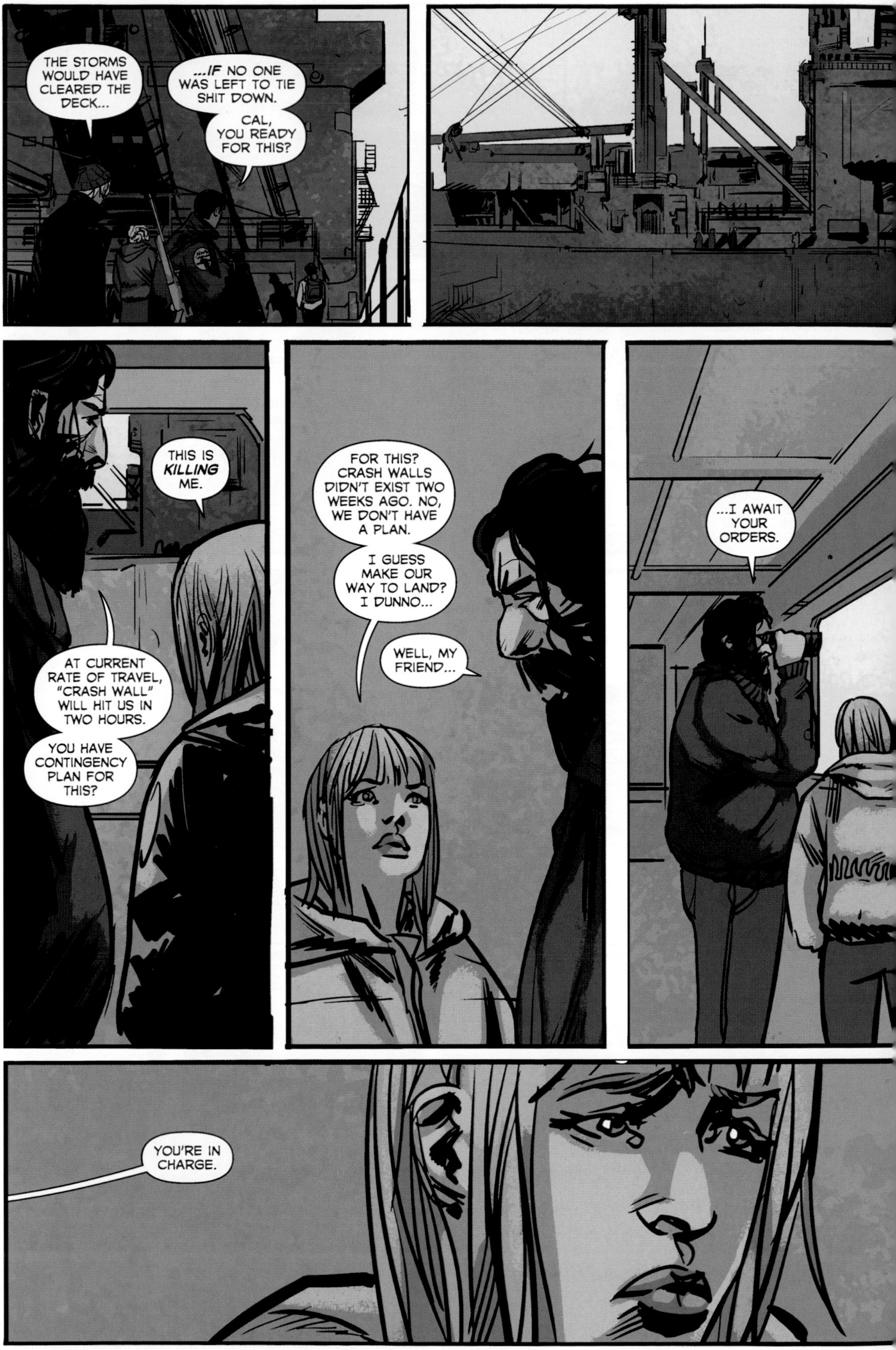
THE STORMS WOULD HAVE CLEARED THE DECK...
...IF NO ONE WAS LEFT TO TIE SHIT DOWN.
CAL, YOU READY FOR THIS?
THIS IS KILLING ME.
AT CURRENT RATE OF TRAVEL, "CRASH WALL" WILL HIT US IN TWO HOURS.
YOU HAVE CONTINGENCY PLAN FOR THIS?
FOR THIS? CRASH WALLS DIDN'T EXIST TWO WEEKS AGO. NO, WE DON'T HAVE A PLAN.
I GUESS MAKE OUR WAY TO LAND? I DUNNO...
WELL, MY FRIEND...
...I AWAIT YOUR ORDERS.
YOU'RE IN CHARGE.

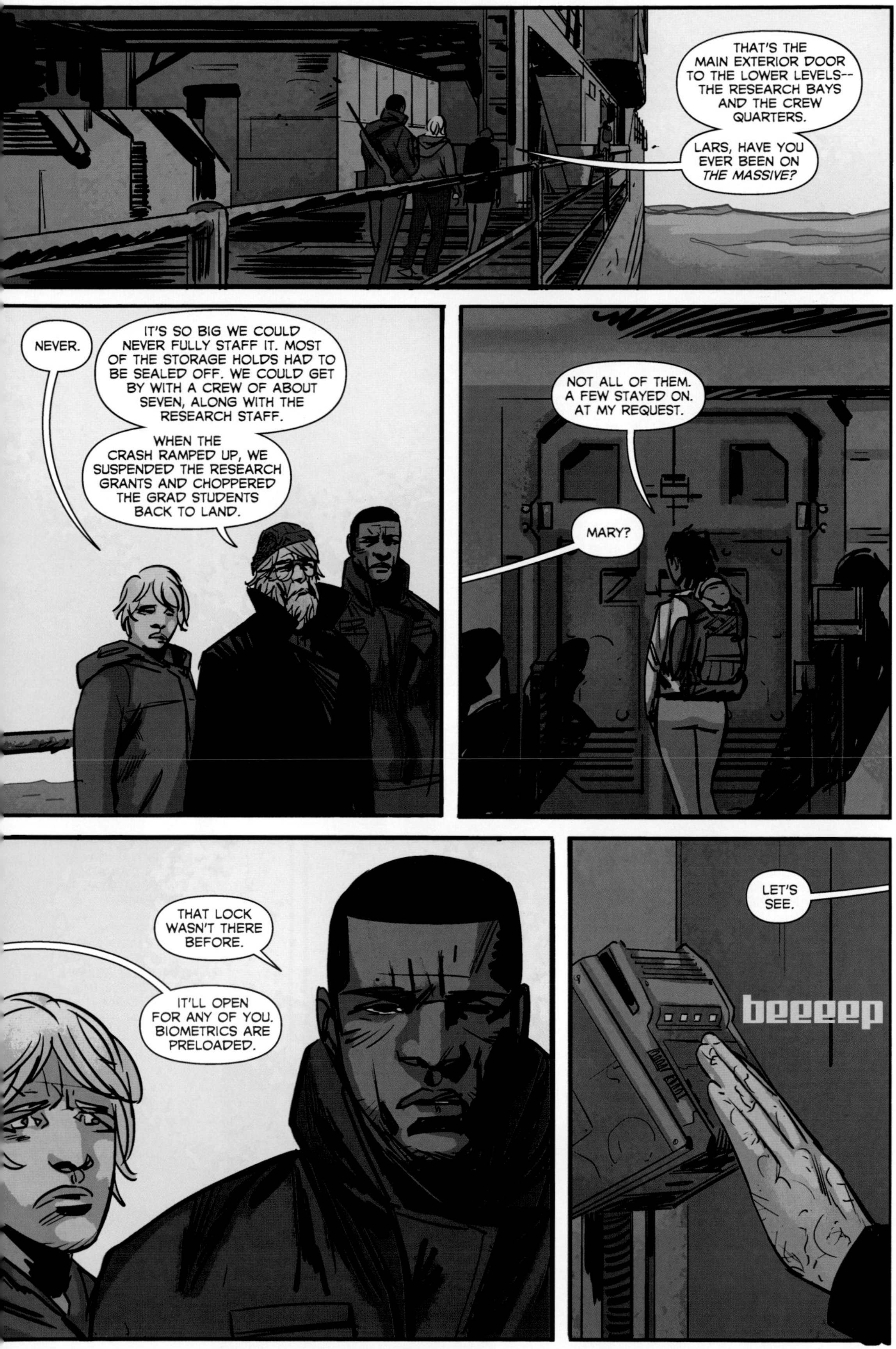
THAT'S THE MAIN EXTERIOR DOOR TO THE LOWER LEVELS-- THE RESEARCH BAYS AND THE CREW QUARTERS.
LARS, HAVE YOU EVER BEEN ON *THE MASSIVE?*
NEVER.
IT'S SO BIG WE COULD NEVER FULLY STAFF IT. MOST OF THE STORAGE HOLDS HAD TO BE SEALED OFF. WE COULD GET BY WITH A CREW OF ABOUT SEVEN, ALONG WITH THE RESEARCH STAFF.
WHEN THE CRASH RAMPED UP, WE SUSPENDED THE RESEARCH GRANTS AND CHOPPERED THE GRAD STUDENTS BACK TO LAND.
NOT ALL OF THEM. A FEW STAYED ON. AT MY REQUEST.
MARY?
THAT LOCK WASN'T THERE BEFORE.
IT'LL OPEN FOR ANY OF YOU. BIOMETRICS ARE PRELOADED.
LET'S SEE.
beeeep

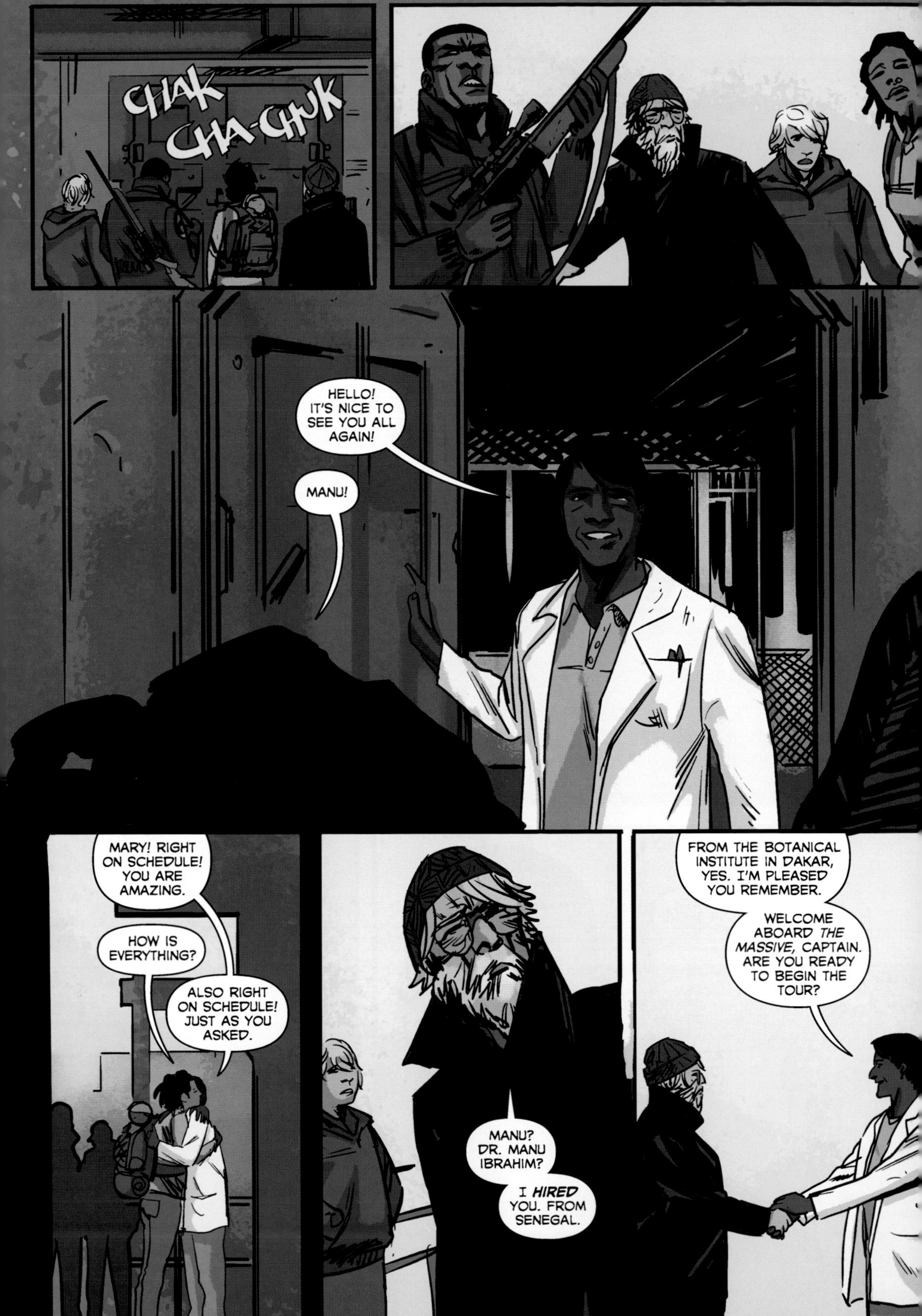
CHAK CHA-CHUK
HELLO! IT'S NICE TO SEE YOU ALL AGAIN!
MANU!
MARY! RIGHT ON SCHEDULE! YOU ARE AMAZING.
HOW IS EVERYTHING?
ALSO RIGHT ON SCHEDULE! JUST AS YOU ASKED.
MANU? DR. MANU IBRAHIM?
I *HIRED* YOU. FROM SENEGAL.
FROM THE BOTANICAL INSTITUTE IN DAKAR, YES. I'M PLEASED YOU REMEMBER.
WELCOME ABOARD *THE MASSIVE,* CAPTAIN. ARE YOU READY TO BEGIN THE TOUR?

THE TOPMOST LEVEL IS OUR GREENHOUSE. WE'VE SELECTED OUR NAVIGATION PATTERNS TO CREATE "SEASONS" OF A SORT, USING THE EXTERIOR TEMPERATURE AND WEATHER AS MUCH AS WE CAN.

THE CRASH HAS MADE THIS DIFFICULT, OF COURSE.

BUT WE ESTIMATE WE CAN SUCCESSFULLY HARVEST THE EQUIVALENT OF TWELVE ACRES OF FARMLAND EVERY SIX MONTHS OR SO.

WE'VE MODIFIED THE DECK TO ALLOW FOR FRESH AIR AND SUNLIGHT. WE HAVE STORAGE TANKS TO COLLECT RAINWATER AND AN IRRIGATION SYSTEM.

THE NEXT LEVEL DOWN IS ROOT VEGETABLES AND A SMALL BUT PRODUCTIVE FISH FARM. MOST OF THE CREW IS DOWN THERE.

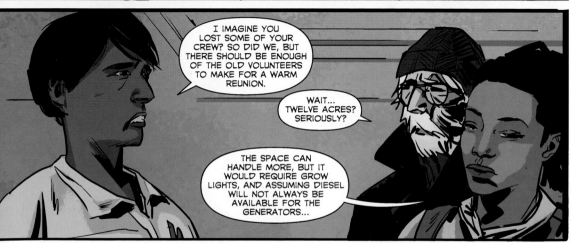

I IMAGINE YOU LOST SOME OF YOUR CREW? SO DID WE, BUT THERE SHOULD BE ENOUGH OF THE OLD VOLUNTEERS TO MAKE FOR A WARM REUNION.

WAIT... TWELVE ACRES? SERIOUSLY?

THE SPACE CAN HANDLE MORE, BUT IT WOULD REQUIRE GROW LIGHTS, AND ASSUMING DIESEL WILL NOT ALWAYS BE AVAILABLE FOR THE GENERATORS...

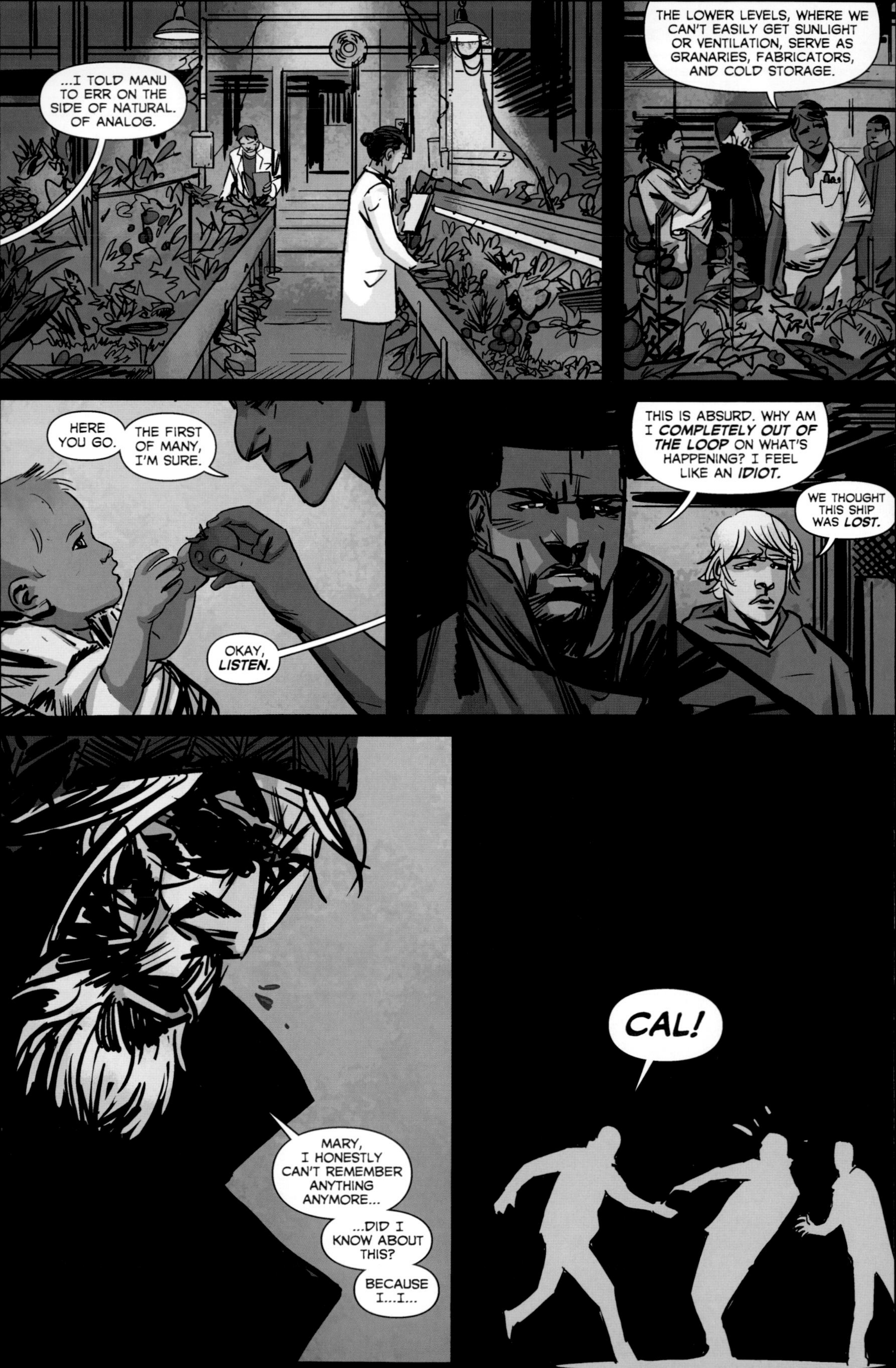
...I TOLD MANU TO ERR ON THE SIDE OF NATURAL. OF ANALOG.
THE LOWER LEVELS, WHERE WE CAN'T EASILY GET SUNLIGHT OR VENTILATION, SERVE AS GRANARIES, FABRICATORS, AND COLD STORAGE.
HERE YOU GO.
THE FIRST OF MANY, I'M SURE.
OKAY, LISTEN.
THIS IS ABSURD. WHY AM I COMPLETELY OUT OF THE LOOP ON WHAT'S HAPPENING? I FEEL LIKE AN IDIOT.
WE THOUGHT THIS SHIP WAS LOST.
MARY, I HONESTLY CAN'T REMEMBER ANYTHING ANYMORE...
...DID I KNOW ABOUT THIS?
BECAUSE I...I...
CAL!

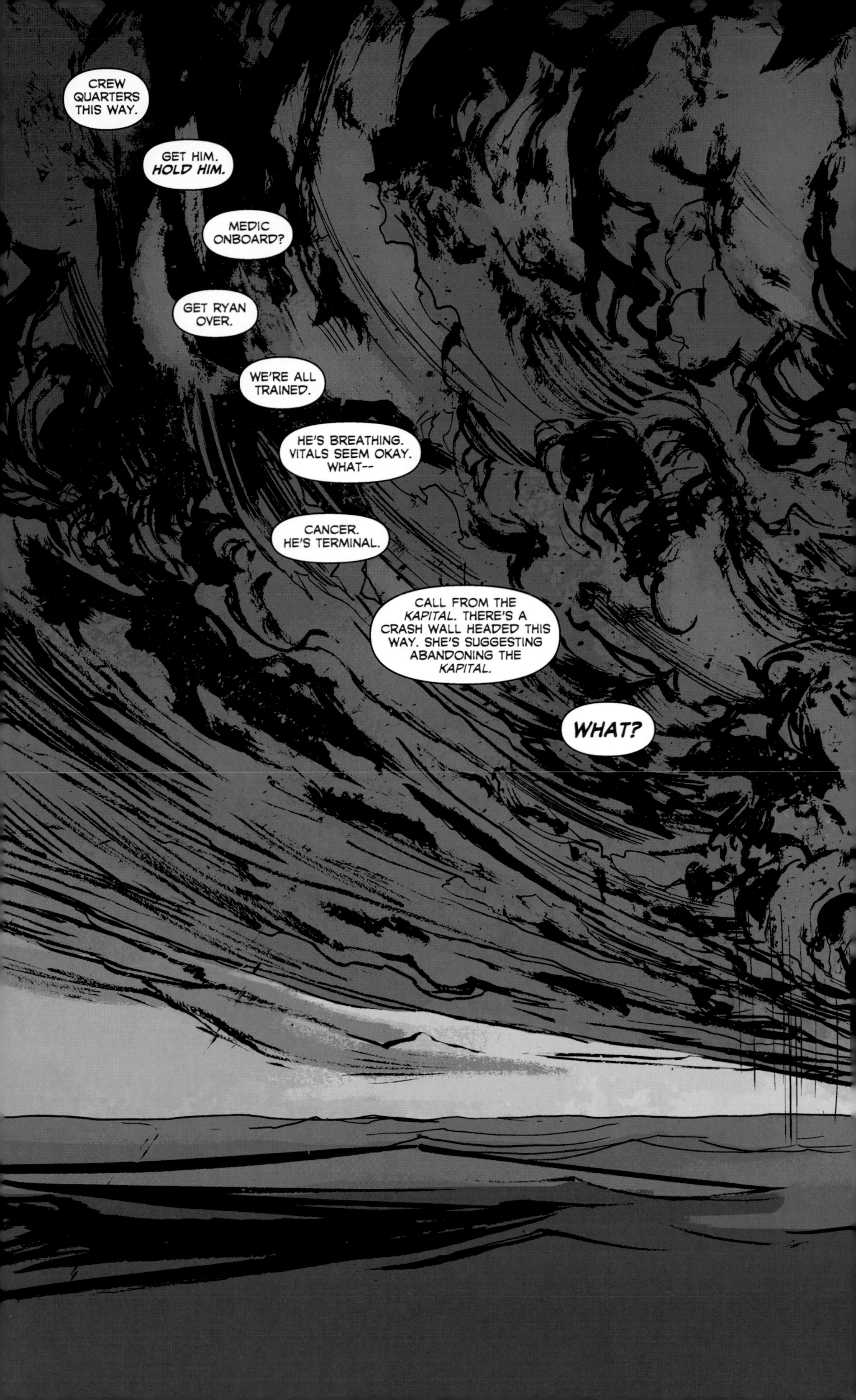

CREW QUARTERS THIS WAY.
GET HIM. *HOLD HIM.*
MEDIC ONBOARD?
GET RYAN OVER.
WE'RE ALL TRAINED.
HE'S BREATHING. VITALS SEEM OKAY. WHAT--
CANCER. HE'S TERMINAL.
CALL FROM THE *KAPITAL.* THERE'S A CRASH WALL HEADED THIS WAY. SHE'S SUGGESTING ABANDONING THE *KAPITAL.*
WHAT?

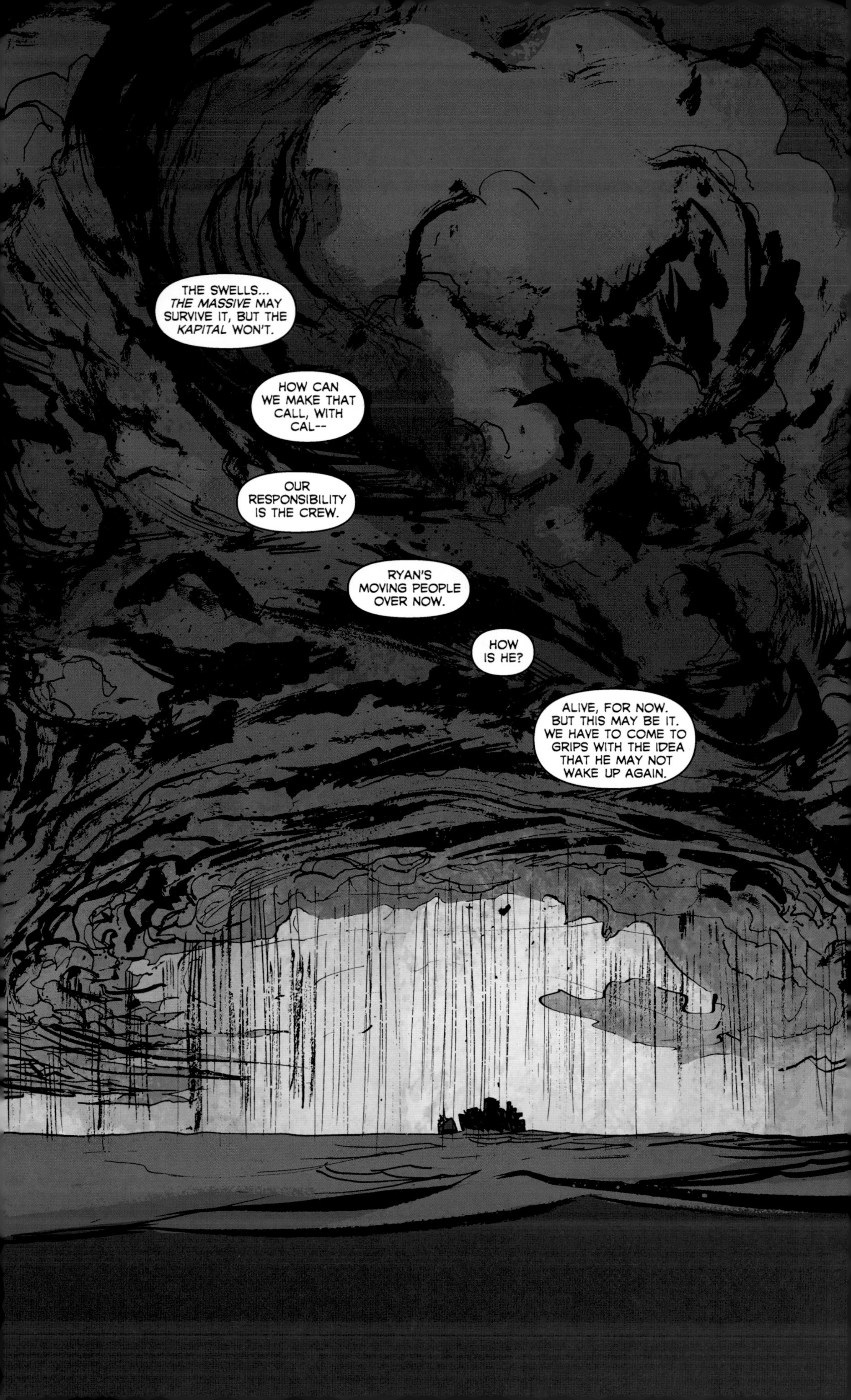
THE SWELLS... *THE MASSIVE* MAY SURVIVE IT, BUT THE *KAPITAL* WON'T.
HOW CAN WE MAKE THAT CALL, WITH CAL--
OUR RESPONSIBILITY IS THE CREW.
RYAN'S MOVING PEOPLE OVER NOW.
HOW IS HE?
ALIVE, FOR NOW. BUT THIS MAY BE IT. WE HAVE TO COME TO GRIPS WITH THE IDEA THAT HE MAY NOT WAKE UP AGAIN.

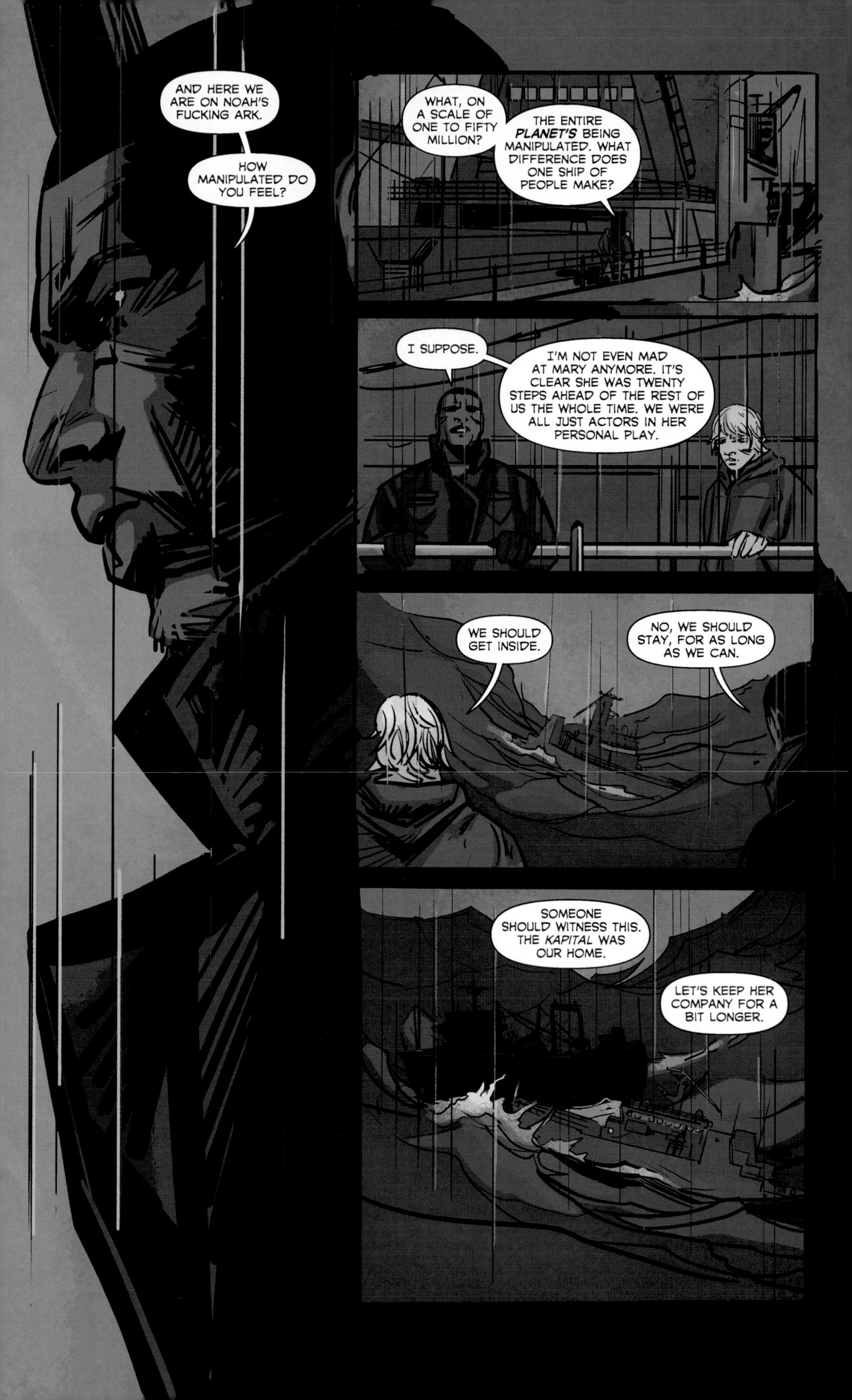
AND HERE WE ARE ON NOAH'S FUCKING ARK.
HOW MANIPULATED DO YOU FEEL?
WHAT, ON A SCALE OF ONE TO FIFTY MILLION?
THE ENTIRE *PLANET'S* BEING MANIPULATED. WHAT DIFFERENCE DOES ONE SHIP OF PEOPLE MAKE?
I SUPPOSE.
I'M NOT EVEN MAD AT MARY ANYMORE. IT'S CLEAR SHE WAS TWENTY STEPS AHEAD OF THE REST OF US THE WHOLE TIME. WE WERE ALL JUST ACTORS IN HER PERSONAL PLAY.
WE SHOULD GET INSIDE.
NO, WE SHOULD STAY, FOR AS LONG AS WE CAN.
SOMEONE SHOULD WITNESS THIS. THE *KAPITAL* WAS OUR HOME.
LET'S KEEP HER COMPANY FOR A BIT LONGER.

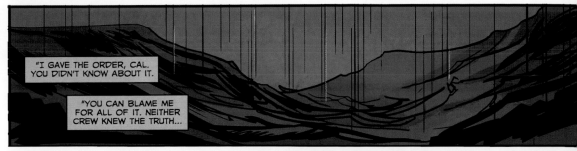

"I GAVE THE ORDER, CAL. YOU DIDN'T KNOW ABOUT IT.

"YOU CAN BLAME ME FOR ALL OF IT. NEITHER CREW KNEW THE TRUTH...

"...THAT THE *KAPITAL* WAS LOOKING FOR *THE MASSIVE*, AND THAT *THE MASSIVE* HAD A SECRET MISSION.

"BUT WOULD ANY OF YOU HAVE BELIEVED ME IF I'D TOLD YOU?

"THIS IS HOW THE WORLD DIES.

"BUT SOME CAN STILL LIVE."

THIS IS MY GIFT TO YOU. NINTH WAVE CAN SURVIVE THIS.

THE MASSIVE IS LARGE ENOUGH AND PREPARED ENOUGH TO BE A SHELTER FROM WHAT'S TO COME.

AND SHE'S FILLED WITH GOOD PEOPLE...

...WHO CAN BE A FAMILY TO OUR DAUGHTER.

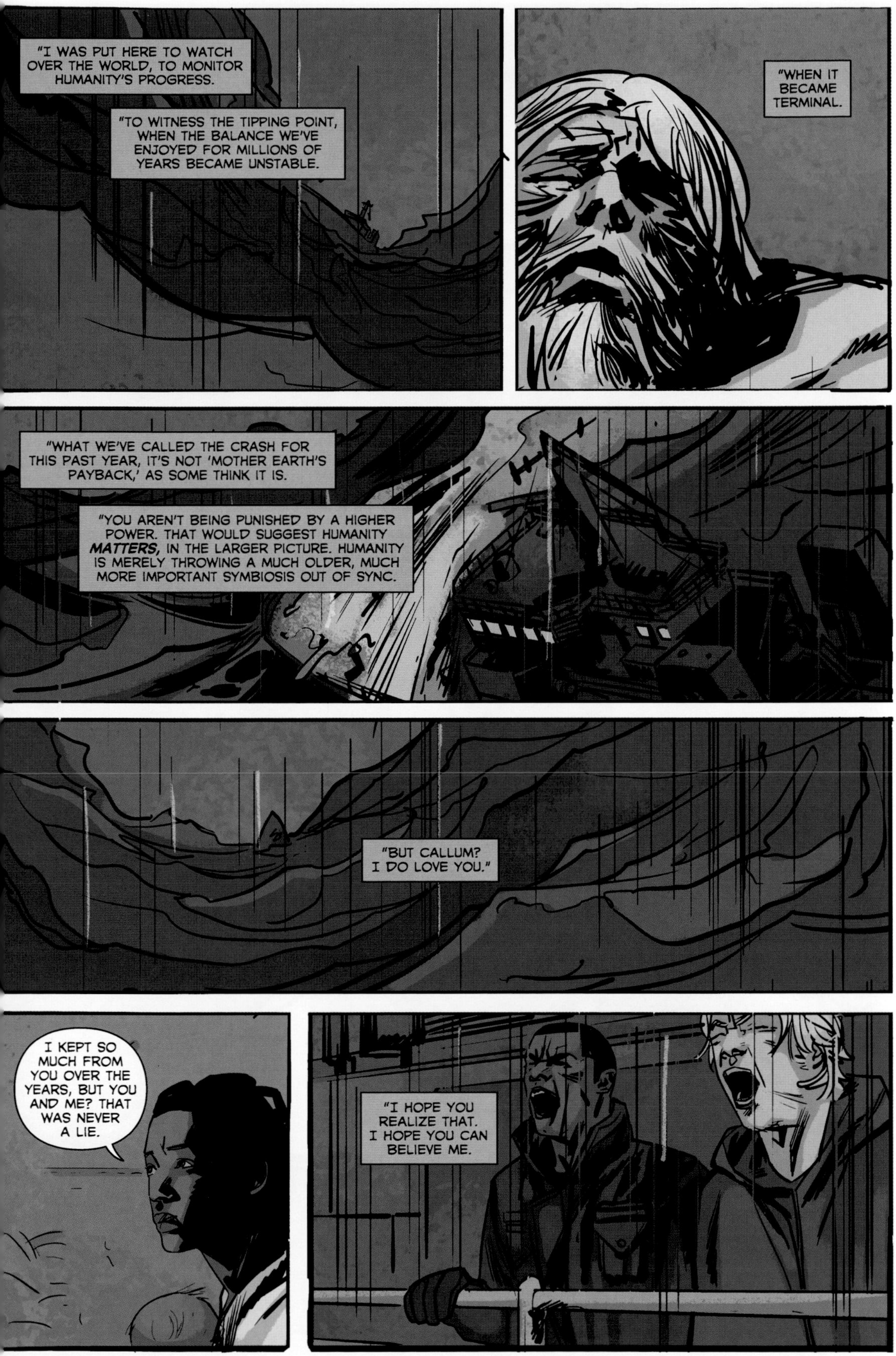
"I WAS PUT HERE TO WATCH OVER THE WORLD, TO MONITOR HUMANITY'S PROGRESS.
"TO WITNESS THE TIPPING POINT, WHEN THE BALANCE WE'VE ENJOYED FOR MILLIONS OF YEARS BECAME UNSTABLE.
"WHEN IT BECAME TERMINAL.
"WHAT WE'VE CALLED THE CRASH FOR THIS PAST YEAR, IT'S NOT 'MOTHER EARTH'S PAYBACK,' AS SOME THINK IT IS.
"YOU AREN'T BEING PUNISHED BY A HIGHER POWER. THAT WOULD SUGGEST HUMANITY ***MATTERS,*** IN THE LARGER PICTURE. HUMANITY IS MERELY THROWING A MUCH OLDER, MUCH MORE IMPORTANT SYMBIOSIS OUT OF SYNC.
"BUT CALLUM? I DO LOVE YOU."
I KEPT SO MUCH FROM YOU OVER THE YEARS, BUT YOU AND ME? THAT WAS NEVER A LIE.
"I HOPE YOU REALIZE THAT. I HOPE YOU CAN BELIEVE ME.

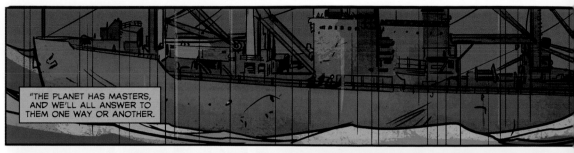

"THE PLANET HAS MASTERS, AND WE'LL ALL ANSWER TO THEM ONE WAY OR ANOTHER.

"I'LL PAY A HEAVY PRICE FOR THIS, BUT IT'S WORTH PAYING. YEVA IS WORTH EVERYTHING."

ARE YOU READY?

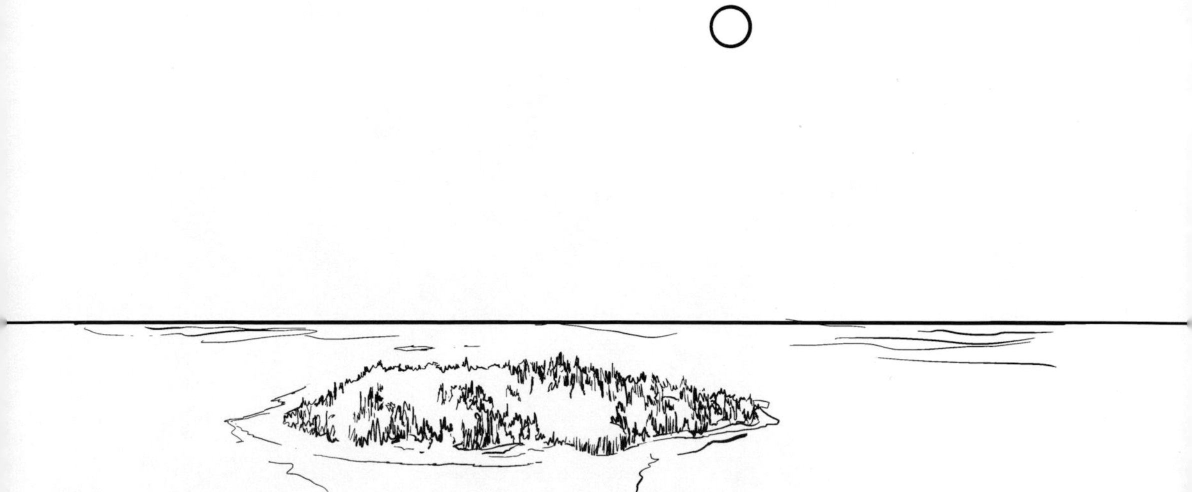

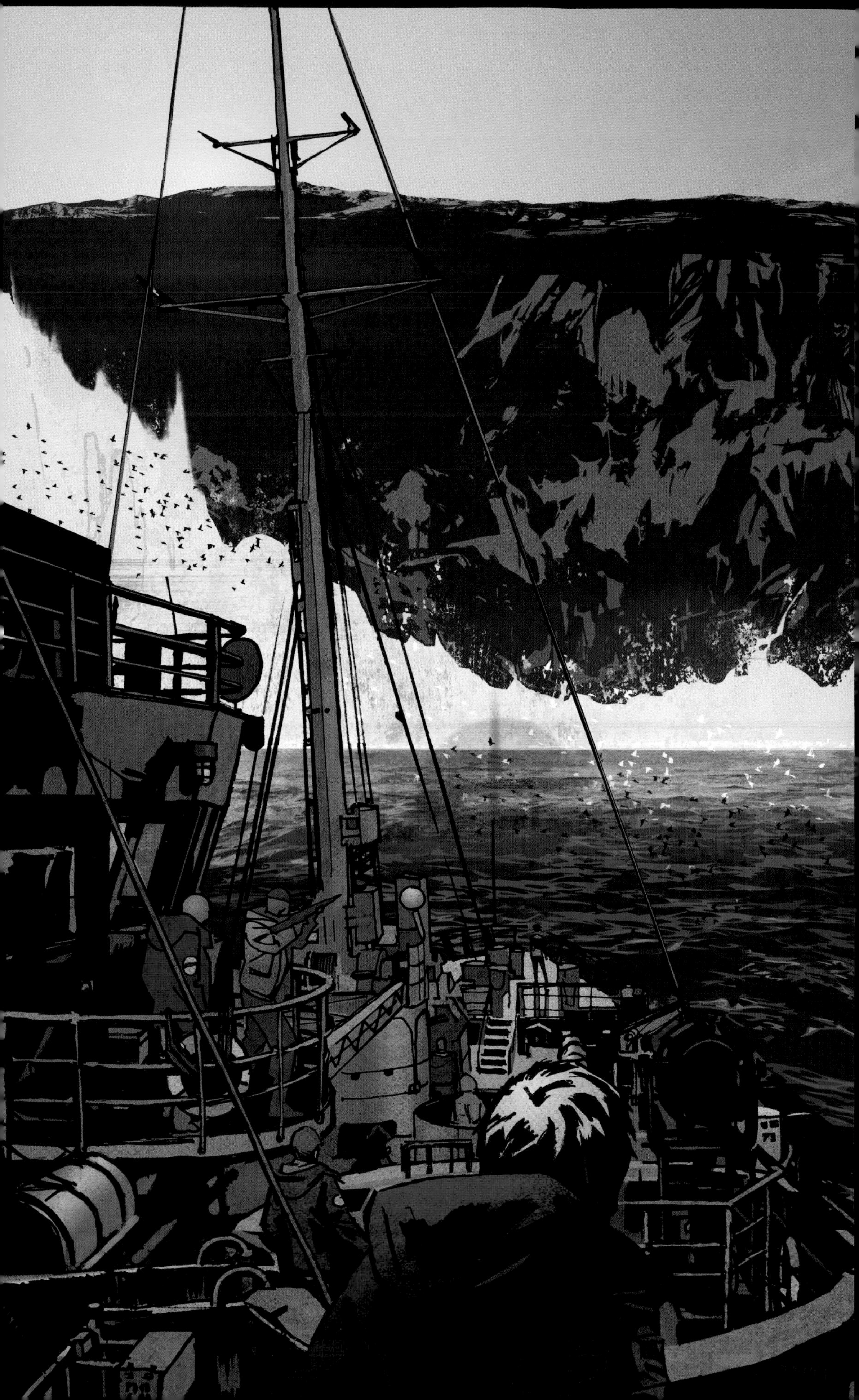

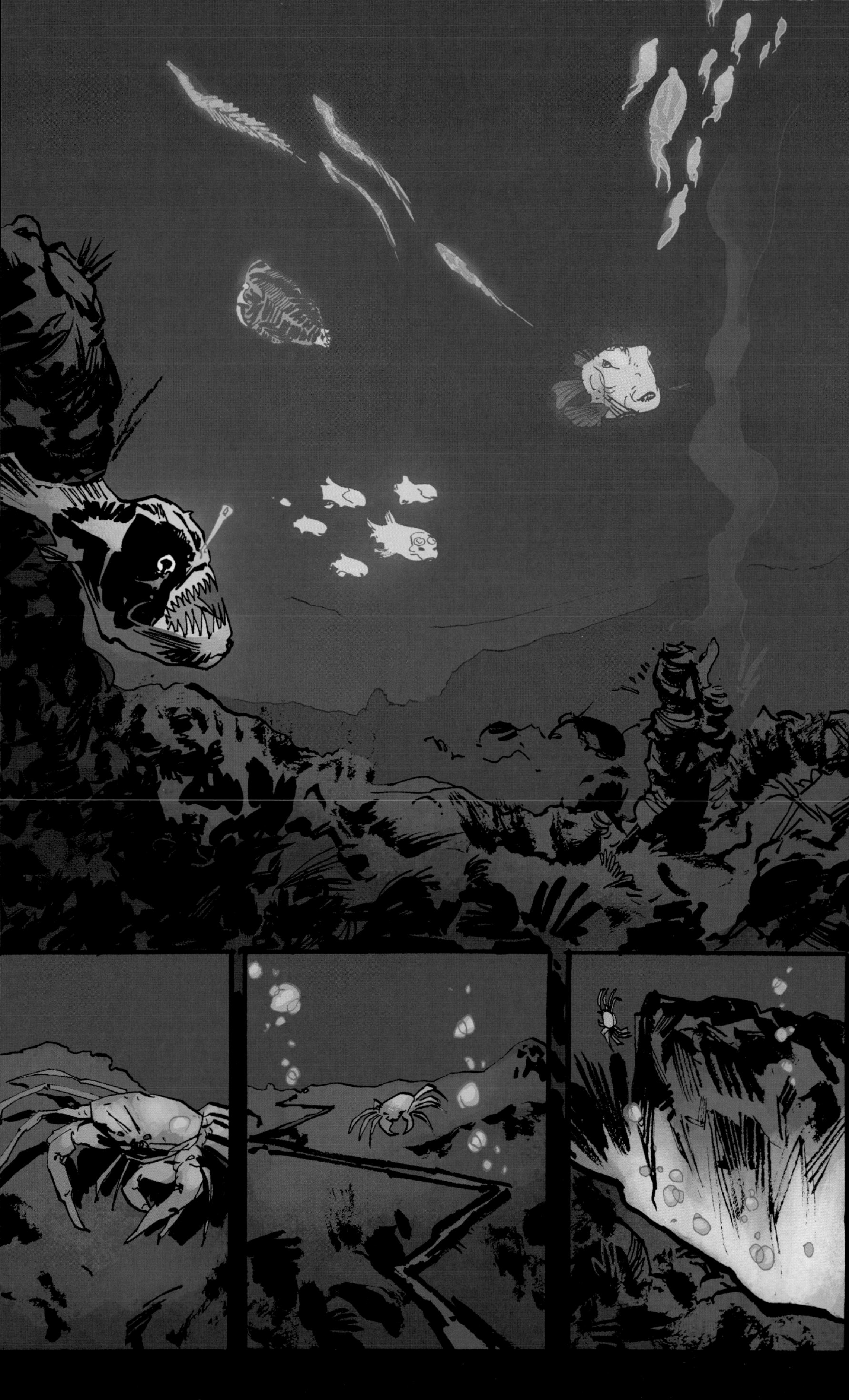

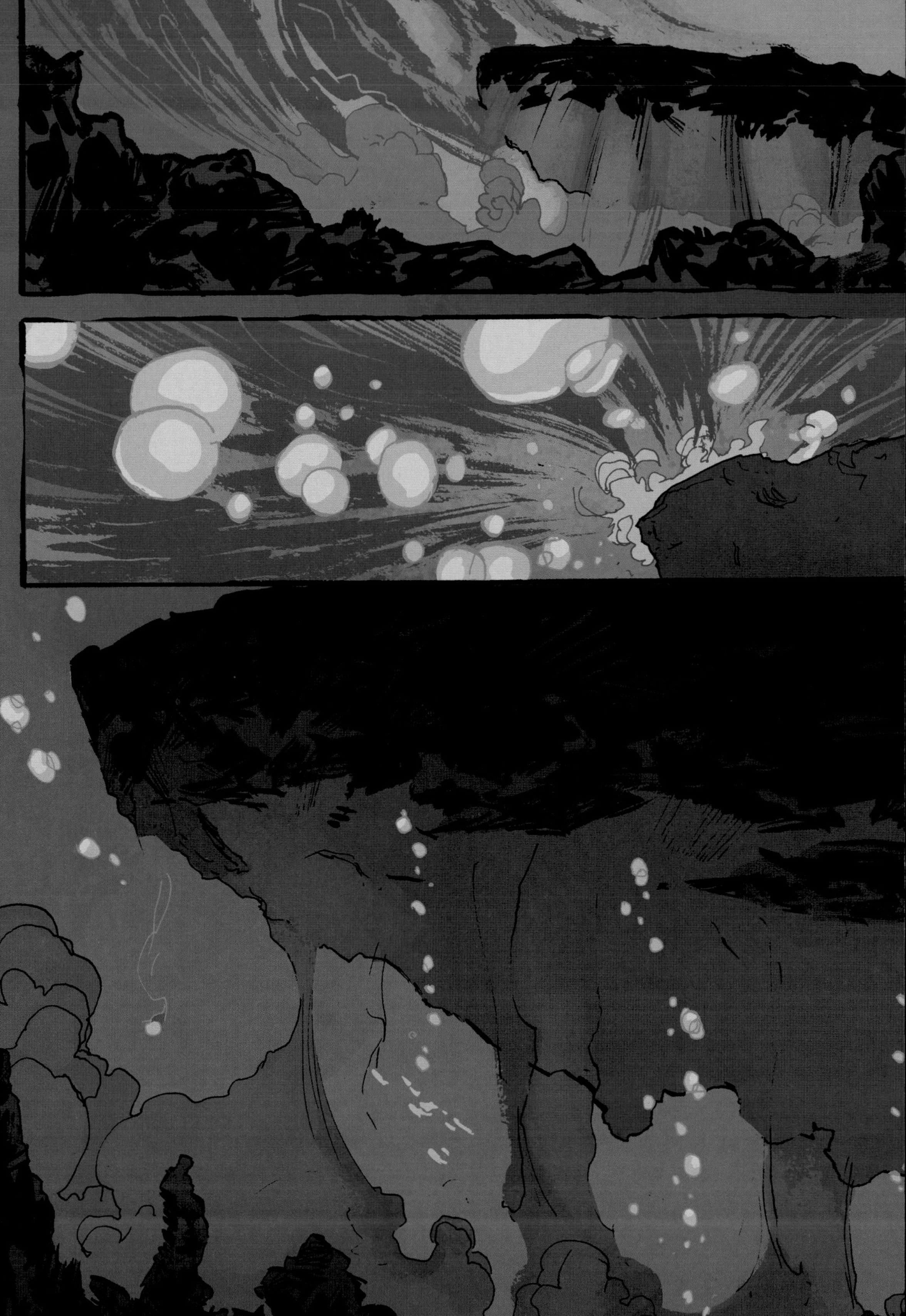

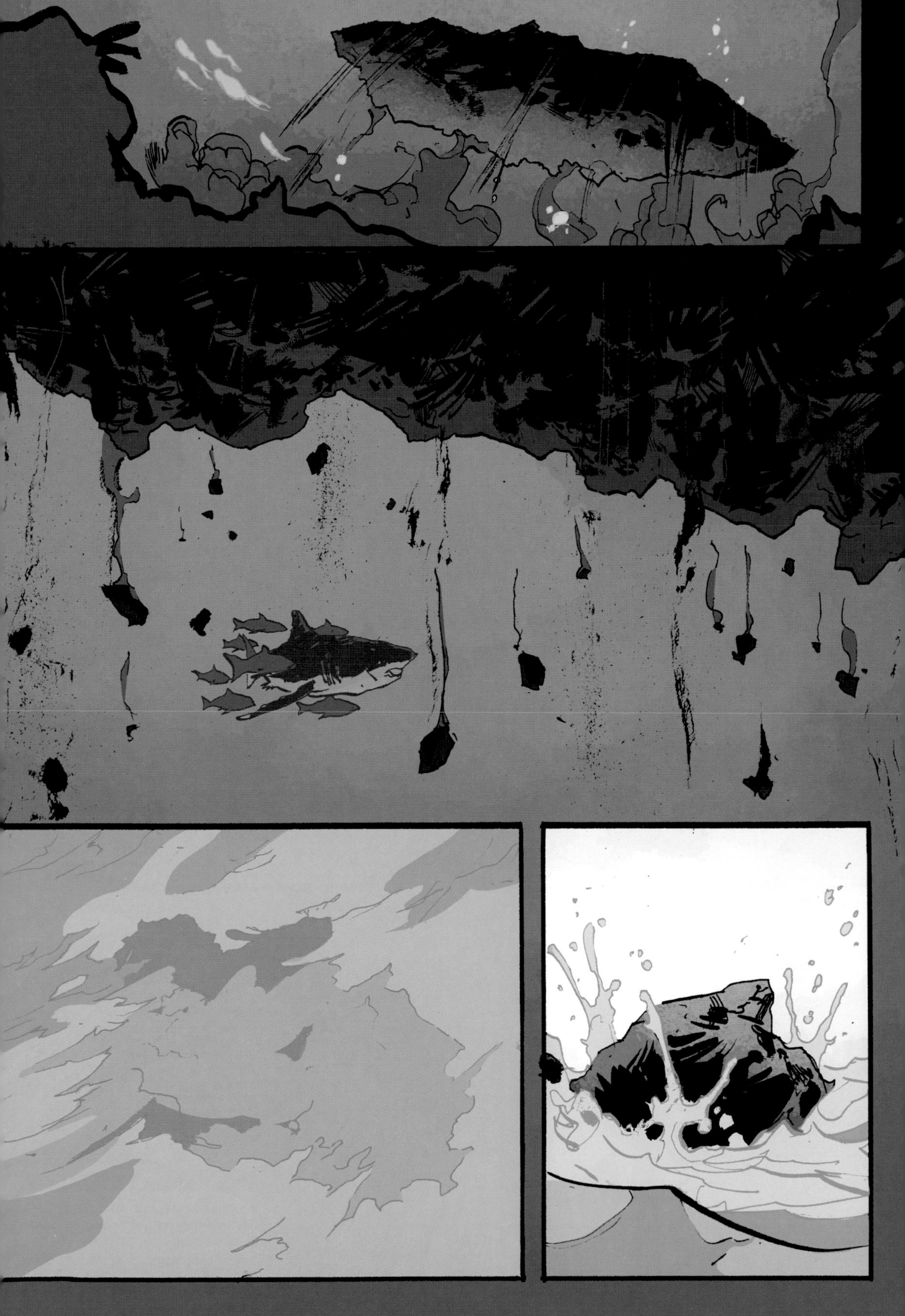

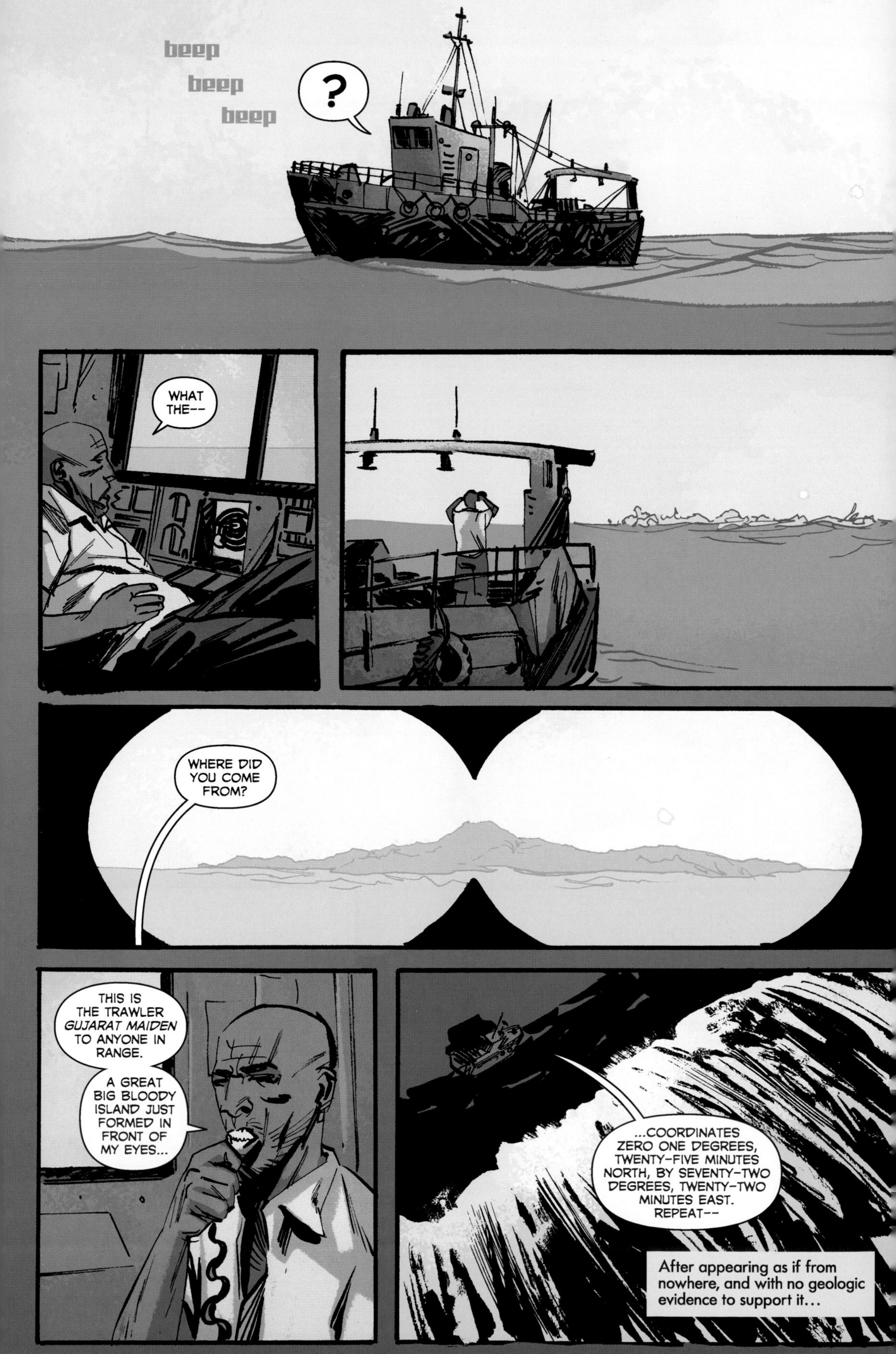
beep
beep
beep
?
WHAT THE--
WHERE DID YOU COME FROM?
THIS IS THE TRAWLER *GUJARAT MAIDEN* TO ANYONE IN RANGE.
A GREAT BIG BLOODY ISLAND JUST FORMED IN FRONT OF MY EYES...
...COORDINATES ZERO ONE DEGREES, TWENTY-FIVE MINUTES NORTH, BY SEVENTY-TWO DEGREES, TWENTY-TWO MINUTES EAST. REPEAT--
After appearing as if from nowhere, and with no geologic evidence to support it...

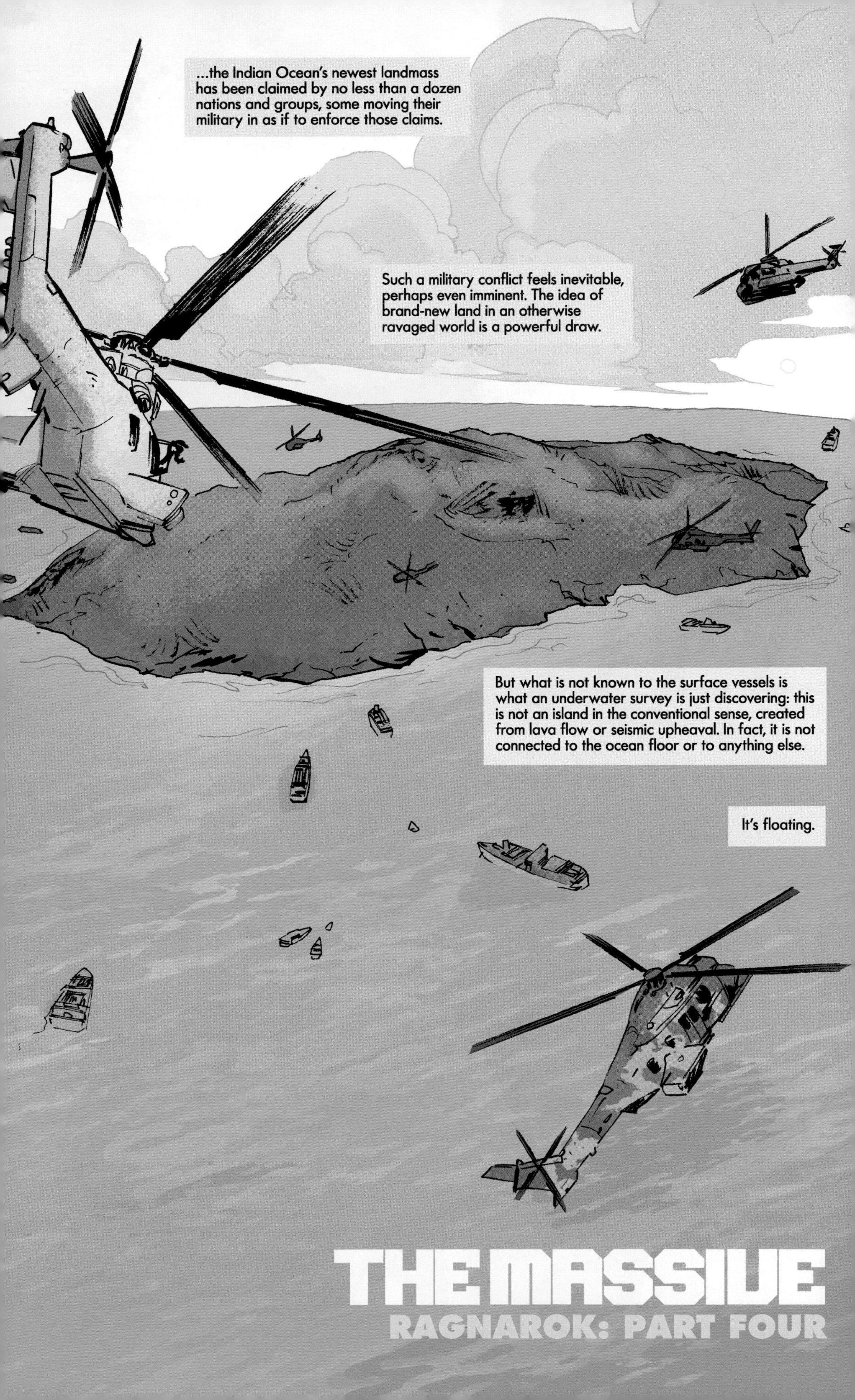
...the Indian Ocean's newest landmass has been claimed by no less than a dozen nations and groups, some moving their military in as if to enforce those claims.
Such a military conflict feels inevitable, perhaps even imminent. The idea of brand-new land in an otherwise ravaged world is a powerful draw.
But what is not known to the surface vessels is what an underwater survey is just discovering: this is not an island in the conventional sense, created from lava flow or seismic upheaval. In fact, it is not connected to the ocean floor or to anything else.
It's floating.
THE MASSIVE
RAGNAROK: PART FOUR

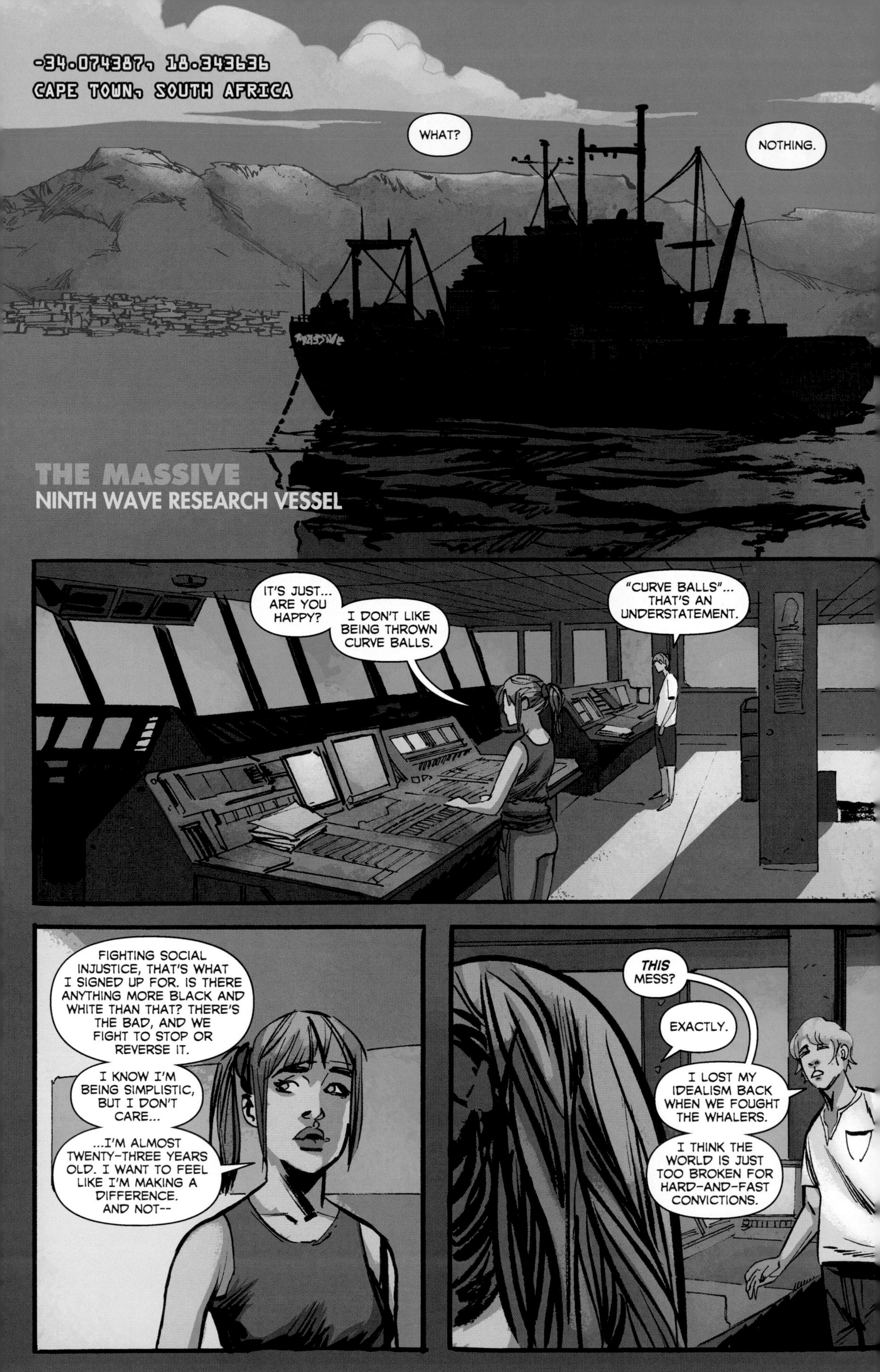
-34.074387, 18.343636
CAPE TOWN, SOUTH AFRICA
WHAT?
NOTHING.
THE MASSIVE
NINTH WAVE RESEARCH VESSEL
IT'S JUST... ARE YOU HAPPY?
I DON'T LIKE BEING THROWN CURVE BALLS.
"CURVE BALLS"... THAT'S AN UNDERSTATEMENT.
FIGHTING SOCIAL INJUSTICE, THAT'S WHAT I SIGNED UP FOR. IS THERE ANYTHING MORE BLACK AND WHITE THAN THAT? THERE'S THE BAD, AND WE FIGHT TO STOP OR REVERSE IT.
I KNOW I'M BEING SIMPLISTIC, BUT I DON'T CARE...
...I'M ALMOST TWENTY-THREE YEARS OLD. I WANT TO FEEL LIKE I'M MAKING A DIFFERENCE. AND NOT--
THIS MESS?
EXACTLY.
I LOST MY IDEALISM BACK WHEN WE FOUGHT THE WHALERS.
I THINK THE WORLD IS JUST TOO BROKEN FOR HARD-AND-FAST CONVICTIONS.

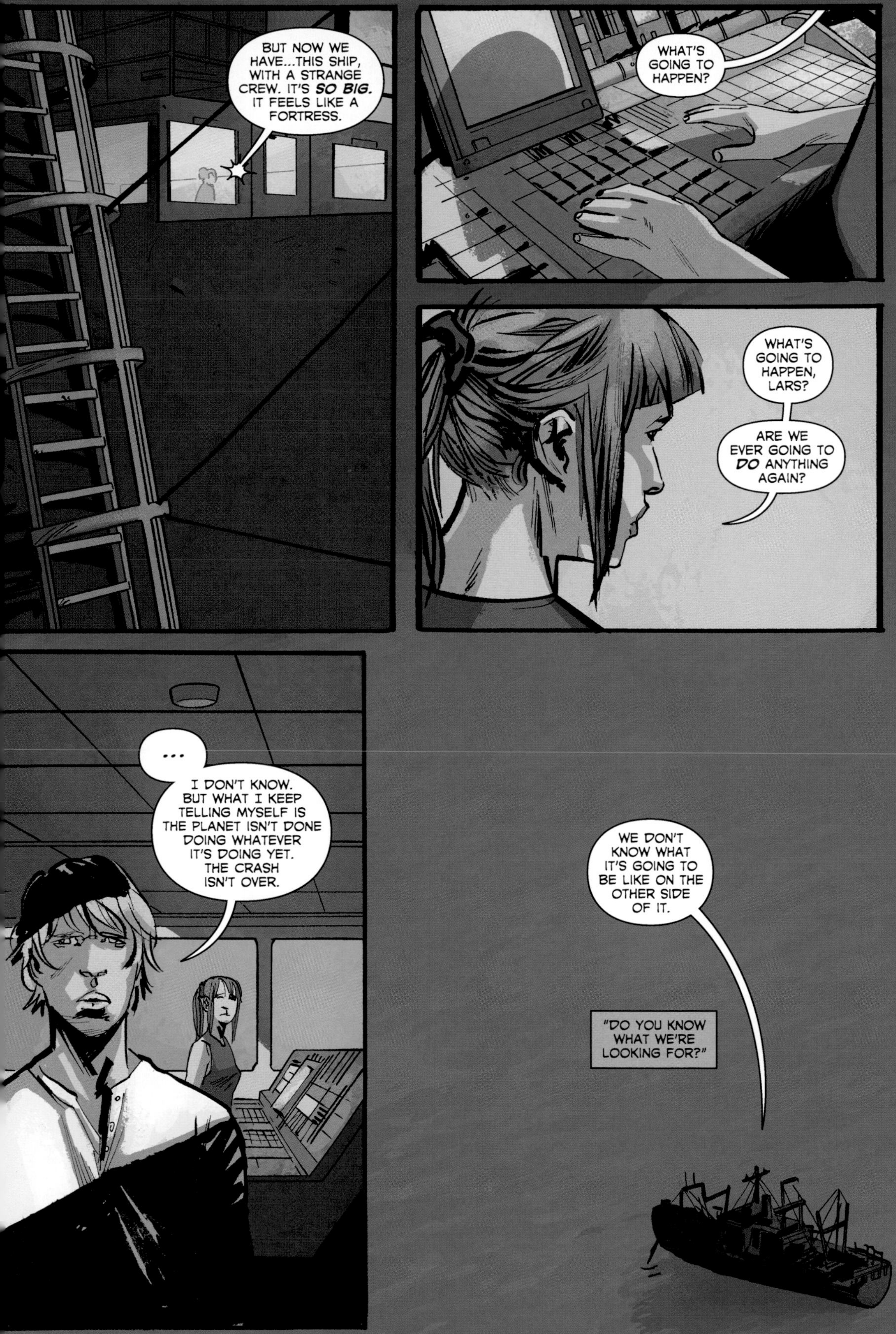

BUT NOW WE HAVE...THIS SHIP, WITH A STRANGE CREW. IT'S SO BIG. IT FEELS LIKE A FORTRESS.
WHAT'S GOING TO HAPPEN?
WHAT'S GOING TO HAPPEN, LARS?
ARE WE EVER GOING TO DO ANYTHING AGAIN?
...
I DON'T KNOW. BUT WHAT I KEEP TELLING MYSELF IS THE PLANET ISN'T DONE DOING WHATEVER IT'S DOING YET. THE CRASH ISN'T OVER.
WE DON'T KNOW WHAT IT'S GOING TO BE LIKE ON THE OTHER SIDE OF IT.
"DO YOU KNOW WHAT WE'RE LOOKING FOR?"

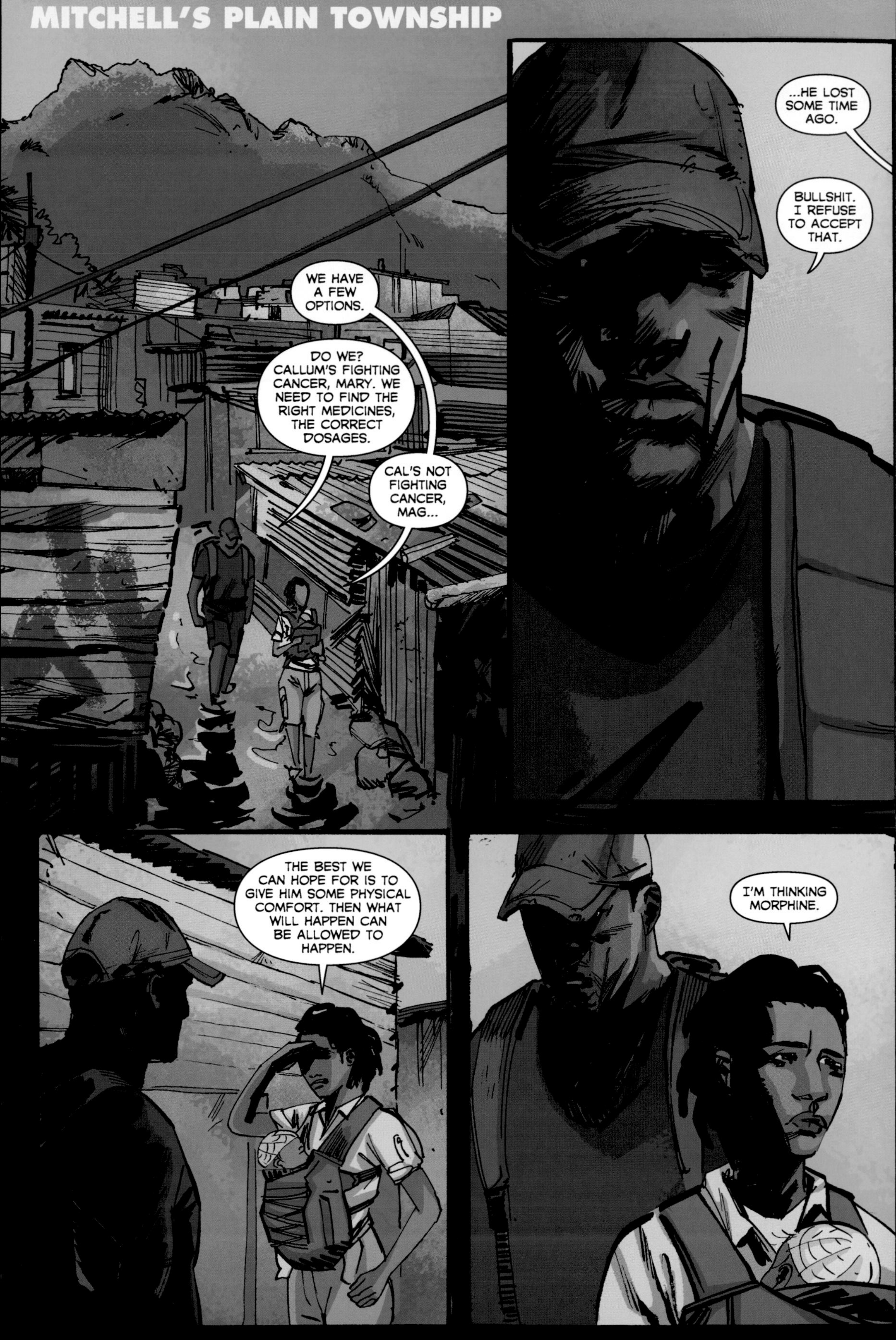
MITCHELL'S PLAIN TOWNSHIP
WE HAVE A FEW OPTIONS.
DO WE? CALLUM'S FIGHTING CANCER, MARY. WE NEED TO FIND THE RIGHT MEDICINES, THE CORRECT DOSAGES.
CAL'S NOT FIGHTING CANCER, MAG...
...HE LOST SOME TIME AGO.
BULLSHIT. I REFUSE TO ACCEPT THAT.
THE BEST WE CAN HOPE FOR IS TO GIVE HIM SOME PHYSICAL COMFORT. THEN WHAT WILL HAPPEN CAN BE ALLOWED TO HAPPEN.
I'M THINKING MORPHINE.

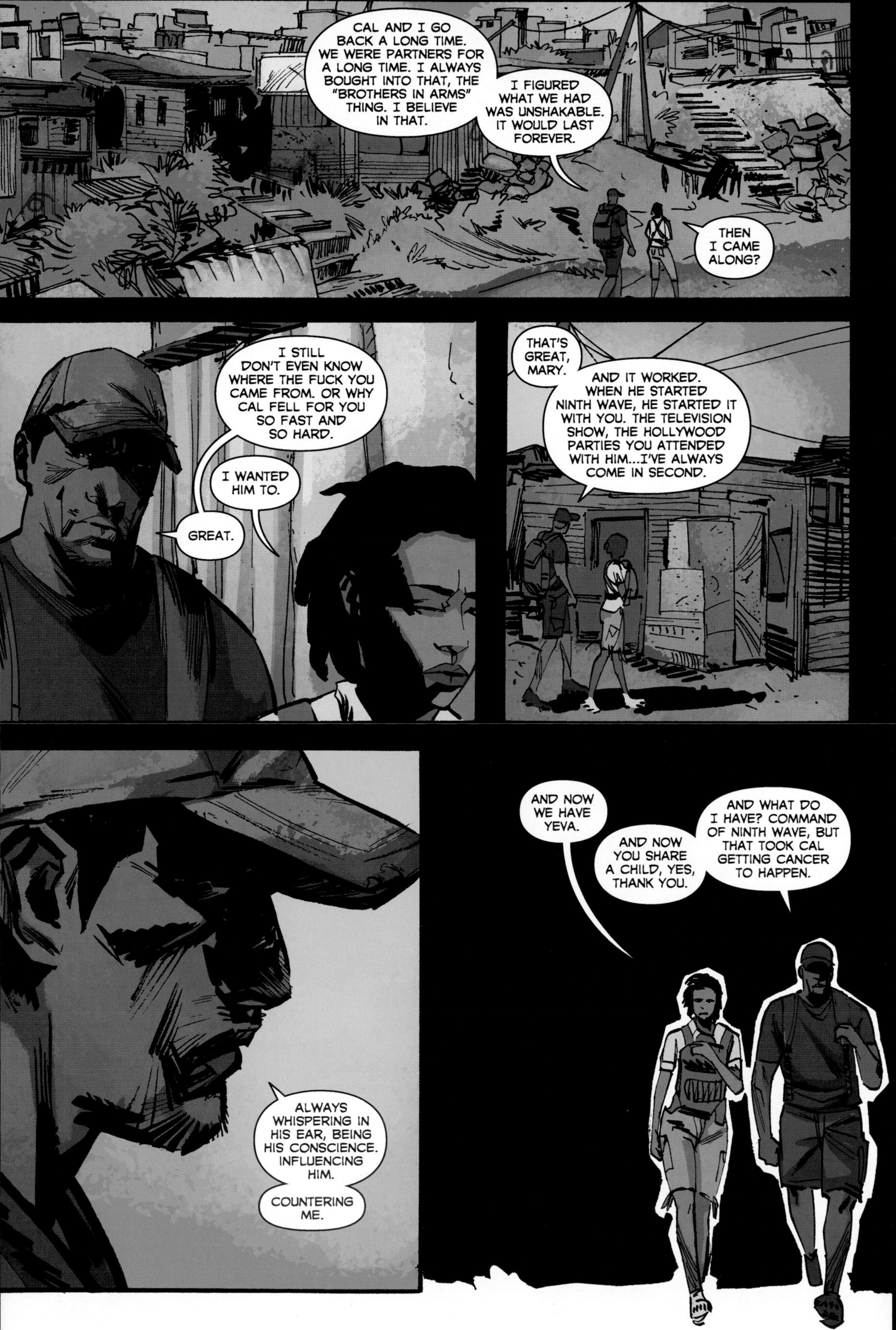

CAL AND I GO BACK A LONG TIME. WE WERE PARTNERS FOR A LONG TIME. I ALWAYS BOUGHT INTO THAT, THE "BROTHERS IN ARMS" THING. I BELIEVE IN THAT.
I FIGURED WHAT WE HAD WAS UNSHAKABLE. IT WOULD LAST FOREVER.
THEN I CAME ALONG?
I STILL DON'T EVEN KNOW WHERE THE FUCK YOU CAME FROM. OR WHY CAL FELL FOR YOU SO FAST AND SO HARD.
I WANTED HIM TO.
GREAT.
THAT'S GREAT, MARY.
AND IT WORKED. WHEN HE STARTED NINTH WAVE, HE STARTED IT WITH YOU. THE TELEVISION SHOW, THE HOLLYWOOD PARTIES YOU ATTENDED WITH HIM...I'VE ALWAYS COME IN SECOND.
ALWAYS WHISPERING IN HIS EAR, BEING HIS CONSCIENCE. INFLUENCING HIM.
COUNTERING ME.
AND NOW WE HAVE YEVA.
AND NOW YOU SHARE A CHILD, YES, THANK YOU.
AND WHAT DO I HAVE? COMMAND OF NINTH WAVE, BUT THAT TOOK CAL GETTING CANCER TO HAPPEN.

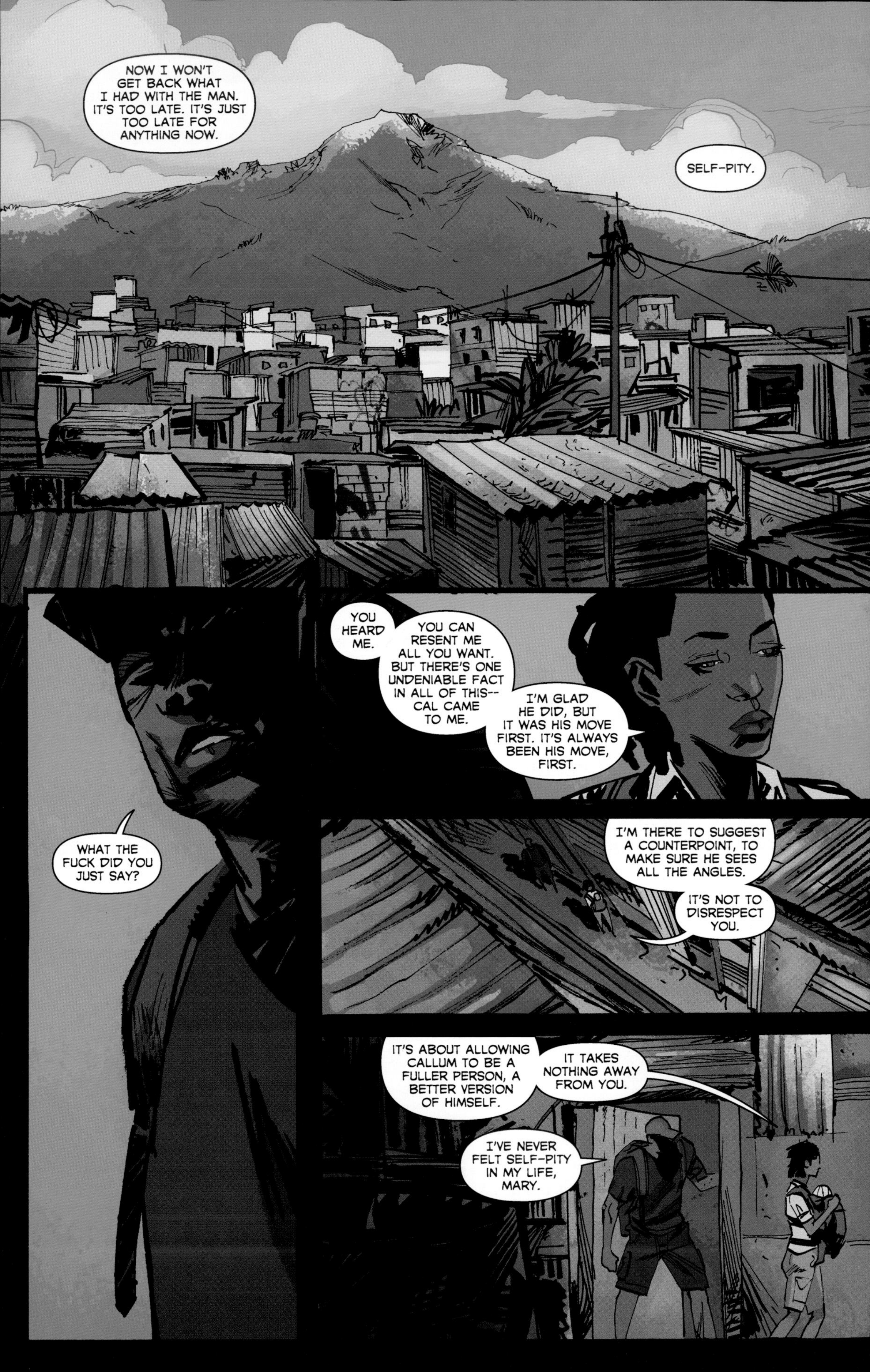
NOW I WON'T GET BACK WHAT I HAD WITH THE MAN. IT'S TOO LATE. IT'S JUST TOO LATE FOR ANYTHING NOW.
SELF-PITY.
WHAT THE FUCK DID YOU JUST SAY?
YOU HEARD ME.
YOU CAN RESENT ME ALL YOU WANT. BUT THERE'S ONE UNDENIABLE FACT IN ALL OF THIS-- CAL CAME TO ME.
I'M GLAD HE DID, BUT IT WAS HIS MOVE FIRST. IT'S ALWAYS BEEN HIS MOVE, FIRST.
I'M THERE TO SUGGEST A COUNTERPOINT, TO MAKE SURE HE SEES ALL THE ANGLES.
IT'S NOT TO DISRESPECT YOU.
IT'S ABOUT ALLOWING CALLUM TO BE A FULLER PERSON, A BETTER VERSION OF HIMSELF.
IT TAKES NOTHING AWAY FROM YOU.
I'VE NEVER FELT SELF-PITY IN MY LIFE, MARY.

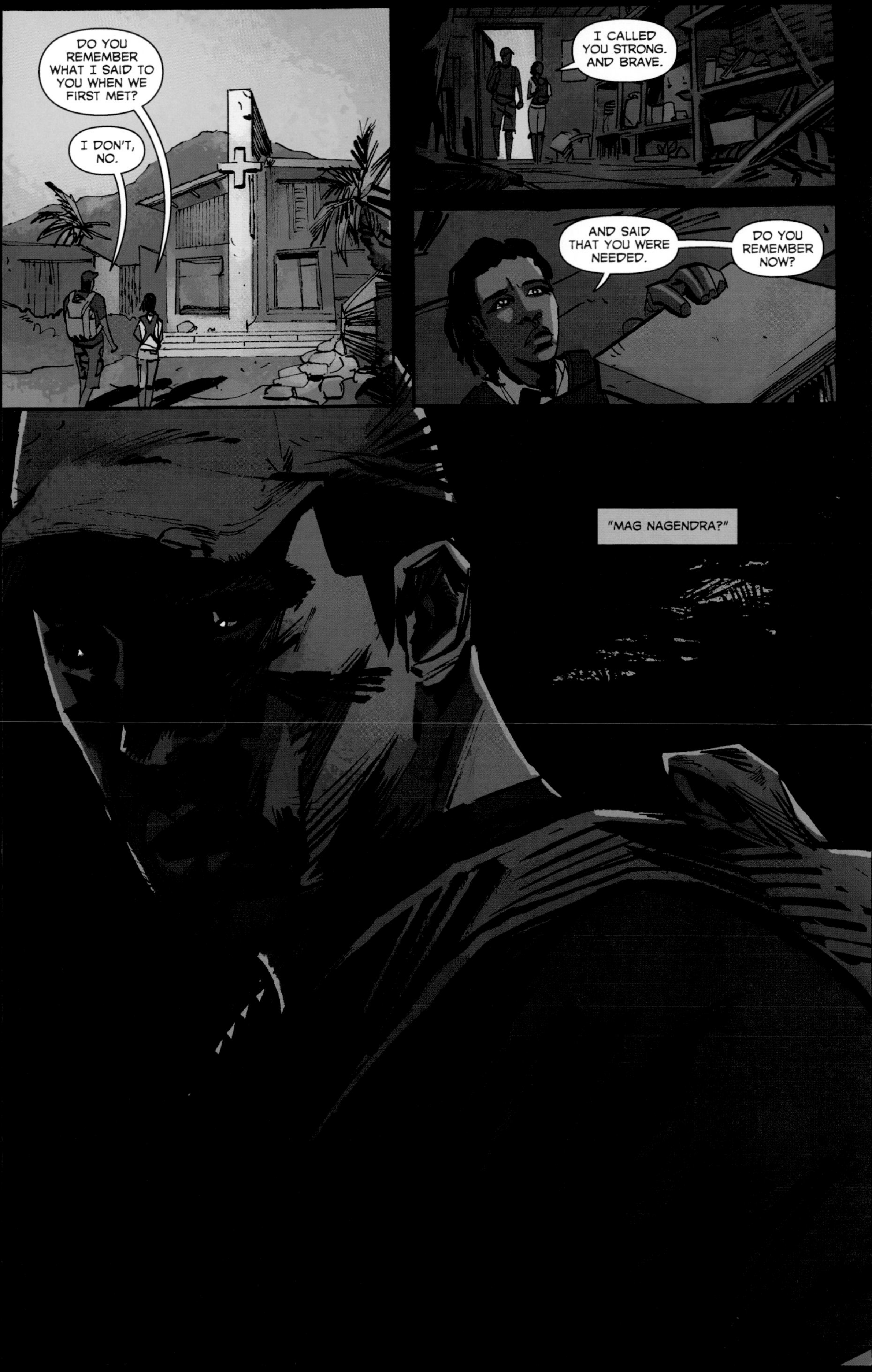
DO YOU REMEMBER WHAT I SAID TO YOU WHEN WE FIRST MET?
I DON'T, NO.
I CALLED YOU STRONG. AND BRAVE.
AND SAID THAT YOU WERE NEEDED.
DO YOU REMEMBER NOW?
"MAG NAGENDRA?"

"I DON'T KNOW HOW I LIVED THAT DAY."

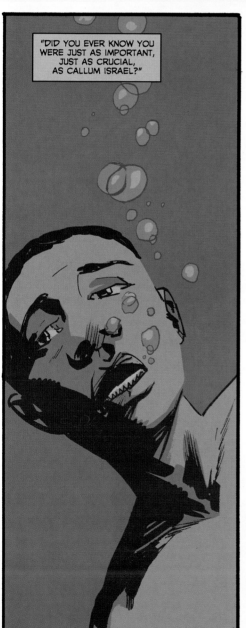

"DID YOU EVER KNOW YOU WERE JUST AS IMPORTANT, JUST AS CRUCIAL, AS CALLUM ISRAEL?"

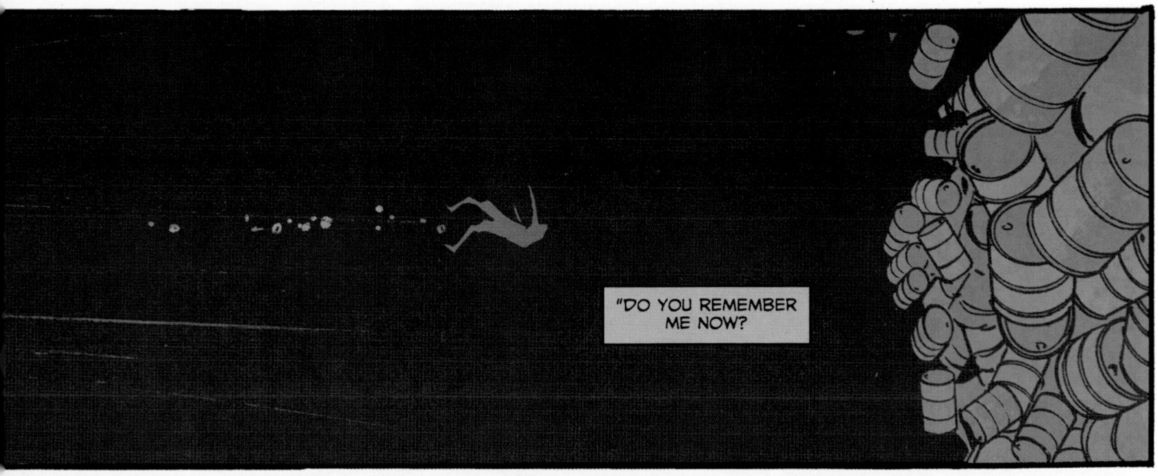
"DO YOU REMEMBER
ME NOW?

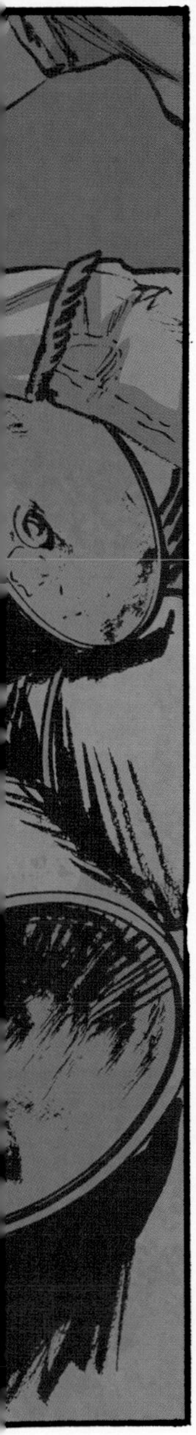

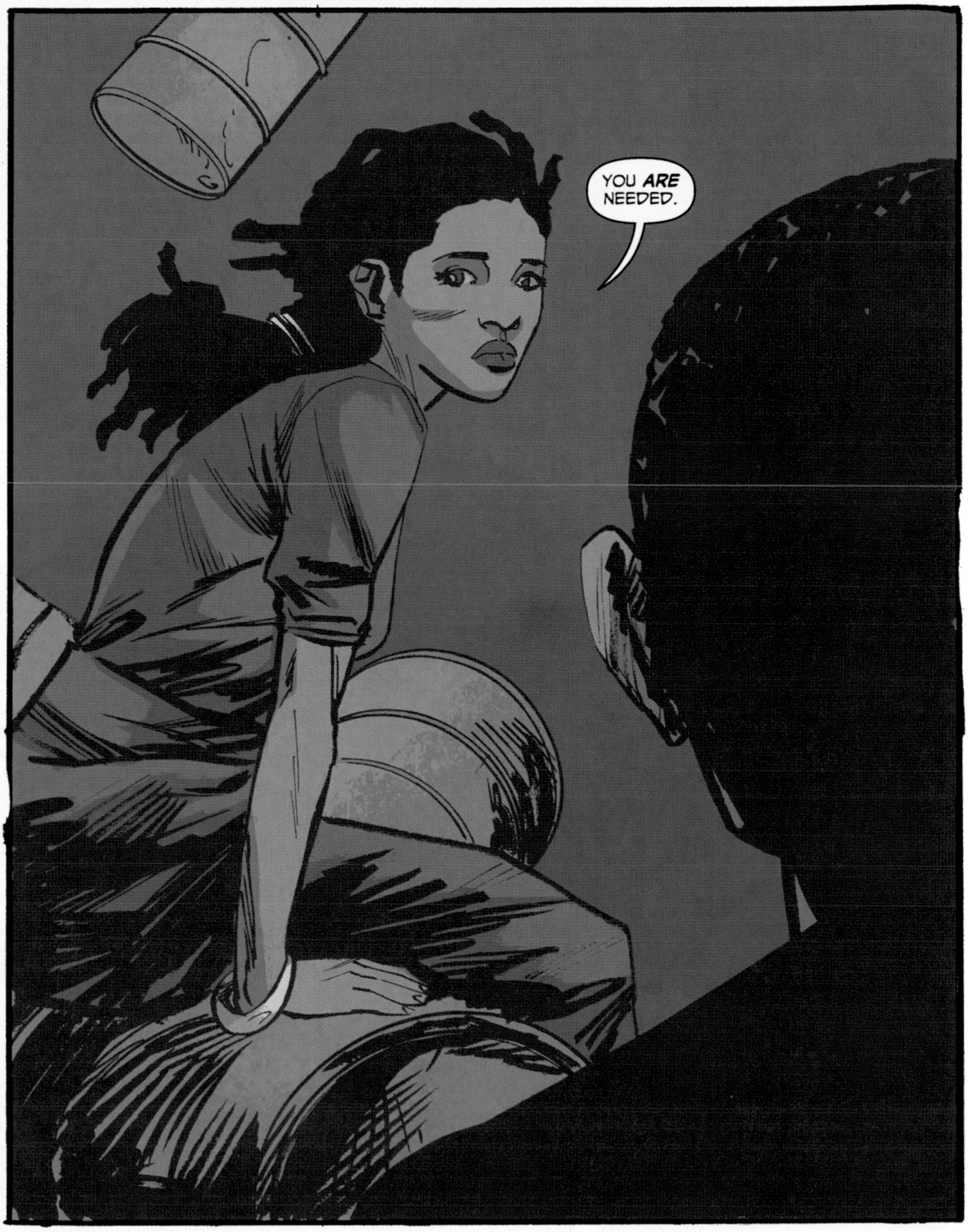
YOU ARE
NEEDED.

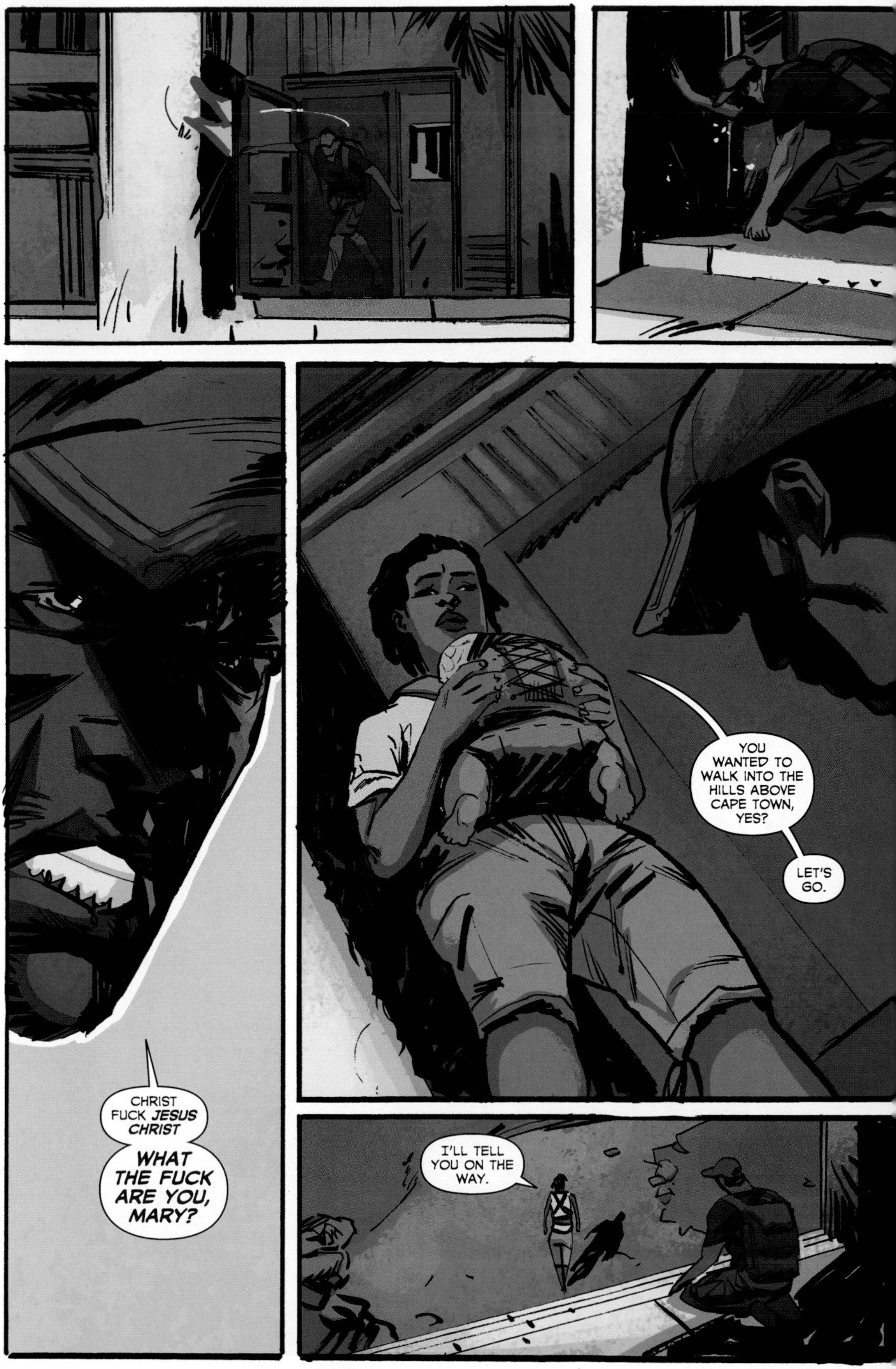
YOU WANTED TO WALK INTO THE HILLS ABOVE CAPE TOWN, YES?
LET'S GO.
CHRIST FUCK *JESUS CHRIST*
WHAT THE FUCK ARE YOU, MARY?
I'LL TELL YOU ON THE WAY.

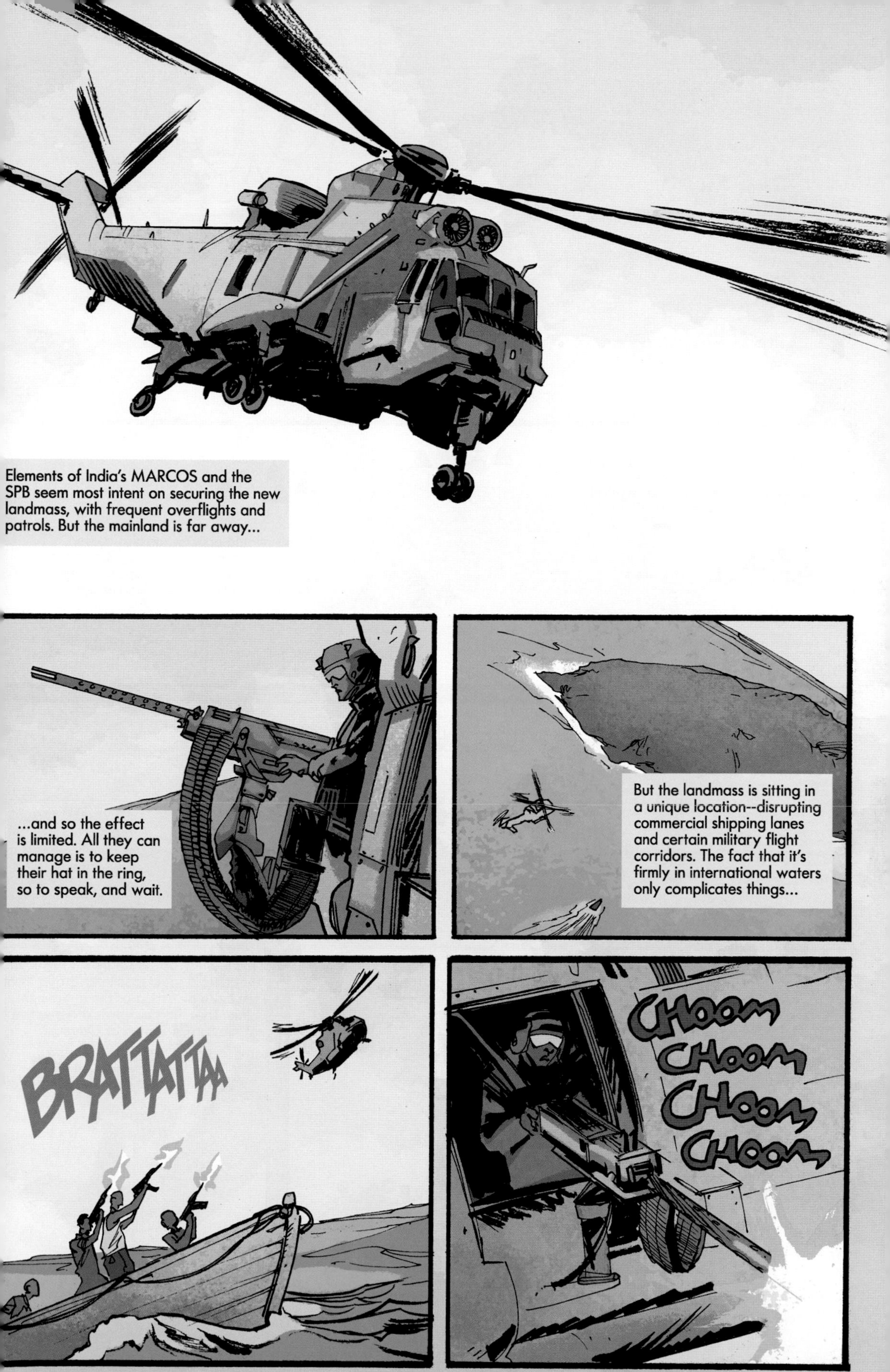
Elements of India's MARCOS and the SPB seem most intent on securing the new landmass, with frequent overflights and patrols. But the mainland is far away...
...and so the effect is limited. All they can manage is to keep their hat in the ring, so to speak, and wait.
But the landmass is sitting in a unique location--disrupting commercial shipping lanes and certain military flight corridors. The fact that it's firmly in international waters only complicates things...
BRATTATTAA
CHOOM
CHOOM
CHOOM
CHOOM

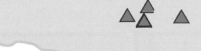

Meanwhile, the landmass seems inert. Visual reconnaissance detects no movement on its surface, no vegetation... Birds don't even land on it.

Crash-related activity has also ceased, completely, around the globe. Like someone hitting a pause button, the appearance of the landmass has had a stilling effect.

Which emboldens some.

The identity of the soldiers is unknown Analysts suspect a splinter group from the Horn of Africa or the al-Batinah plain. Their flag suggests a derivative of the former nation of Oman.

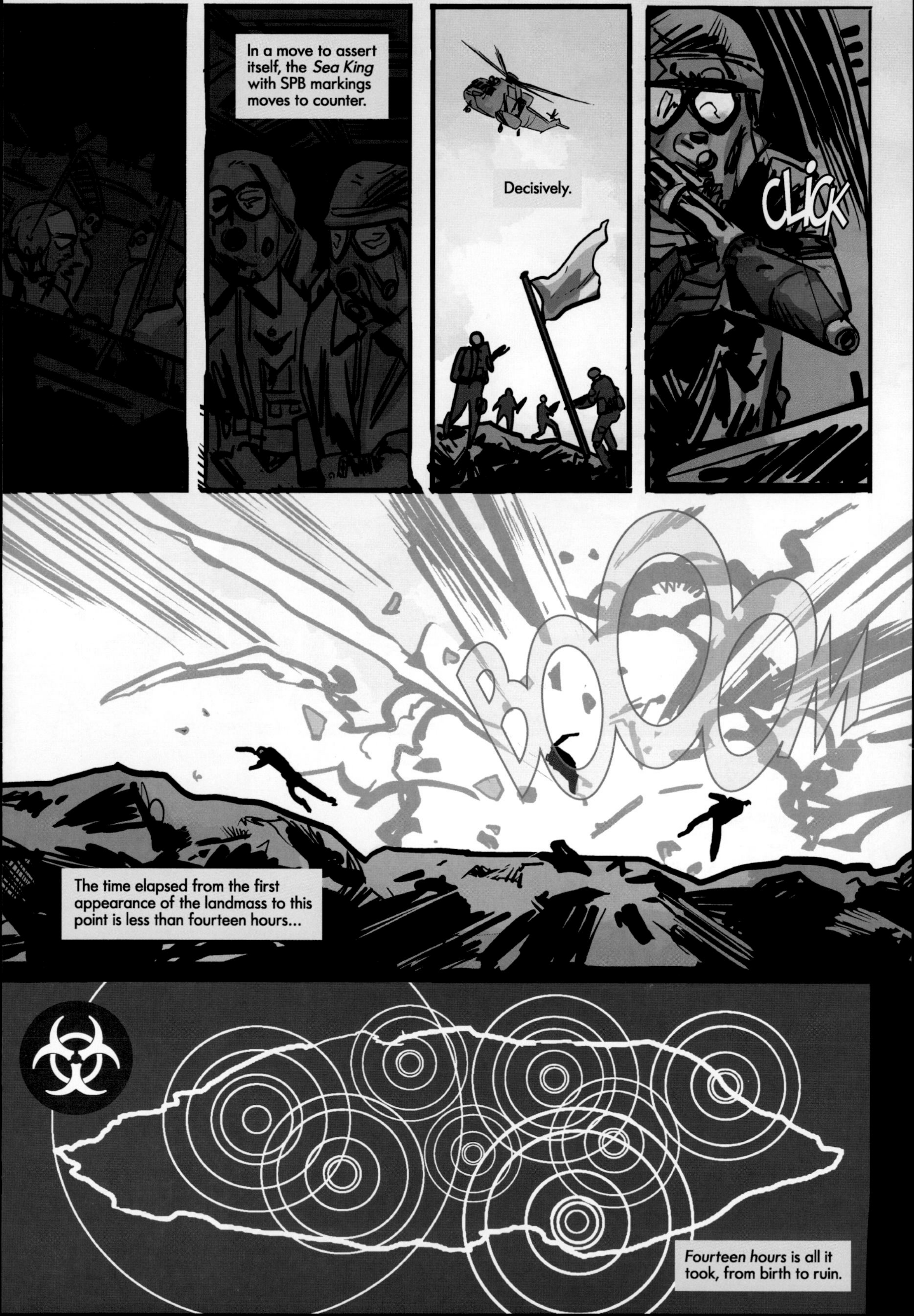
In a move to assert itself, the *Sea King* with SPB markings moves to counter.
Decisively.
CLICK
BOOOM
The time elapsed from the first appearance of the landmass to this point is less than fourteen hours...
Fourteen hours is all it took, from birth to ruin.

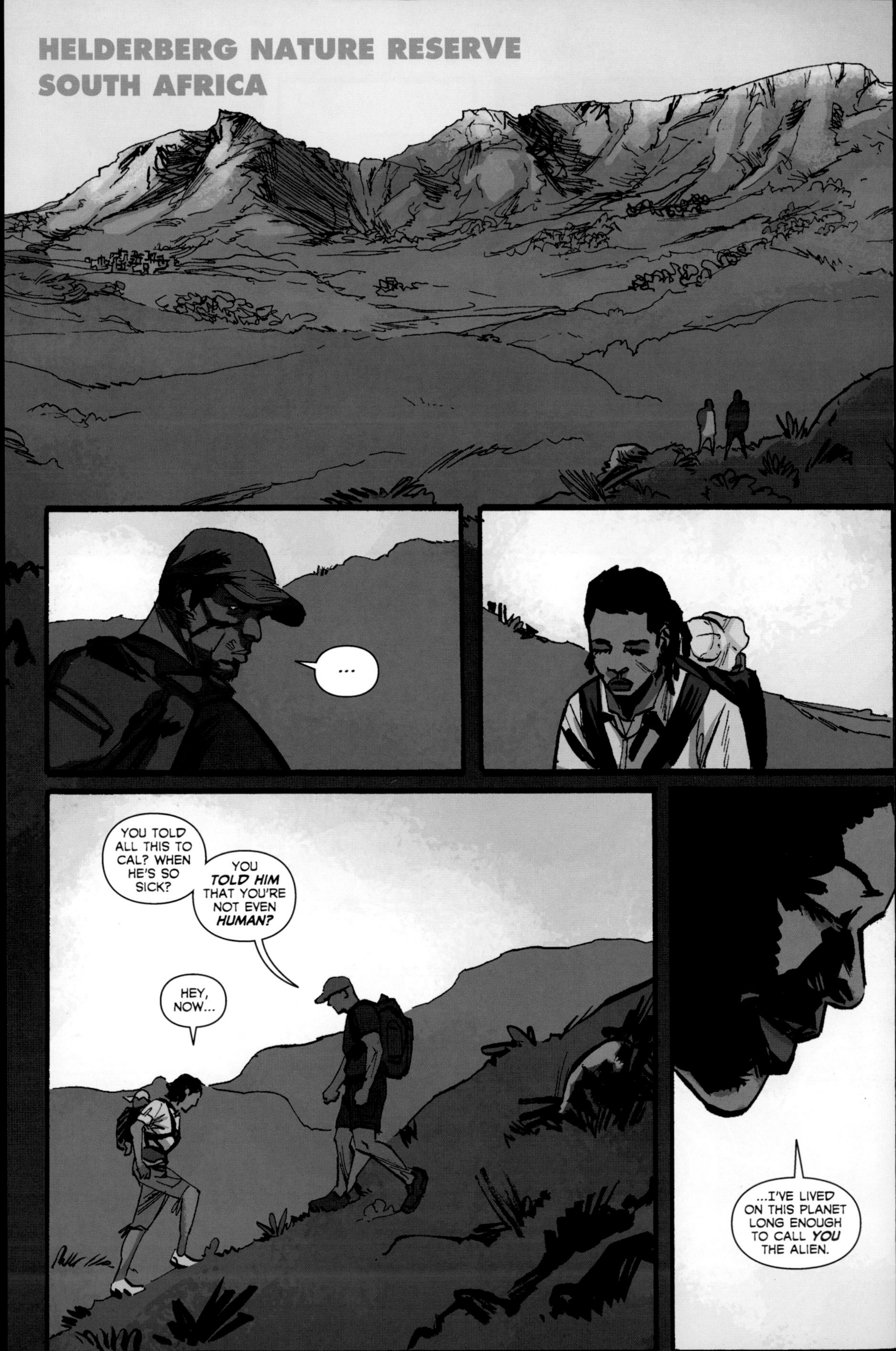
HELDERBERG NATURE RESERVE
SOUTH AFRICA
...
YOU TOLD ALL THIS TO CAL? WHEN HE'S SO SICK?
YOU TOLD HIM THAT YOU'RE NOT EVEN HUMAN?
HEY, NOW...
...I'VE LIVED ON THIS PLANET LONG ENOUGH TO CALL YOU THE ALIEN.

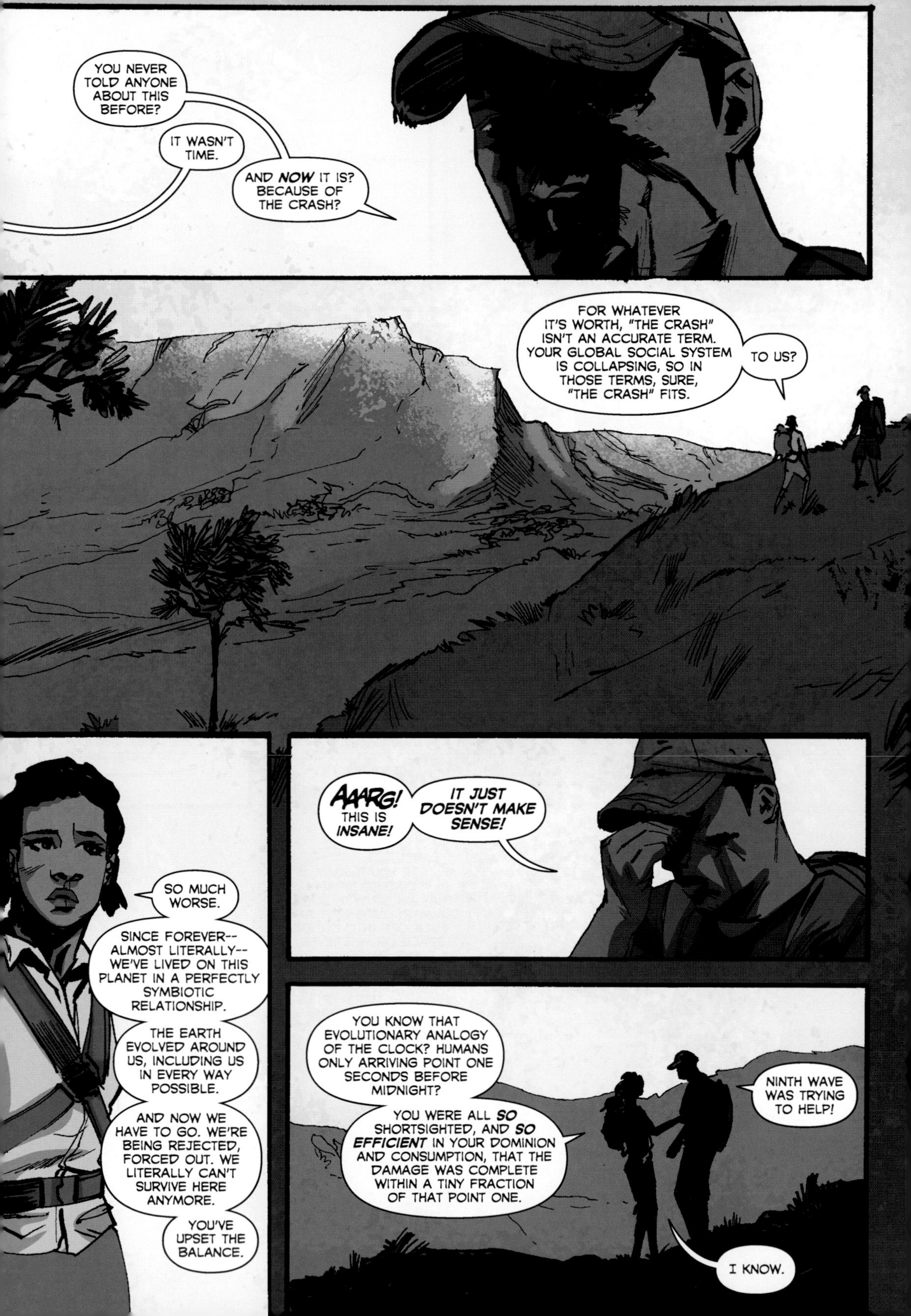
YOU NEVER TOLD ANYONE ABOUT THIS BEFORE?
IT WASN'T TIME.
AND *NOW* IT IS? BECAUSE OF THE CRASH?
FOR WHATEVER IT'S WORTH, "THE CRASH" ISN'T AN ACCURATE TERM. YOUR GLOBAL SOCIAL SYSTEM IS COLLAPSING, SO IN THOSE TERMS, SURE, "THE CRASH" FITS.
TO US?
SO MUCH WORSE.
SINCE FOREVER-- ALMOST LITERALLY-- WE'VE LIVED ON THIS PLANET IN A PERFECTLY SYMBIOTIC RELATIONSHIP.
THE EARTH EVOLVED AROUND US, INCLUDING US IN EVERY WAY POSSIBLE.
AND NOW WE HAVE TO GO. WE'RE BEING REJECTED, FORCED OUT. WE LITERALLY CAN'T SURVIVE HERE ANYMORE.
YOU'VE UPSET THE BALANCE.
AAARG! THIS IS *INSANE!*
IT JUST DOESN'T MAKE SENSE!
YOU KNOW THAT EVOLUTIONARY ANALOGY OF THE CLOCK? HUMANS ONLY ARRIVING POINT ONE SECONDS BEFORE MIDNIGHT?
YOU WERE ALL *SO* SHORTSIGHTED, AND *SO EFFICIENT* IN YOUR DOMINION AND CONSUMPTION, THAT THE DAMAGE WAS COMPLETE WITHIN A TINY FRACTION OF THAT POINT ONE.
NINTH WAVE WAS TRYING TO HELP!
I KNOW.

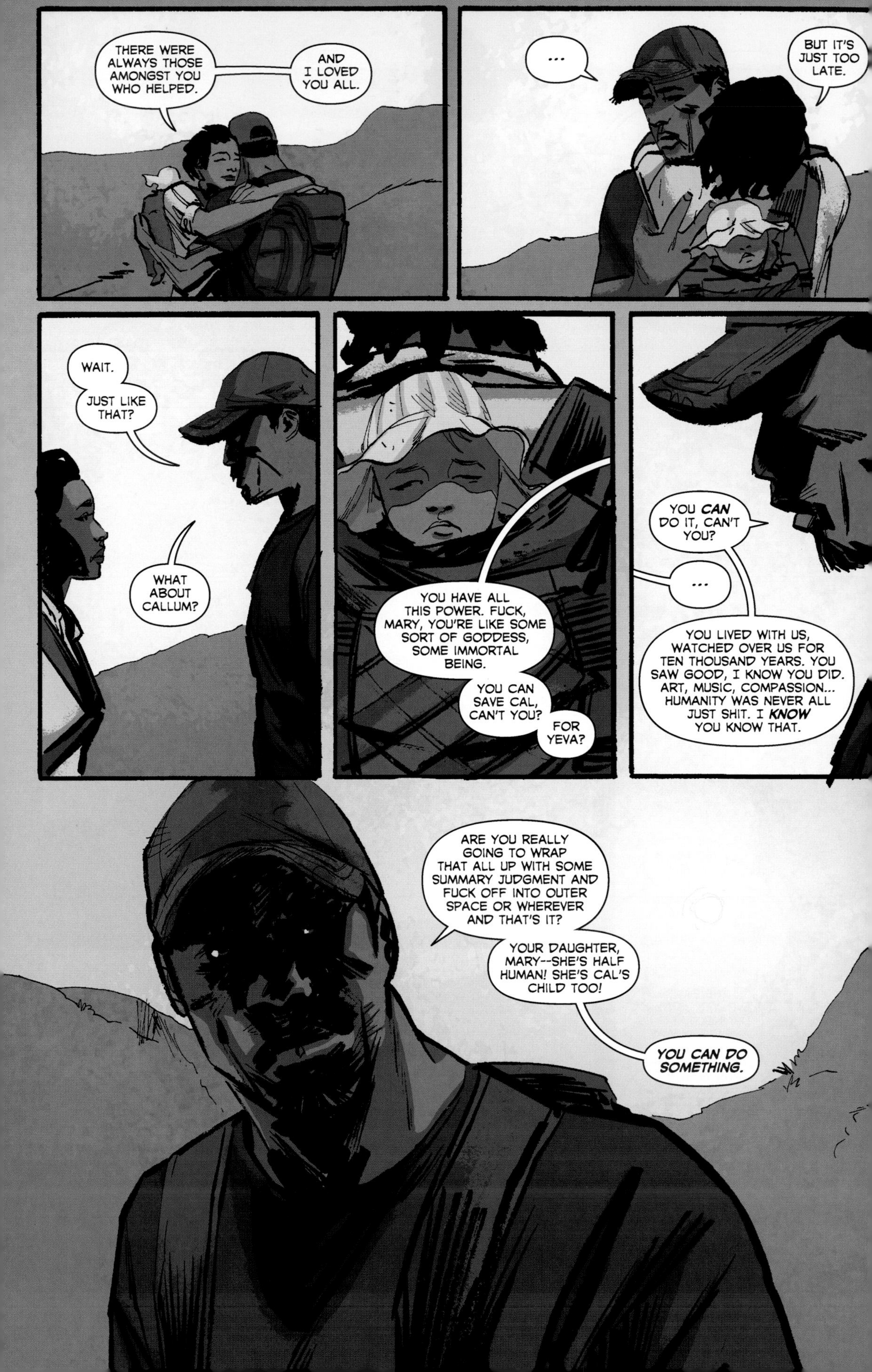
THERE WERE ALWAYS THOSE AMONGST YOU WHO HELPED.
AND I LOVED YOU ALL.
...
BUT IT'S JUST TOO LATE.
WAIT.
JUST LIKE THAT?
WHAT ABOUT CALLUM?
YOU HAVE ALL THIS POWER. FUCK, MARY, YOU'RE LIKE SOME SORT OF GODDESS, SOME IMMORTAL BEING.
YOU CAN SAVE CAL, CAN'T YOU?
FOR YEVA?
YOU *CAN* DO IT, CAN'T YOU?
...
YOU LIVED WITH US, WATCHED OVER US FOR TEN THOUSAND YEARS. YOU SAW GOOD, I KNOW YOU DID. ART, MUSIC, COMPASSION... HUMANITY WAS NEVER ALL JUST SHIT. I ***KNOW*** YOU KNOW THAT.
ARE YOU REALLY GOING TO WRAP THAT ALL UP WITH SOME SUMMARY JUDGMENT AND FUCK OFF INTO OUTER SPACE OR WHEREVER AND THAT'S IT?
YOUR DAUGHTER, MARY--SHE'S HALF HUMAN! SHE'S CAL'S CHILD TOO!
YOU CAN DO SOMETHING.

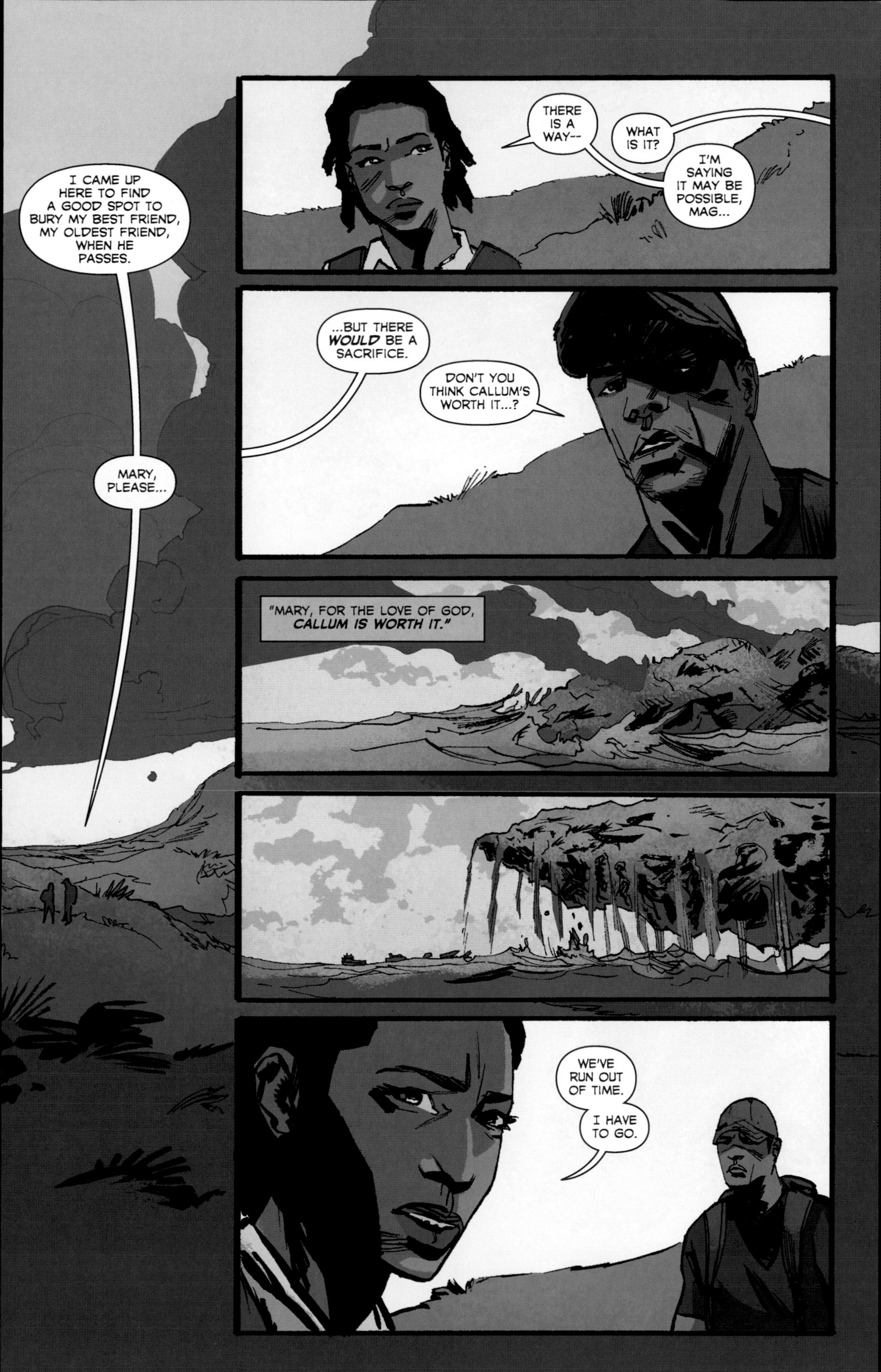

I CAME UP HERE TO FIND A GOOD SPOT TO BURY MY BEST FRIEND, MY OLDEST FRIEND, WHEN HE PASSES.
THERE IS A WAY--
WHAT IS IT?
I'M SAYING IT MAY BE POSSIBLE, MAG...
...BUT THERE *WOULD* BE A SACRIFICE.
DON'T YOU THINK CALLUM'S WORTH IT...?
MARY, PLEASE...
"MARY, FOR THE LOVE OF GOD, ***CALLUM IS WORTH IT.***"
WE'VE RUN OUT OF TIME.
I HAVE TO GO.

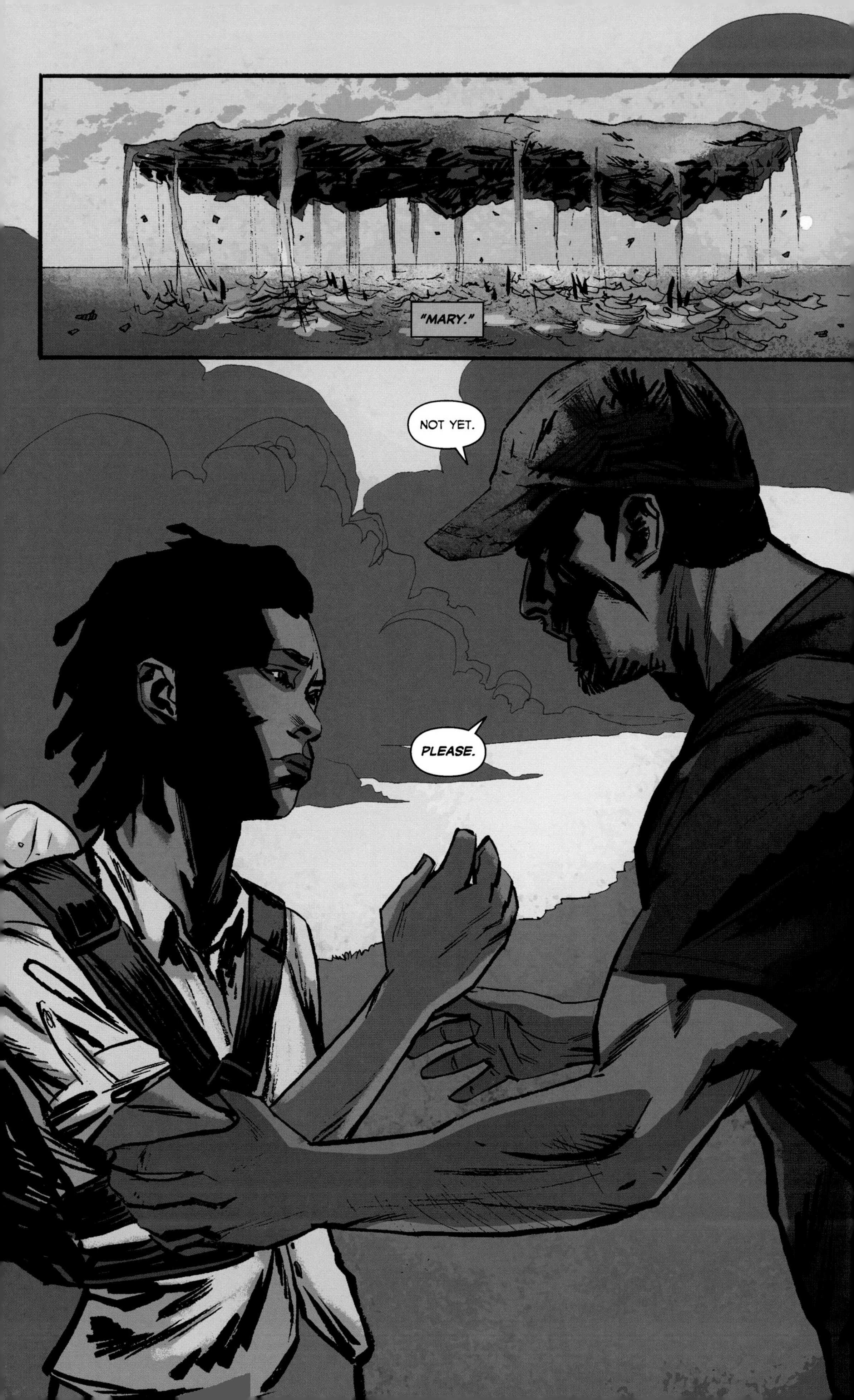
"MARY."
NOT YET.
PLEASE.

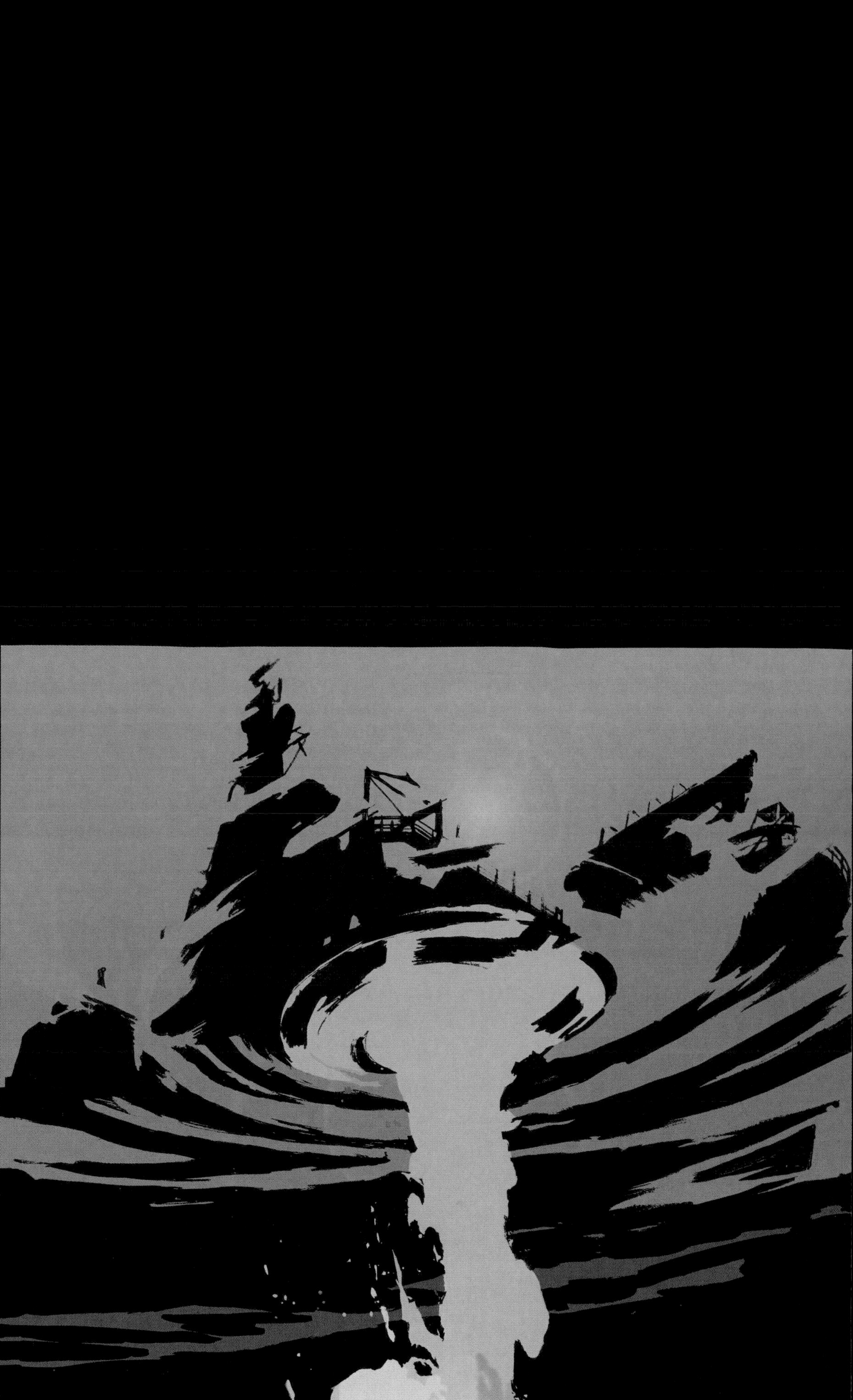

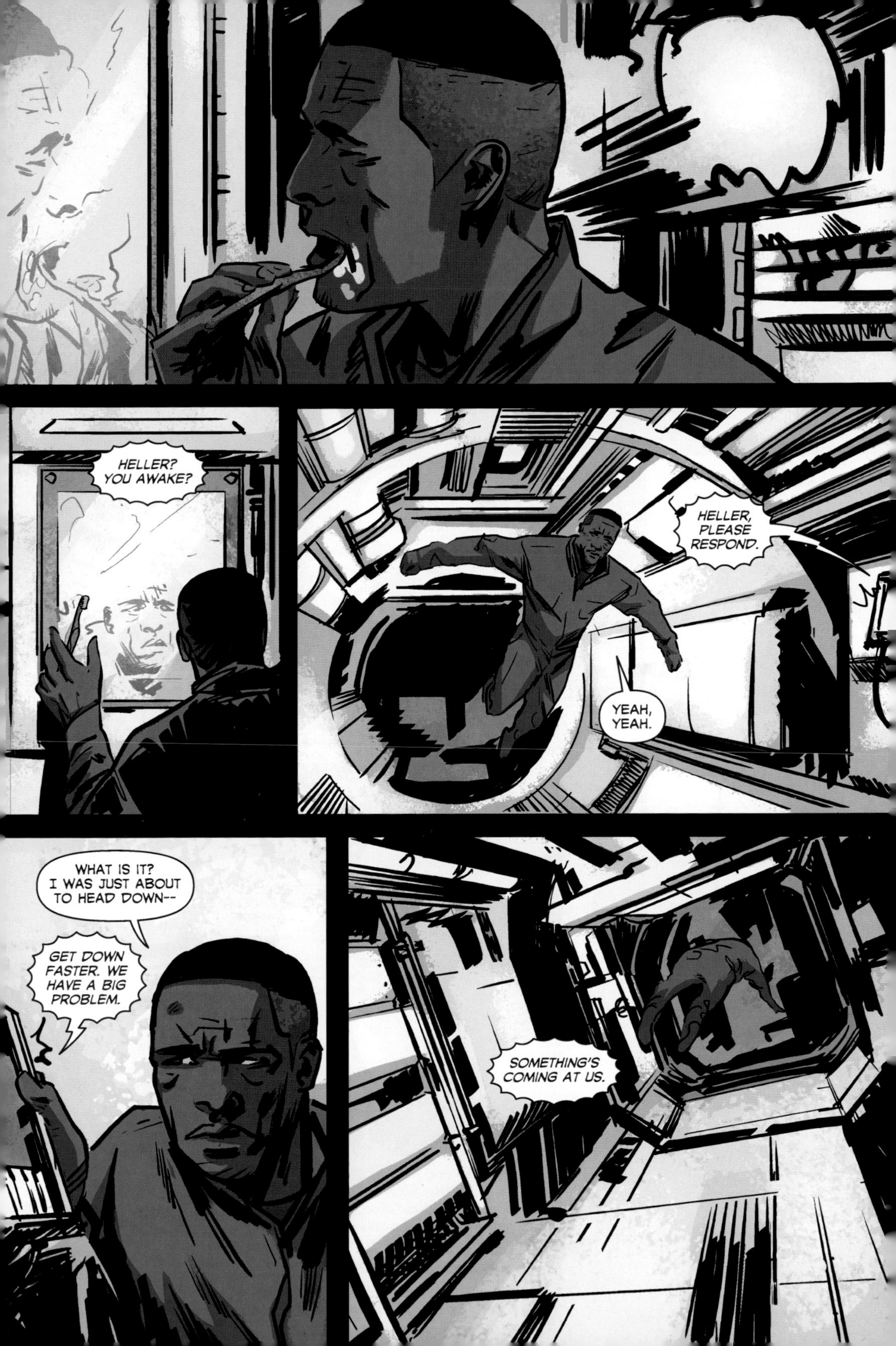
HELLER? YOU AWAKE?
HELLER, PLEASE RESPOND.
YEAH, YEAH.
WHAT IS IT? I WAS JUST ABOUT TO HEAD DOWN--
GET DOWN FASTER. WE HAVE A BIG PROBLEM.
SOMETHING'S COMING AT US.

SCHEISSE!

WHAT IS IT? A LAUNCH? IS IT AN ATTACK?

TOO BIG. HAS TO BE A GLITCH.

THIS IS NO GLITCH.

I CAN *SEE* IT.

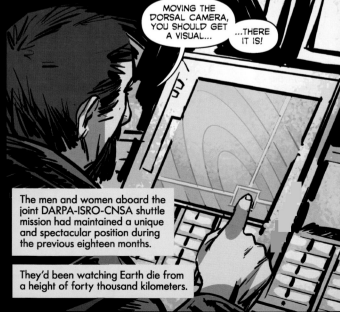

MOVING THE DORSAL CAMERA, YOU SHOULD GET A VISUAL...

...THERE IT IS!

The men and women aboard the joint DARPA-ISRO-CNSA shuttle mission had maintained a unique and spectacular position during the previous eighteen months.

They'd been watching Earth die from a height of forty thousand kilometers.

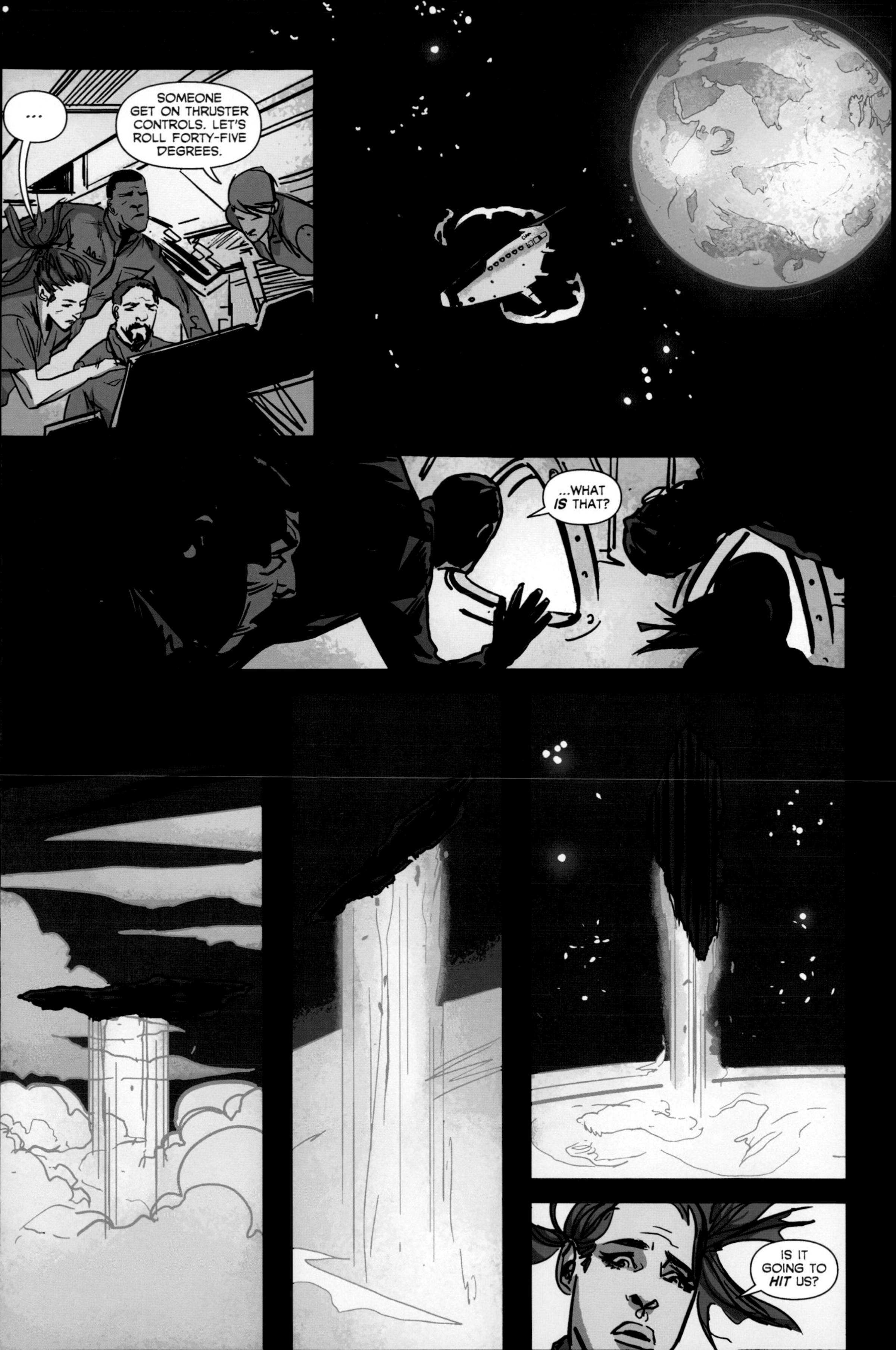
...
SOMEONE GET ON THRUSTER CONTROLS. LET'S ROLL FORTY-FIVE DEGREES.
...WHAT IS THAT?
IS IT GOING TO HIT US?

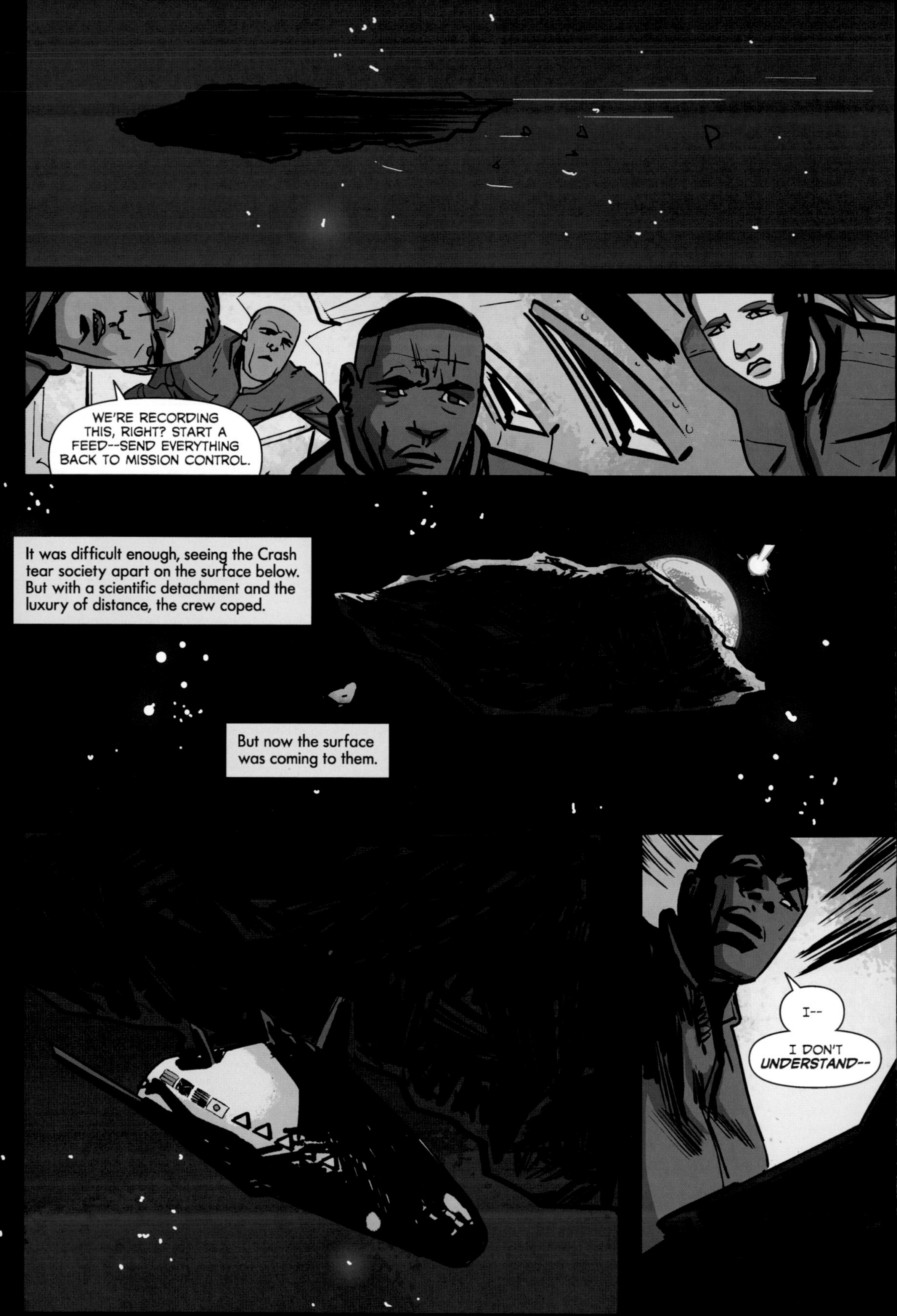
WE'RE RECORDING THIS, RIGHT? START A FEED--SEND EVERYTHING BACK TO MISSION CONTROL.
It was difficult enough, seeing the Crash tear society apart on the surface below. But with a scientific detachment and the luxury of distance, the crew coped.
But now the surface was coming to them.
I--
I DON'T *UNDERSTAND--*

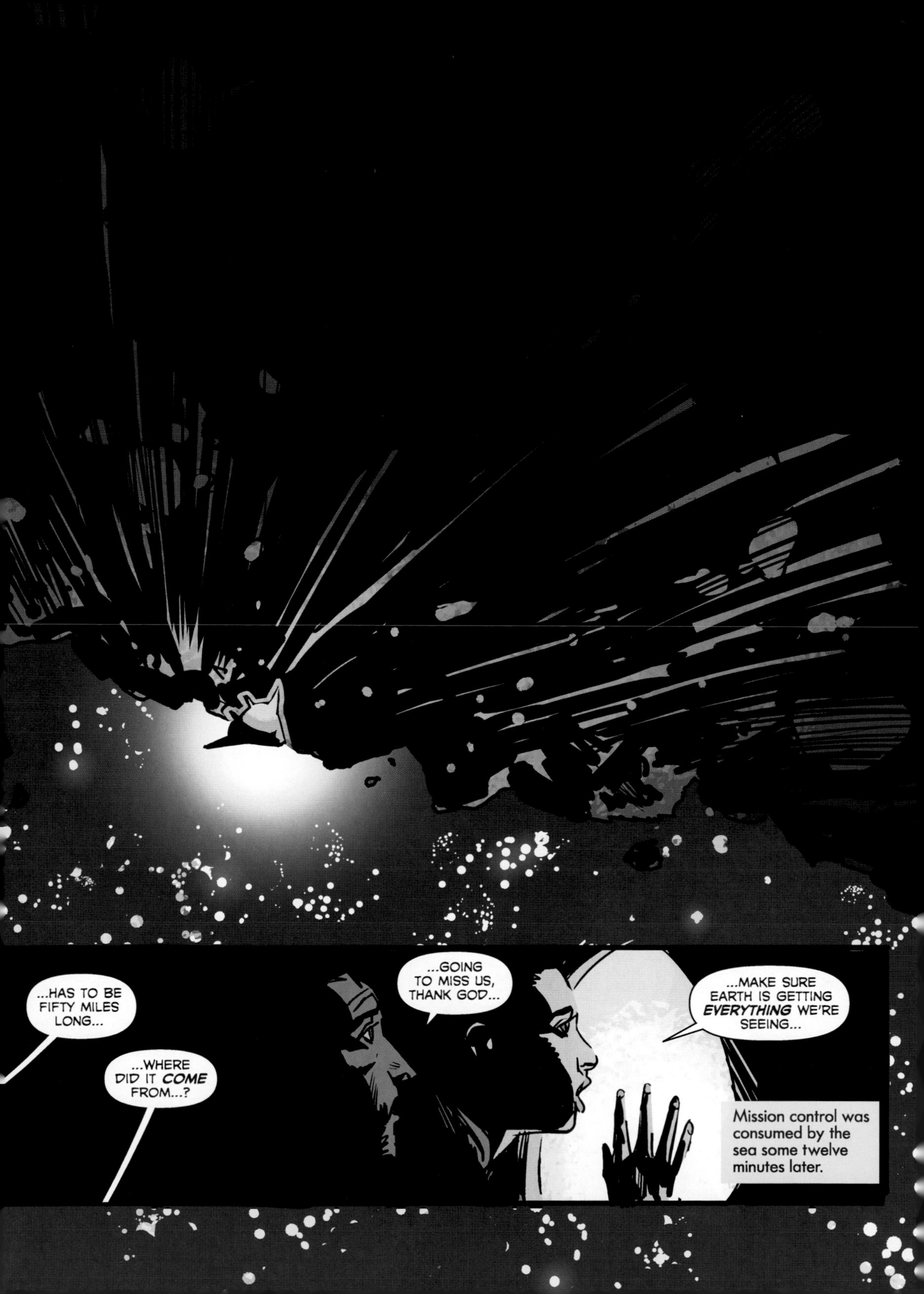
...HAS TO BE FIFTY MILES LONG...
...WHERE DID IT COME FROM...?
...GOING TO MISS US, THANK GOD...
...MAKE SURE EARTH IS GETTING EVERYTHING WE'RE SEEING...
Mission control was consumed by the sea some twelve minutes later.

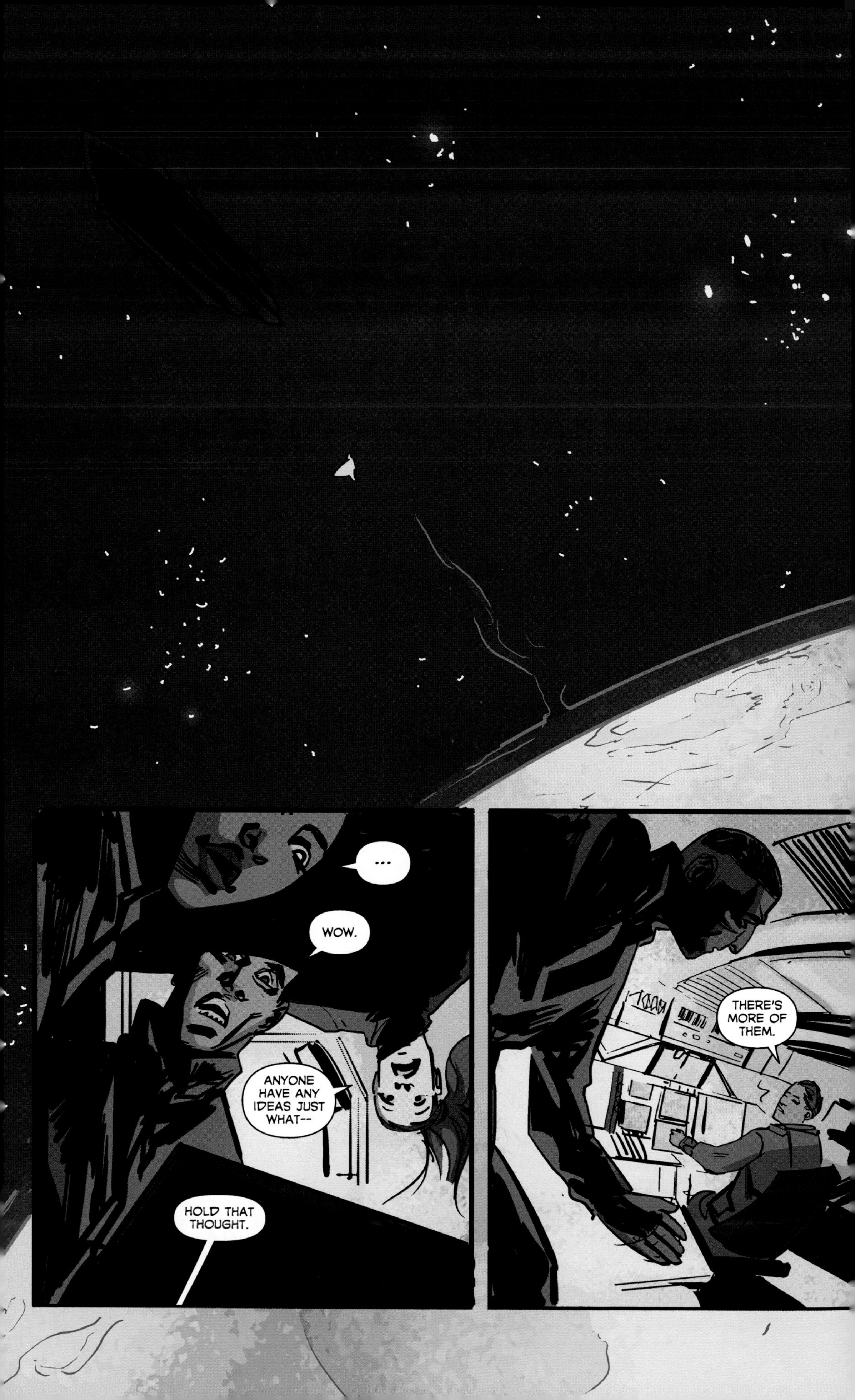
...
WOW.
ANYONE HAVE ANY IDEAS JUST WHAT--
HOLD THAT THOUGHT.
THERE'S MORE OF THEM.

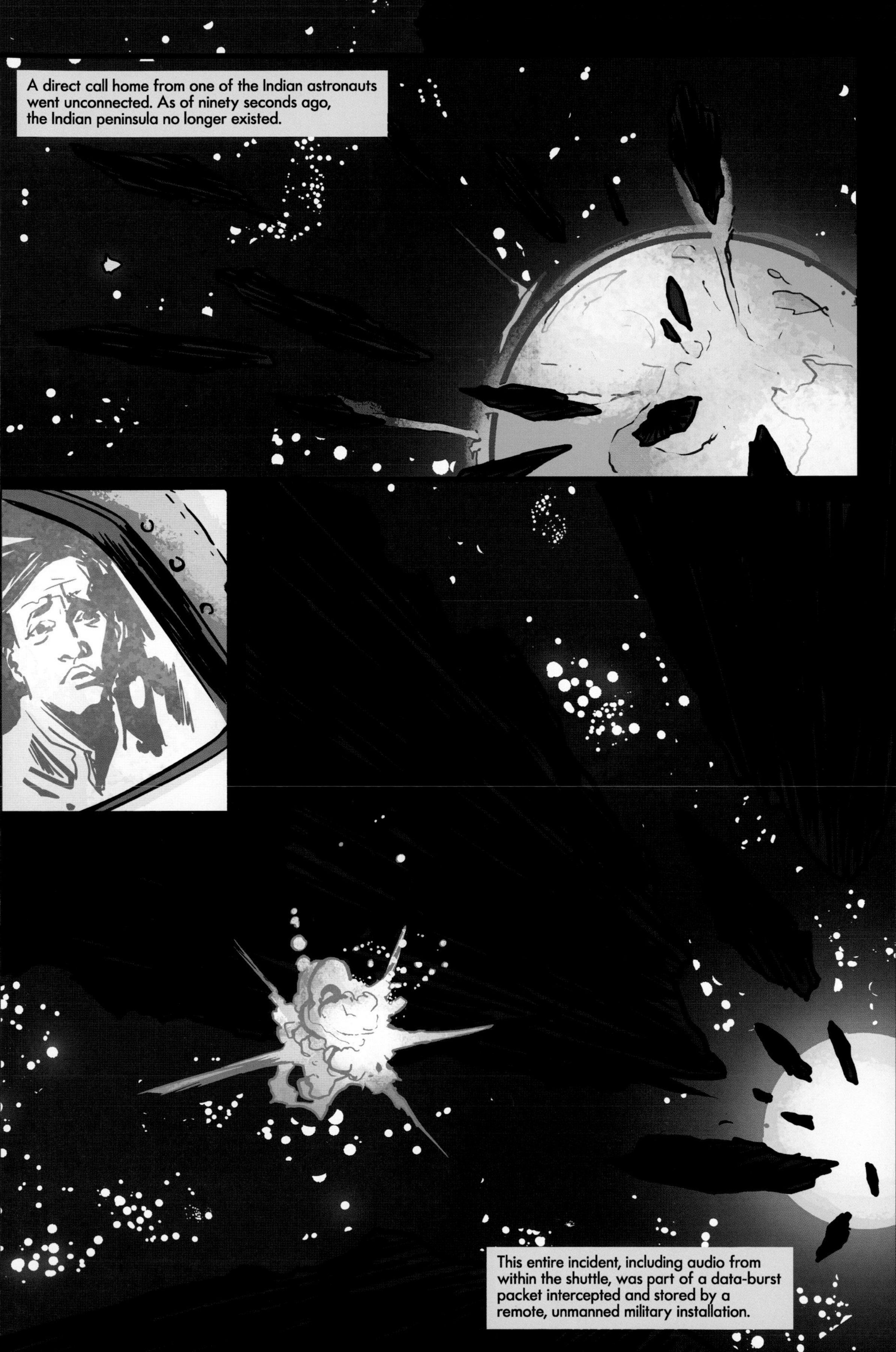
A direct call home from one of the Indian astronauts went unconnected. As of ninety seconds ago, the Indian peninsula no longer existed.
This entire incident, including audio from within the shuttle, was part of a data-burst packet intercepted and stored by a remote, unmanned military installation.

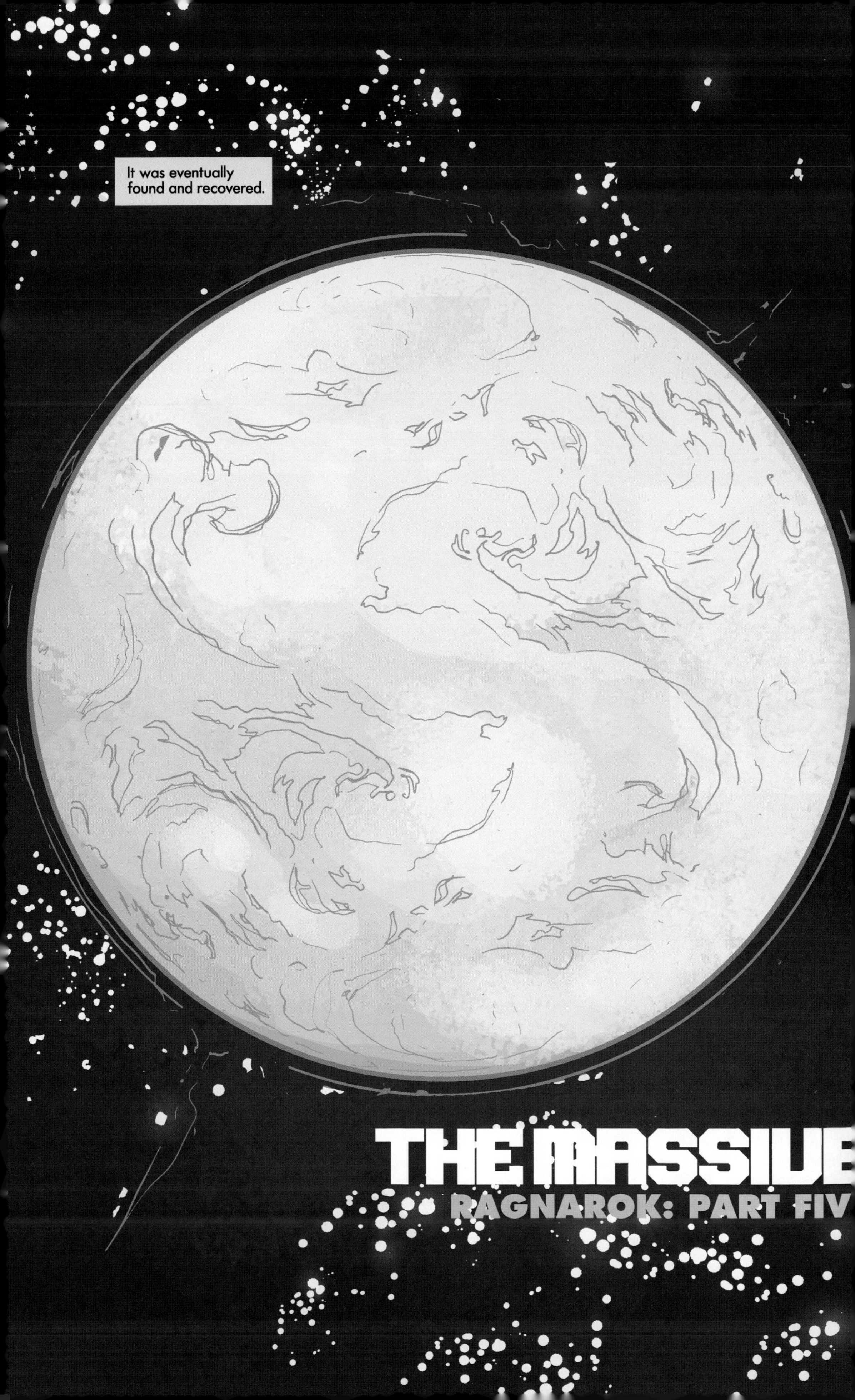
It was eventually found and recovered.
THE MASSIVE
RAGNAROK: PART FIV

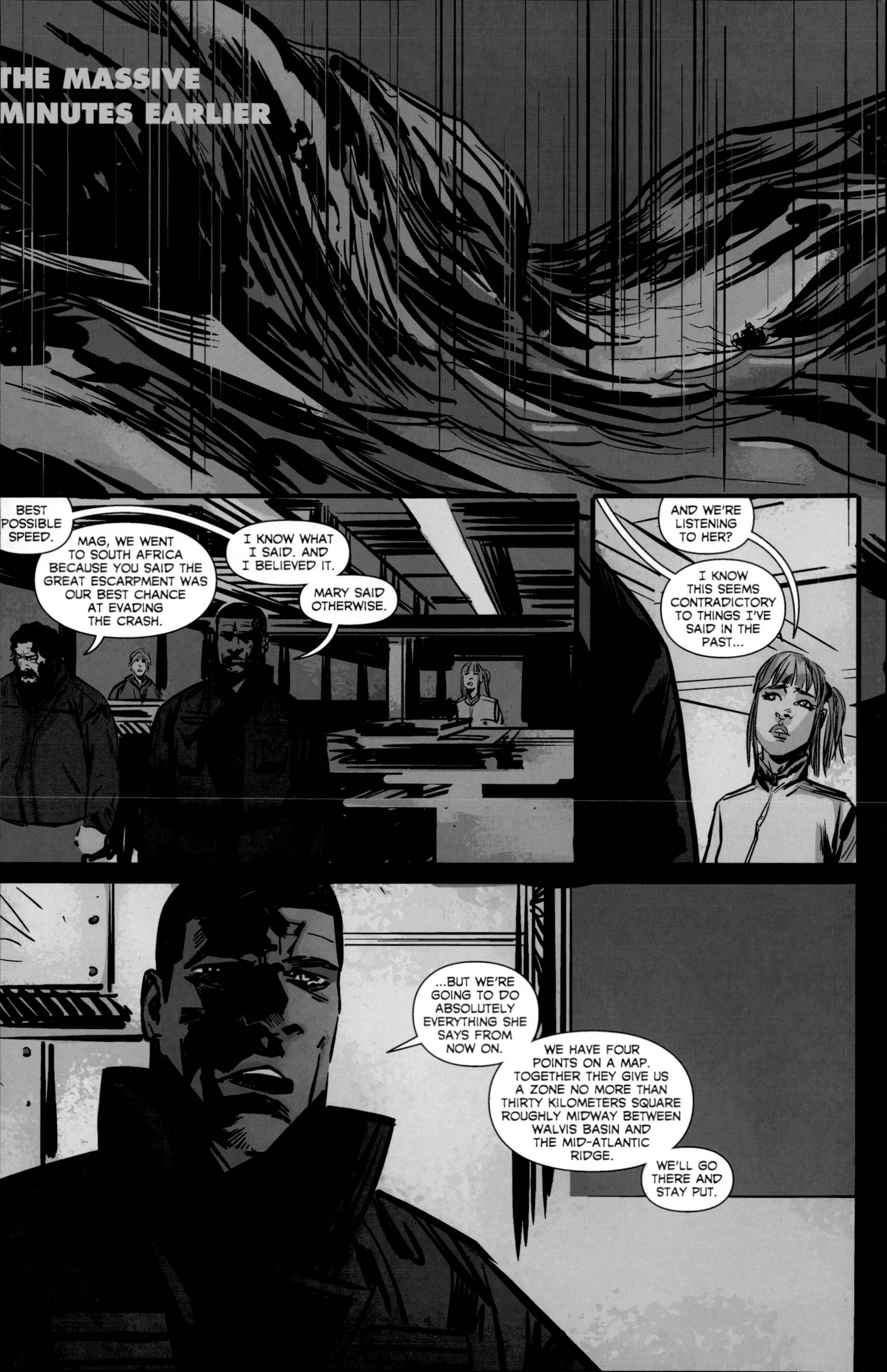
THE MASSIVE
MINUTES EARLIER
BEST POSSIBLE SPEED.
MAG, WE WENT TO SOUTH AFRICA BECAUSE YOU SAID THE GREAT ESCARPMENT WAS OUR BEST CHANCE AT EVADING THE CRASH.
I KNOW WHAT I SAID. AND I BELIEVED IT.
MARY SAID OTHERWISE.
AND WE'RE LISTENING TO HER?
I KNOW THIS SEEMS CONTRADICTORY TO THINGS I'VE SAID IN THE PAST...
...BUT WE'RE GOING TO DO ABSOLUTELY EVERYTHING SHE SAYS FROM NOW ON.
WE HAVE FOUR POINTS ON A MAP. TOGETHER THEY GIVE US A ZONE NO MORE THAN THIRTY KILOMETERS SQUARE ROUGHLY MIDWAY BETWEEN WALVIS BASIN AND THE MID-ATLANTIC RIDGE.
WE'LL GO THERE AND STAY PUT.

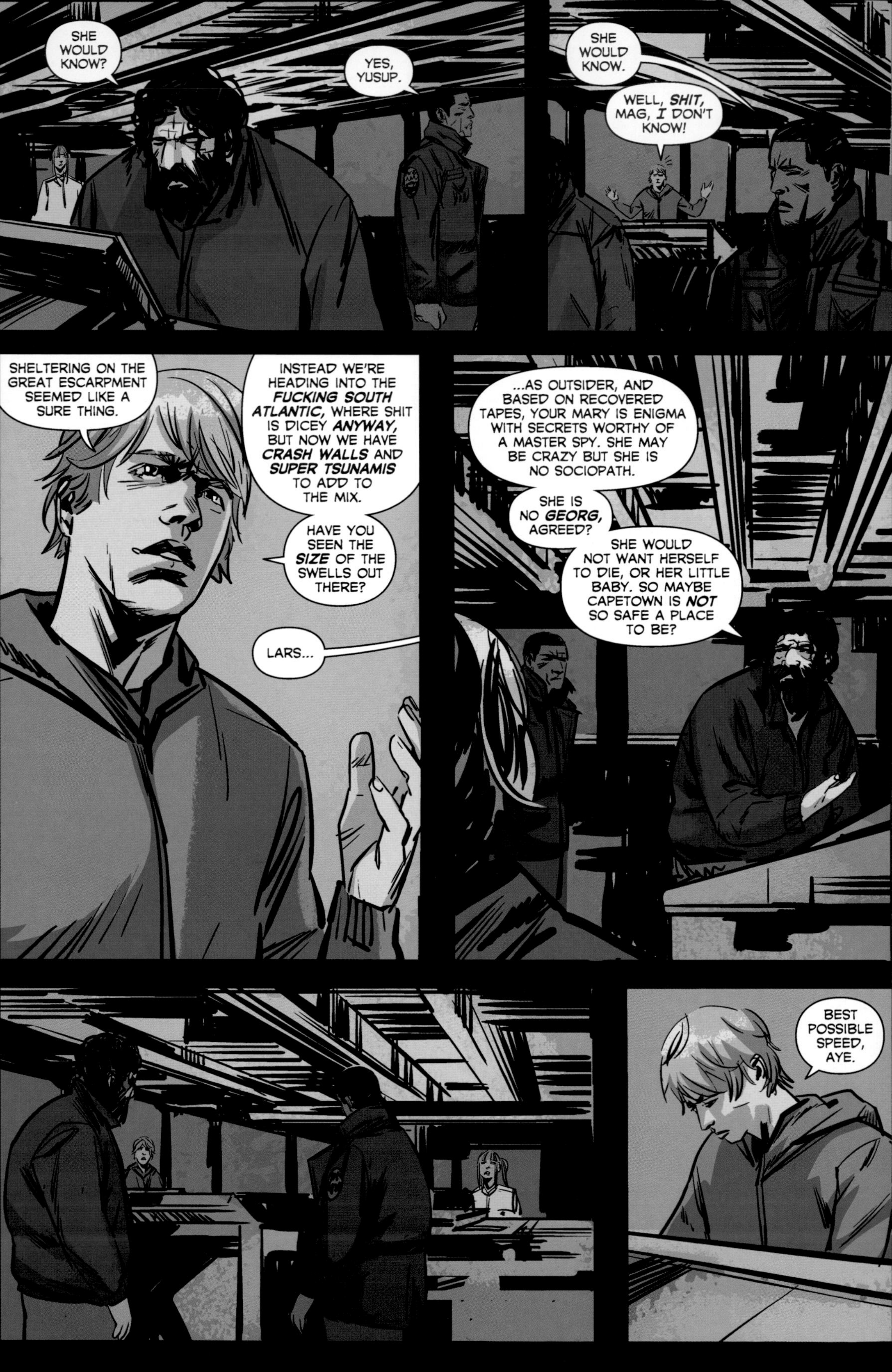
SHE WOULD KNOW?
YES, YUSUP.
SHE WOULD KNOW.
WELL, SHIT, MAG, I DON'T KNOW!
SHELTERING ON THE GREAT ESCARPMENT SEEMED LIKE A SURE THING.
INSTEAD WE'RE HEADING INTO THE FUCKING SOUTH ATLANTIC, WHERE SHIT IS DICEY ANYWAY, BUT NOW WE HAVE CRASH WALLS AND SUPER TSUNAMIS TO ADD TO THE MIX.
HAVE YOU SEEN THE SIZE OF THE SWELLS OUT THERE?
LARS...
...AS OUTSIDER, AND BASED ON RECOVERED TAPES, YOUR MARY IS ENIGMA WITH SECRETS WORTHY OF A MASTER SPY. SHE MAY BE CRAZY BUT SHE IS NO SOCIOPATH.
SHE IS NO GEORG, AGREED?
SHE WOULD NOT WANT HERSELF TO DIE, OR HER LITTLE BABY. SO MAYBE CAPETOWN IS NOT SO SAFE A PLACE TO BE?
BEST POSSIBLE SPEED, AYE.

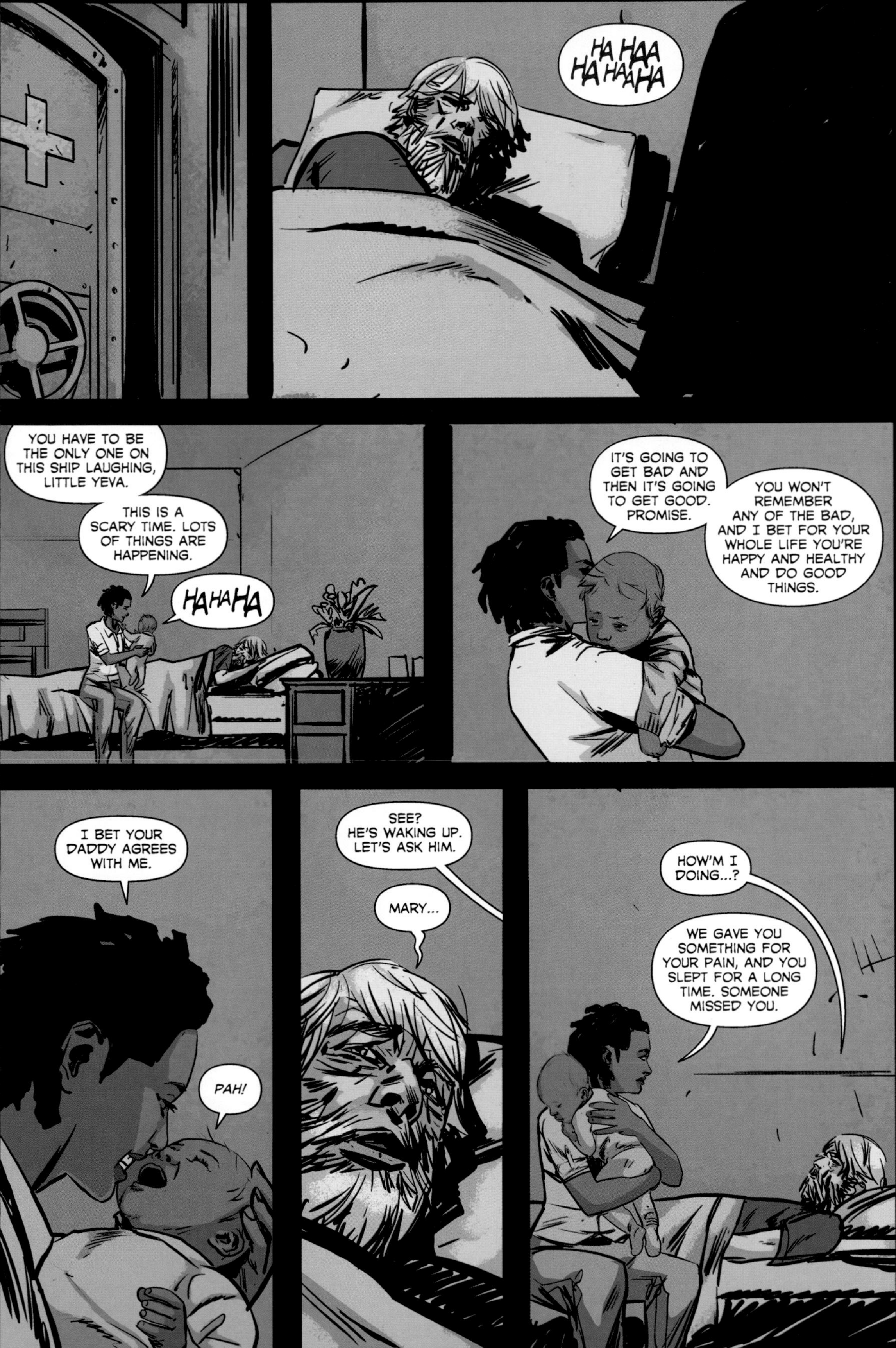
HA HAA HA HAAHA
YOU HAVE TO BE THE ONLY ONE ON THIS SHIP LAUGHING, LITTLE YEVA.
THIS IS A SCARY TIME. LOTS OF THINGS ARE HAPPENING.
HAHAHA
IT'S GOING TO GET BAD AND THEN IT'S GOING TO GET GOOD. PROMISE.
YOU WON'T REMEMBER ANY OF THE BAD, AND I BET FOR YOUR WHOLE LIFE YOU'RE HAPPY AND HEALTHY AND DO GOOD THINGS.
I BET YOUR DADDY AGREES WITH ME.
PAH!
SEE? HE'S WAKING UP. LET'S ASK HIM.
MARY...
HOW'M I DOING...?
WE GAVE YOU SOMETHING FOR YOUR PAIN, AND YOU SLEPT FOR A LONG TIME. SOMEONE MISSED YOU.

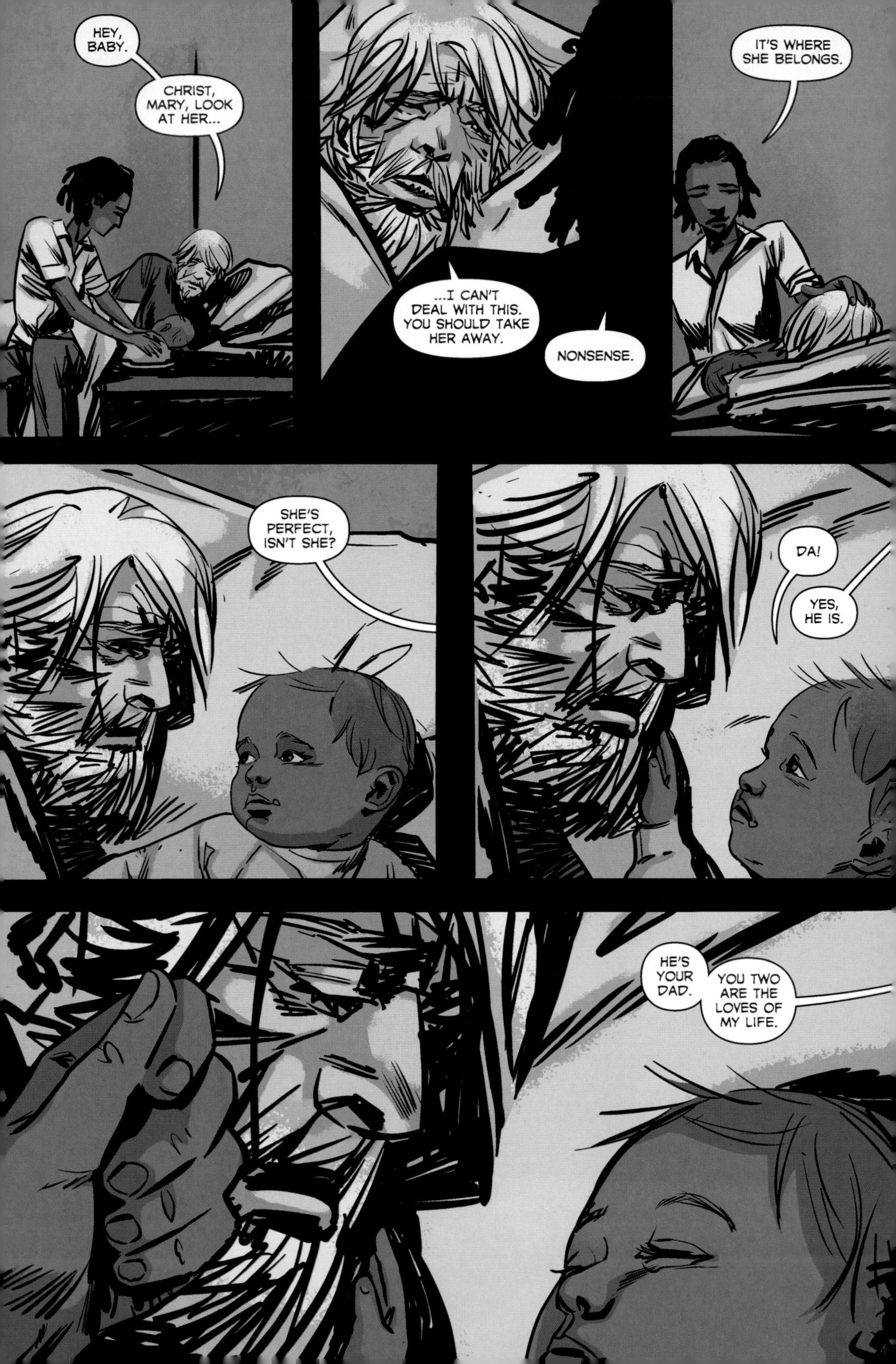
HEY, BABY.
CHRIST, MARY, LOOK AT HER...
...I CAN'T DEAL WITH THIS. YOU SHOULD TAKE HER AWAY.
NONSENSE.
IT'S WHERE SHE BELONGS.
SHE'S PERFECT, ISN'T SHE?
DA!
YES, HE IS.
HE'S YOUR DAD.
YOU TWO ARE THE LOVES OF MY LIFE.

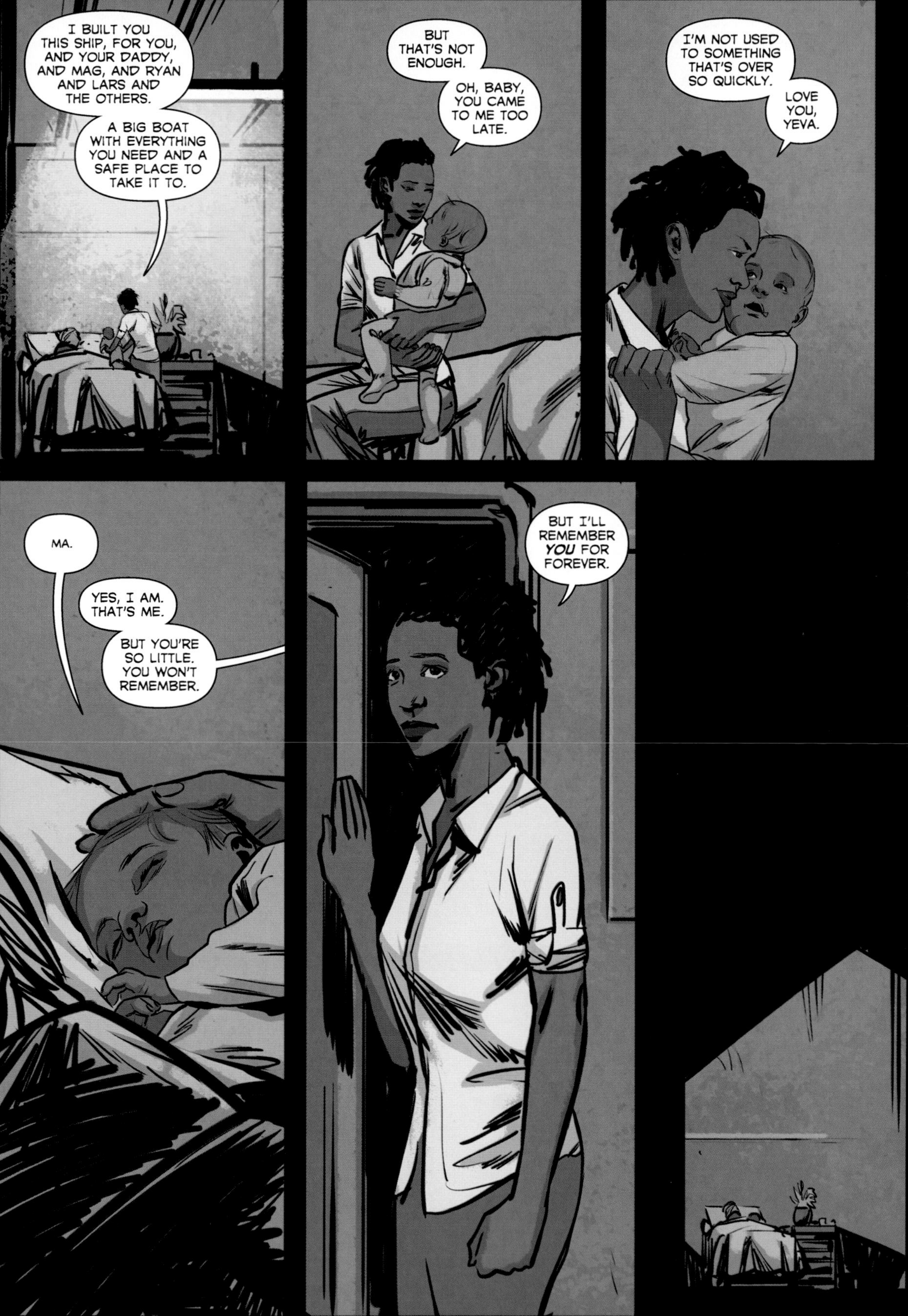
I BUILT YOU THIS SHIP, FOR YOU, AND YOUR DADDY, AND MAG, AND RYAN AND LARS AND THE OTHERS.
A BIG BOAT WITH EVERYTHING YOU NEED AND A SAFE PLACE TO TAKE IT TO.
BUT THAT'S NOT ENOUGH.
OH, BABY, YOU CAME TO ME TOO LATE.
I'M NOT USED TO SOMETHING THAT'S OVER SO QUICKLY.
LOVE YOU, YEVA.
MA.
YES, I AM. THAT'S ME.
BUT YOU'RE SO LITTLE. YOU WON'T REMEMBER.
BUT I'LL REMEMBER *YOU* FOR FOREVER.

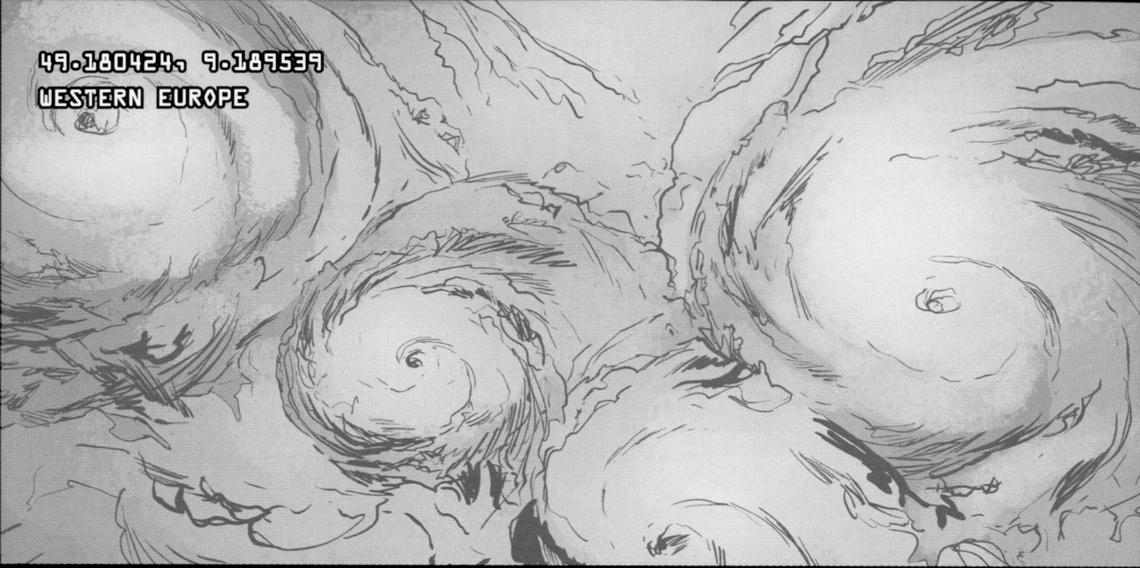
49.180424, 9.189539
WESTERN EUROPE

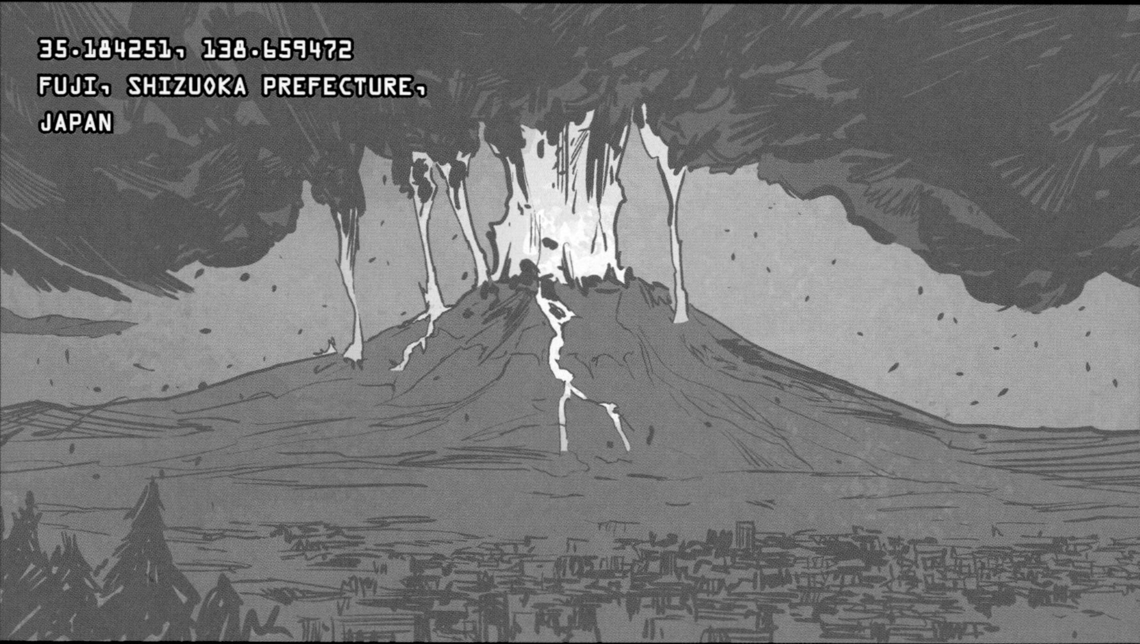
35.184251, 138.659472
FUJI, SHIZUOKA PREFECTURE,
JAPAN

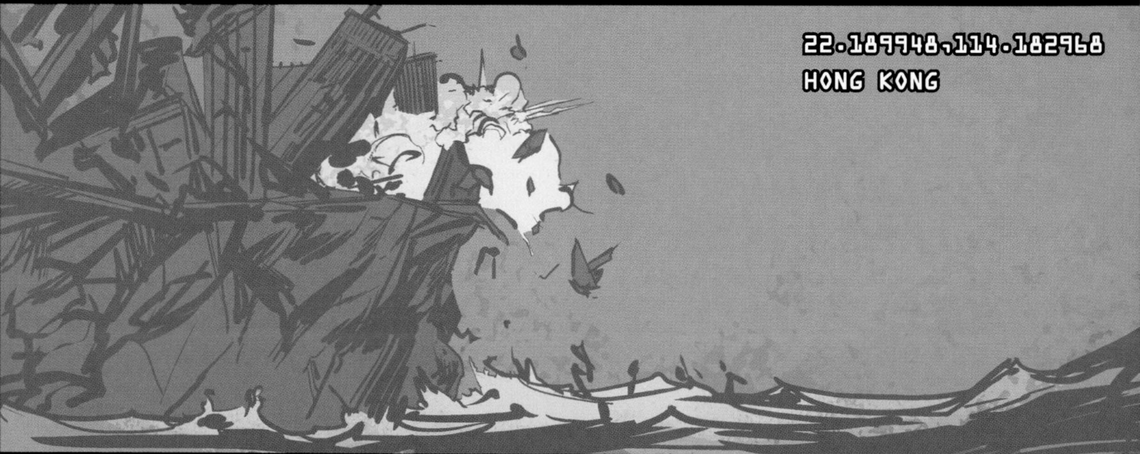
22.189948,114.182968
HONG KONG

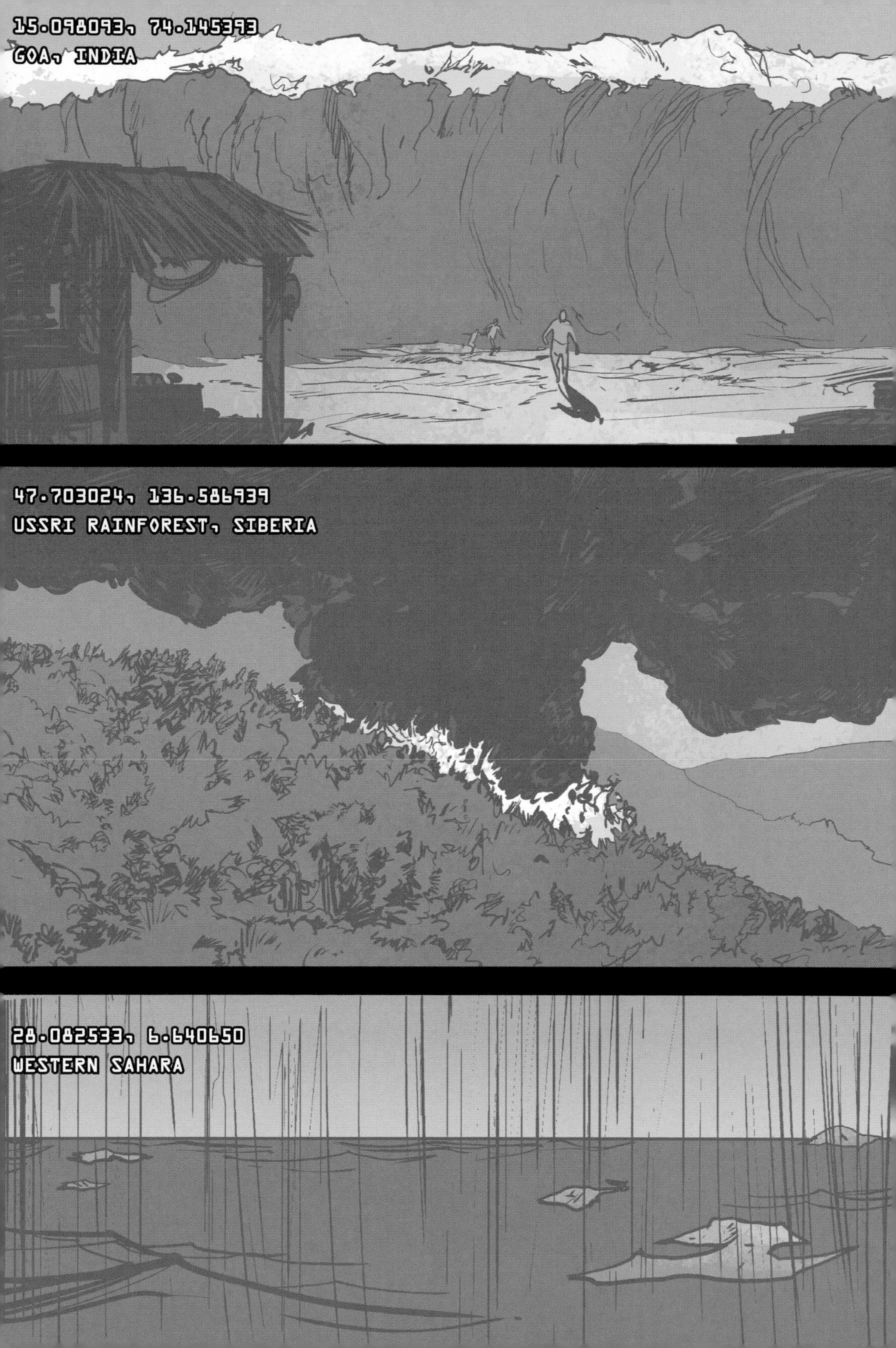
15.098093, 74.145393
GOA, INDIA
47.703024, 136.586939
USSRI RAINFOREST, SIBERIA
28.082533, 6.640650
WESTERN SAHARA

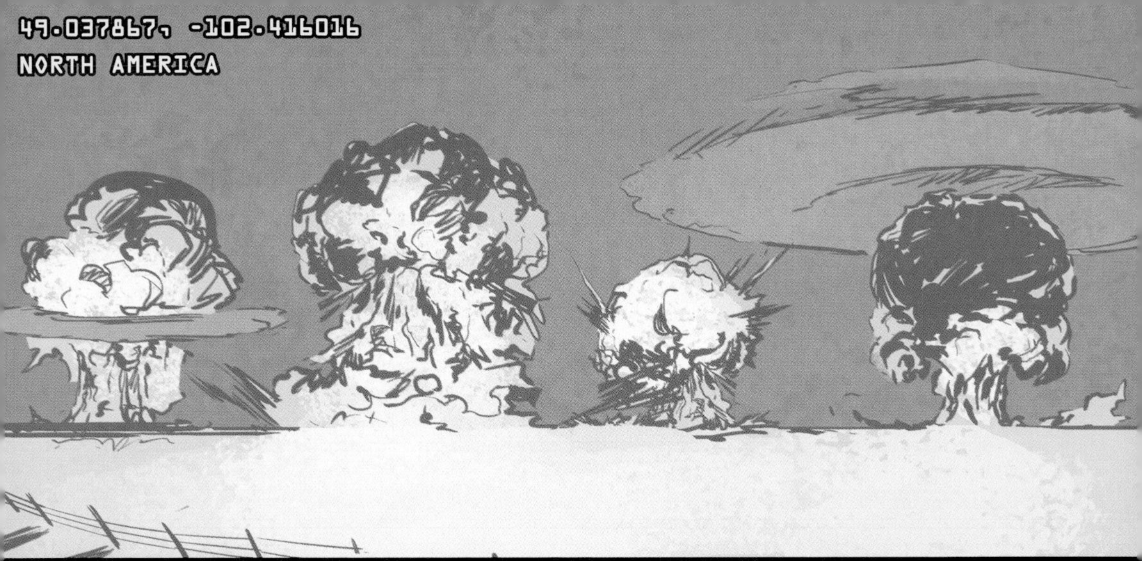
49.037867, -102.416016
NORTH AMERICA

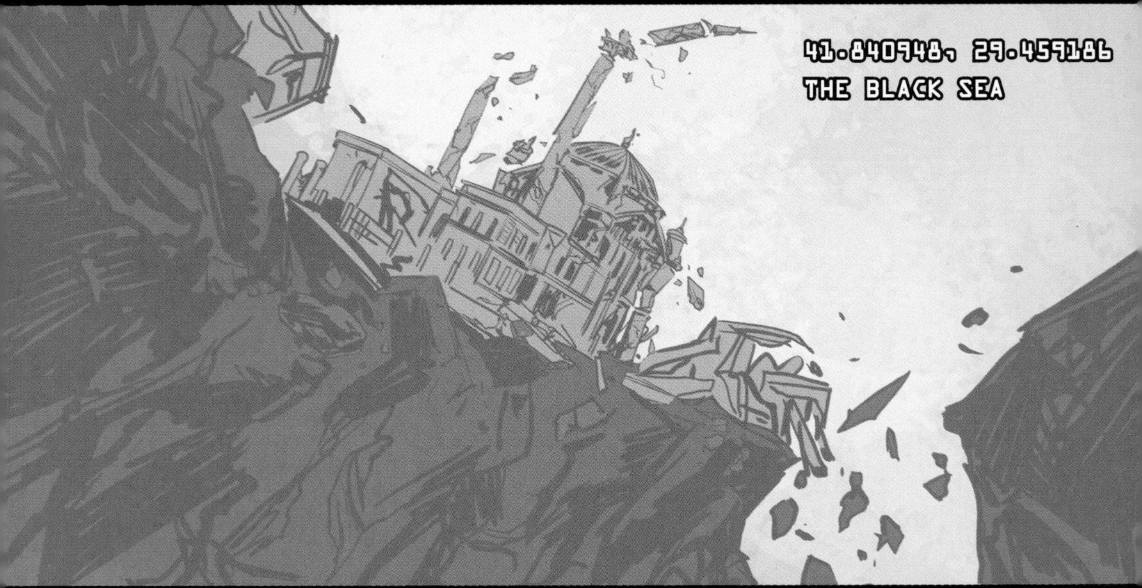
41.840948, 29.459186
THE BLACK SEA

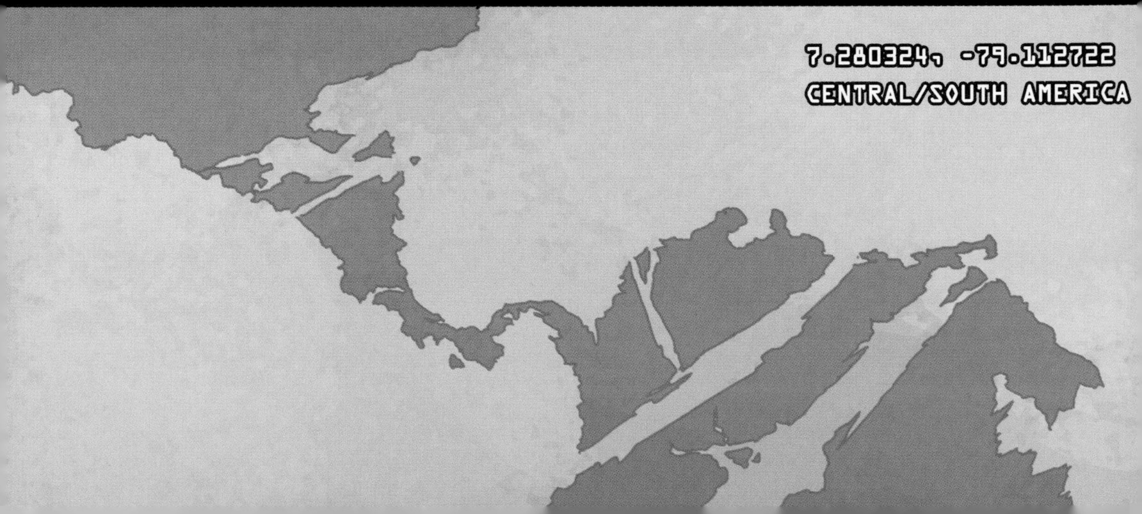
7.280324, -79.112722
CENTRAL/SOUTH AMERICA

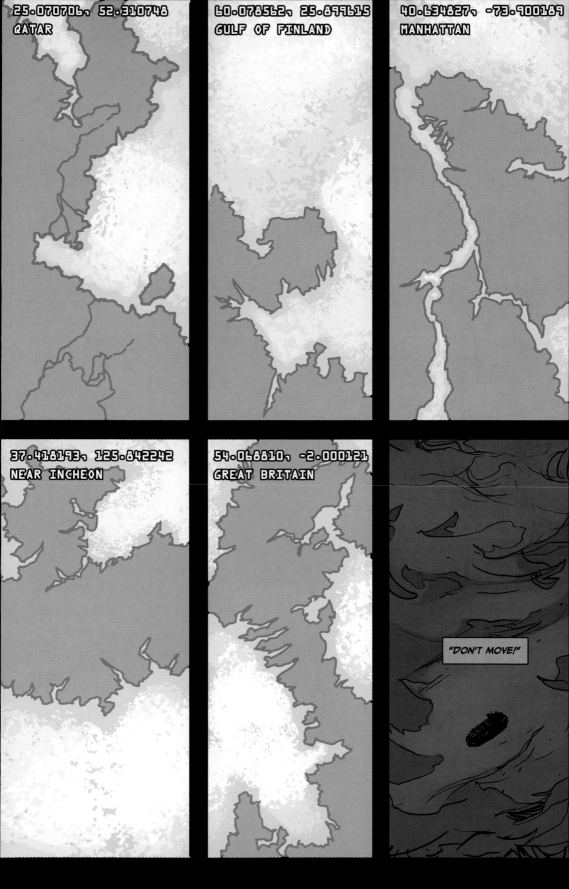

25.070706, 52.310748
QATAR

60.078562, 25.899615
GULF OF FINLAND

40.634827, -73.900189
MANHATTAN

37.418193, 125.842242
NEAR INCHEON

54.068810, -2.000121
GREAT BRITAIN

"DON'T MOVE!"

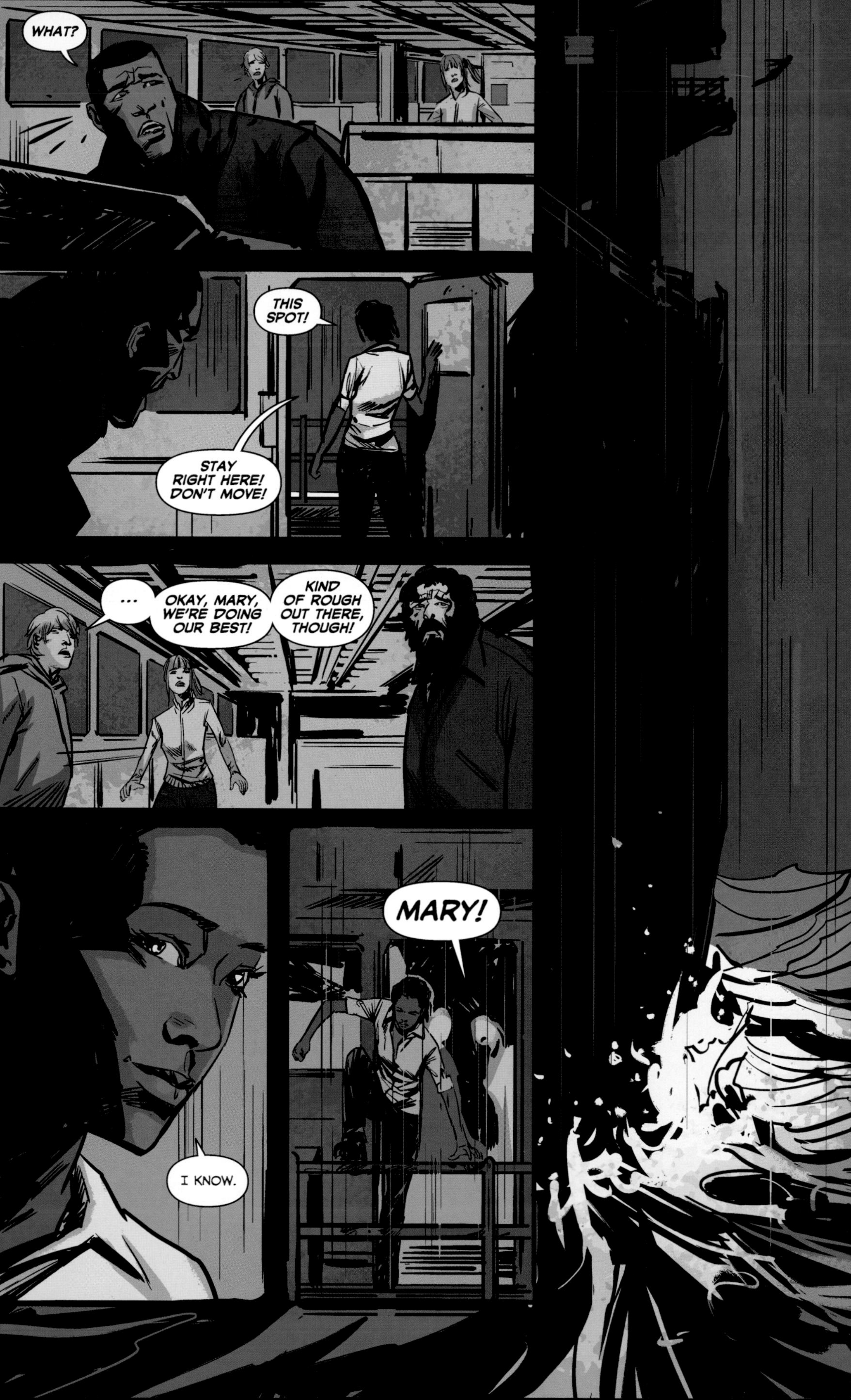
WHAT?
THIS SPOT!
STAY RIGHT HERE! DON'T MOVE!
...
OKAY, MARY, WE'RE DOING OUR BEST!
KIND OF ROUGH OUT THERE, THOUGH!
I KNOW.
MARY!

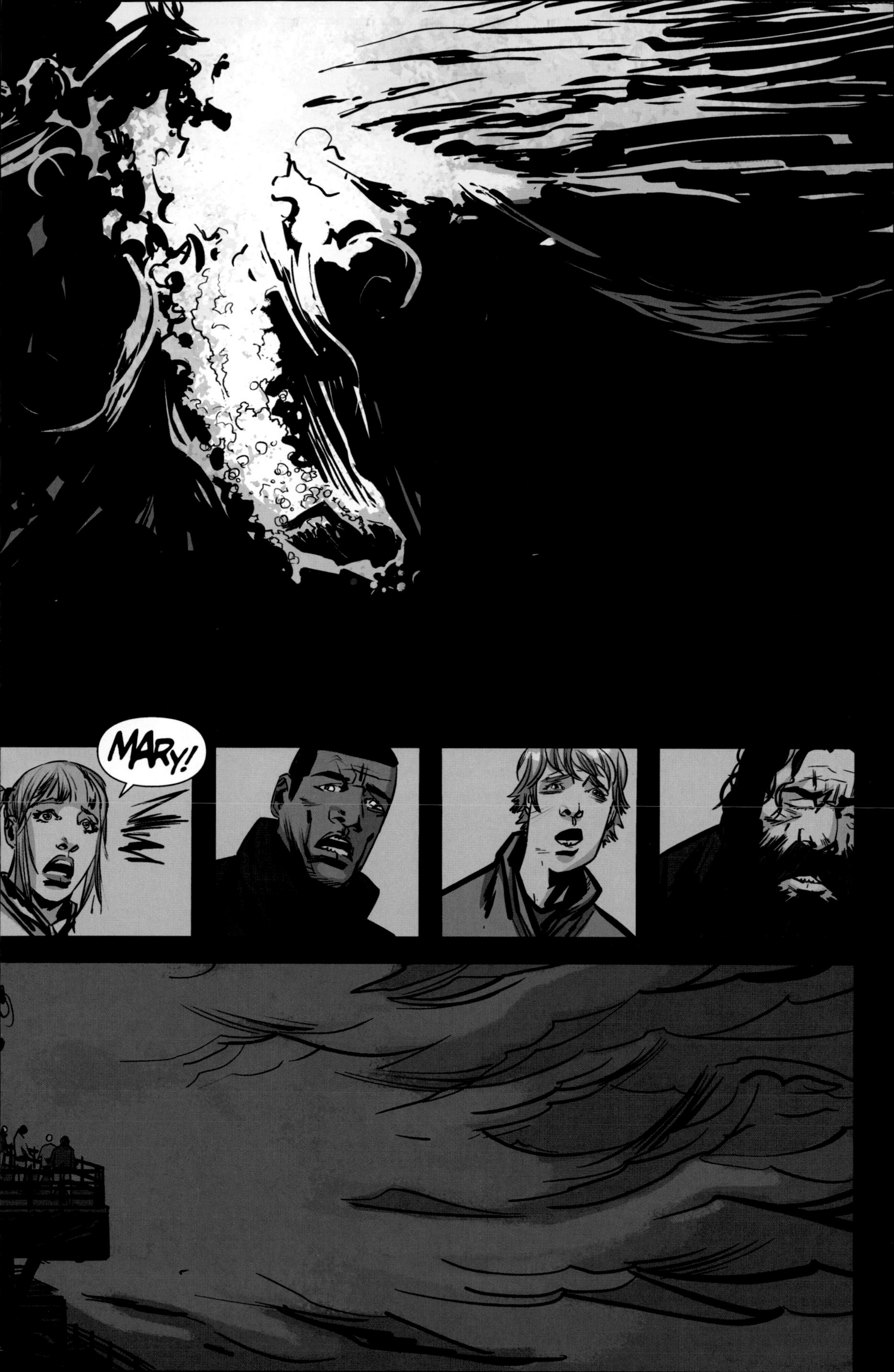
MARY!

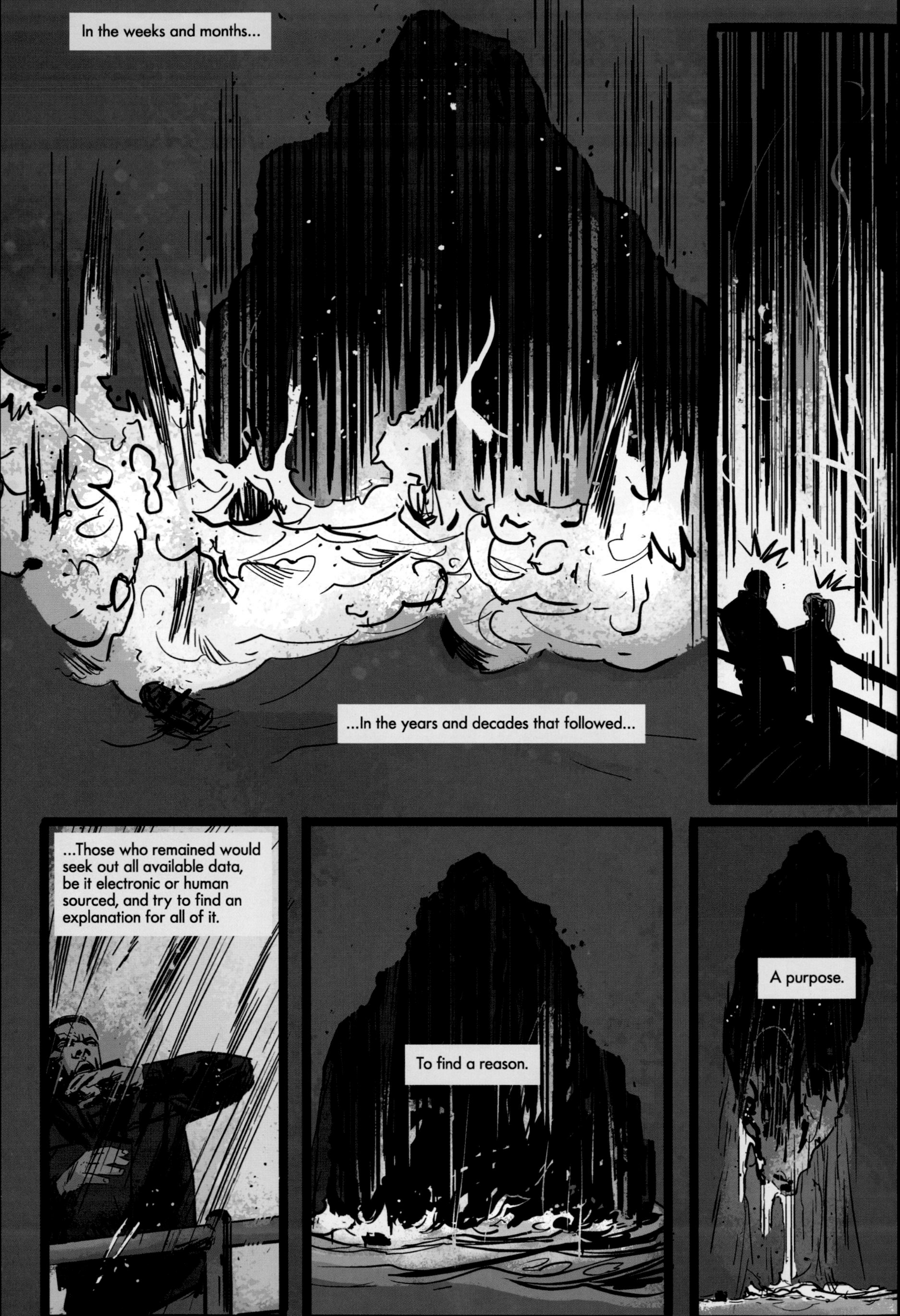
In the weeks and months...
...In the years and decades that followed...
...Those who remained would seek out all available data, be it electronic or human sourced, and try to find an explanation for all of it.
To find a reason.
A purpose.

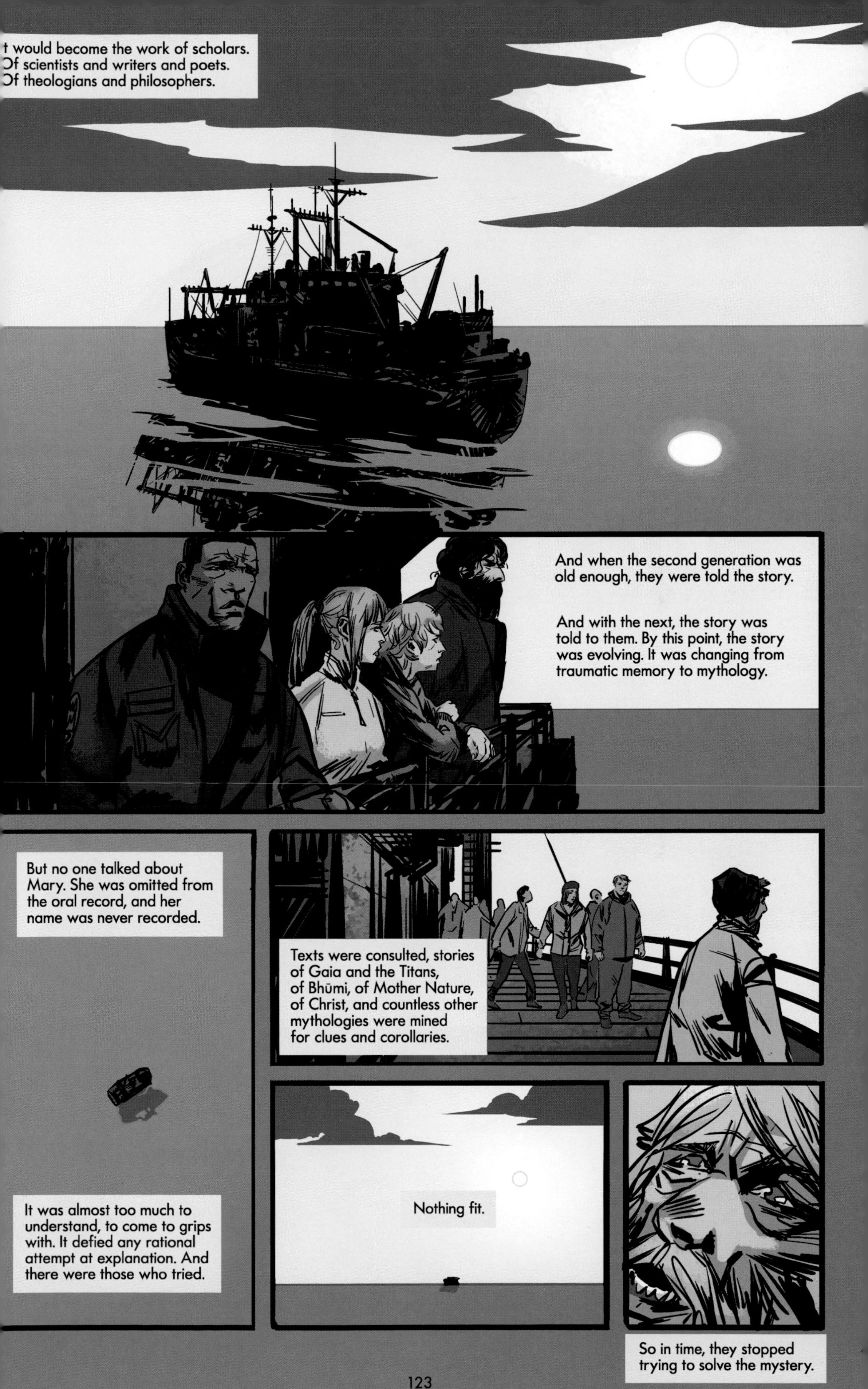
t would become the work of scholars. Of scientists and writers and poets. Of theologians and philosophers.
And when the second generation was old enough, they were told the story.
And with the next, the story was told to them. By this point, the story was evolving. It was changing from traumatic memory to mythology.
But no one talked about Mary. She was omitted from the oral record, and her name was never recorded.
Texts were consulted, stories of Gaia and the Titans, of Bhūmi, of Mother Nature, of Christ, and countless other mythologies were mined for clues and corollaries.
It was almost too much to understand, to come to grips with. It defied any rational attempt at explanation. And there were those who tried.
Nothing fit.
So in time, they stopped trying to solve the mystery.

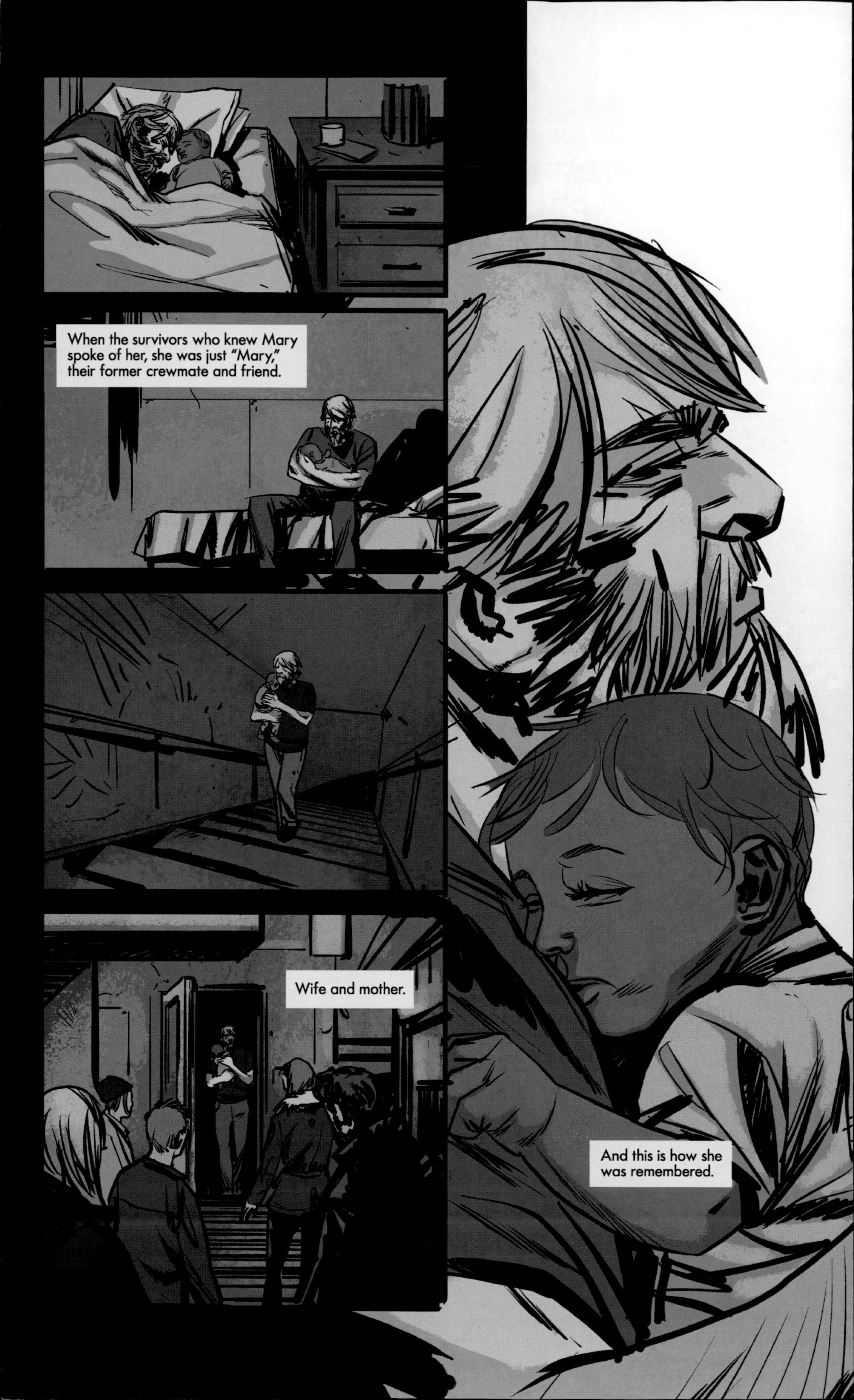

When the survivors who knew Mary spoke of her, she was just "Mary," their former crewmate and friend.
Wife and mother.
And this is how she was remembered.

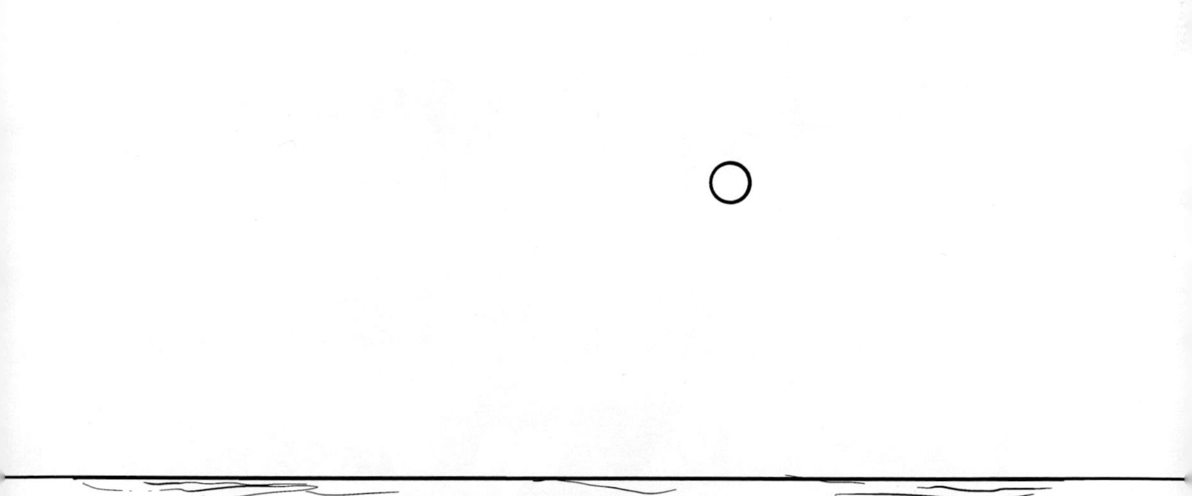

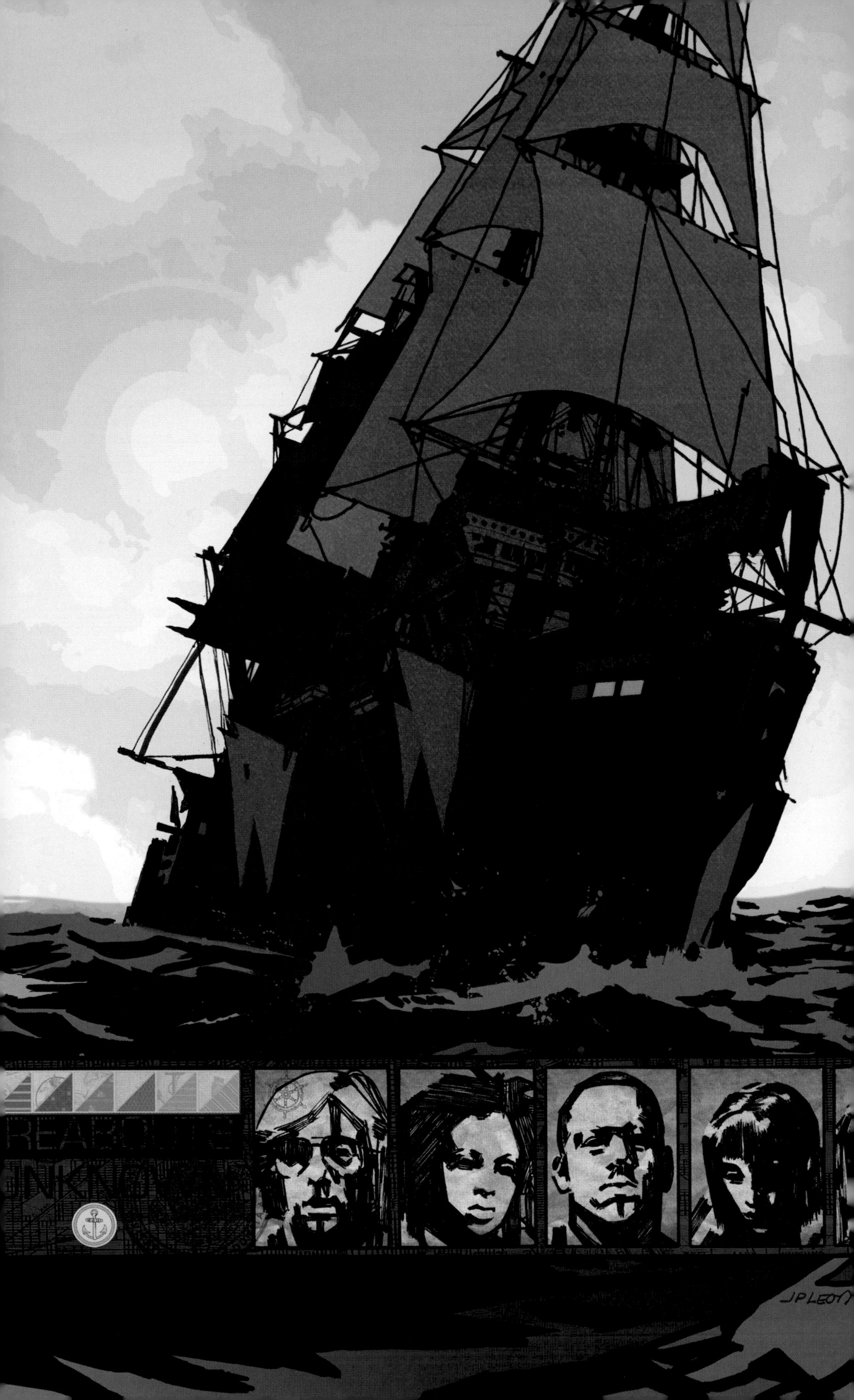

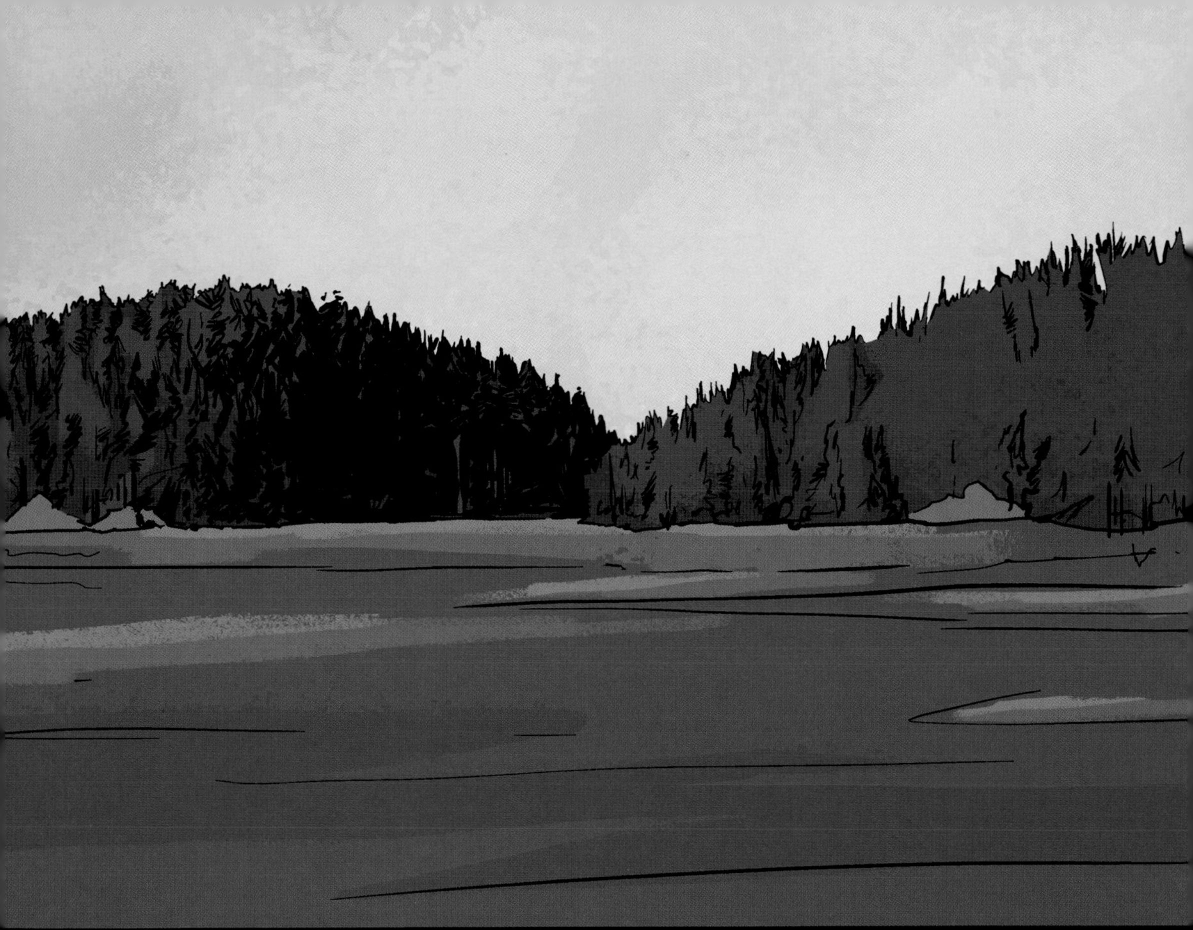
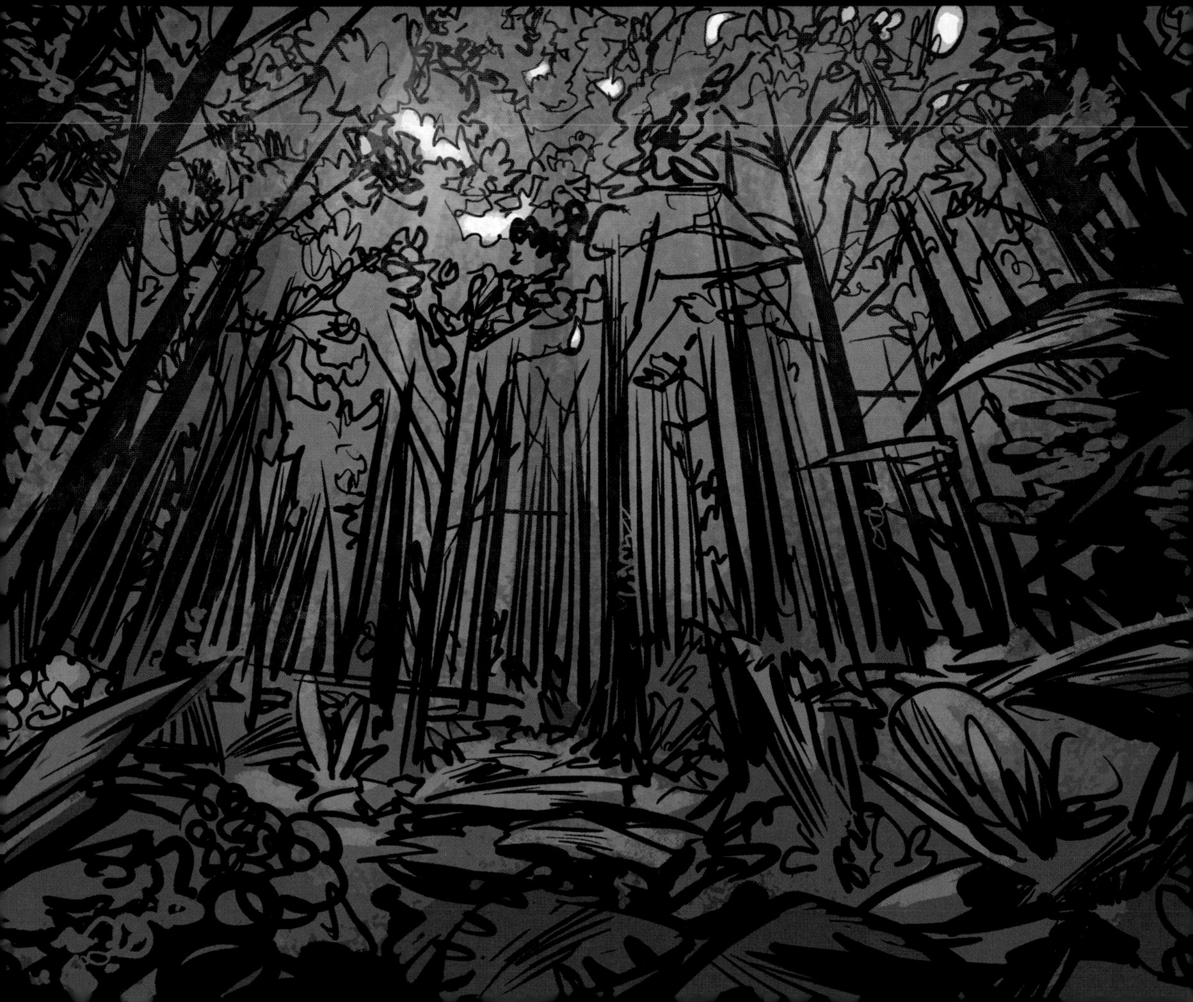

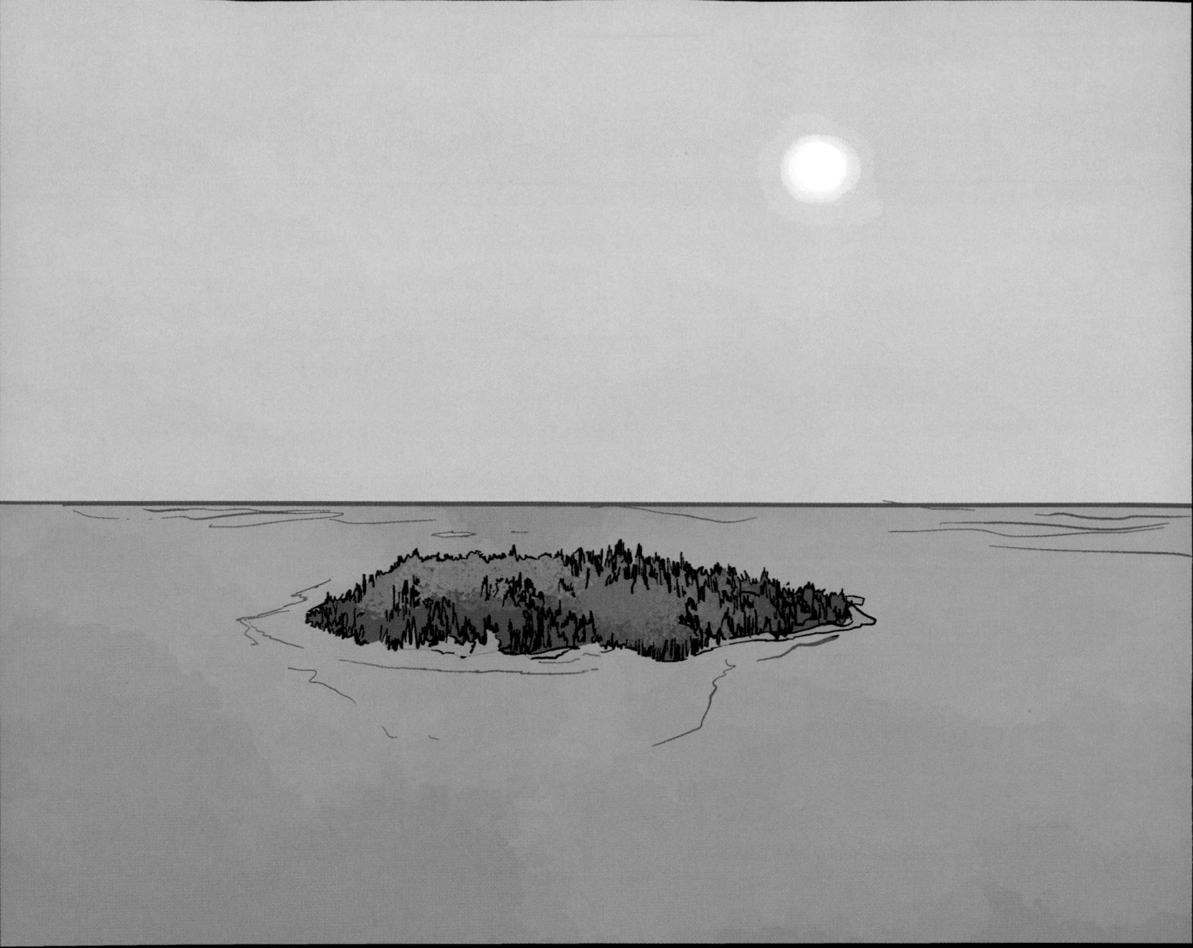
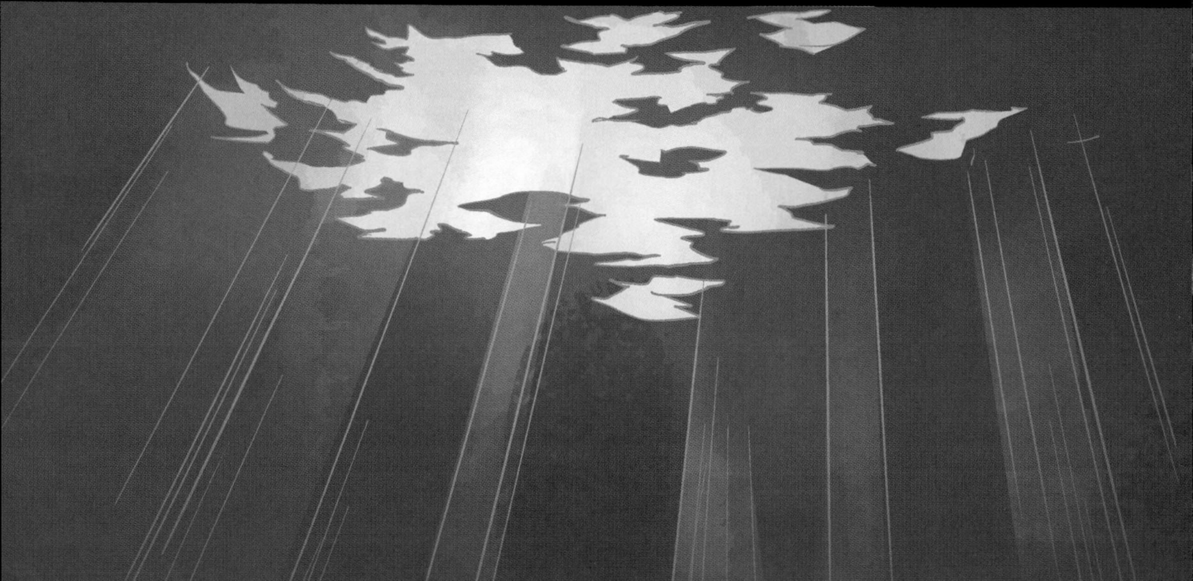

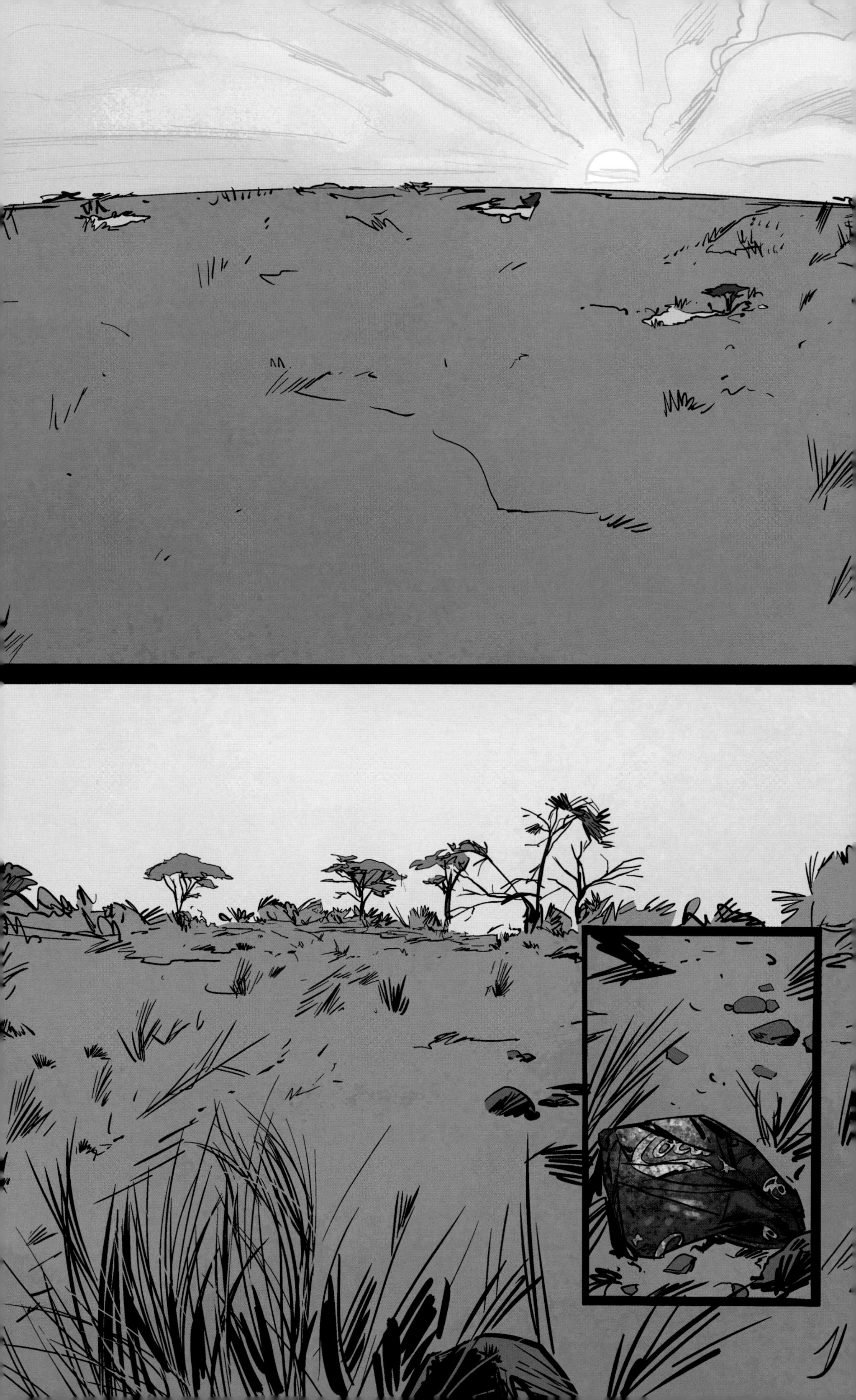

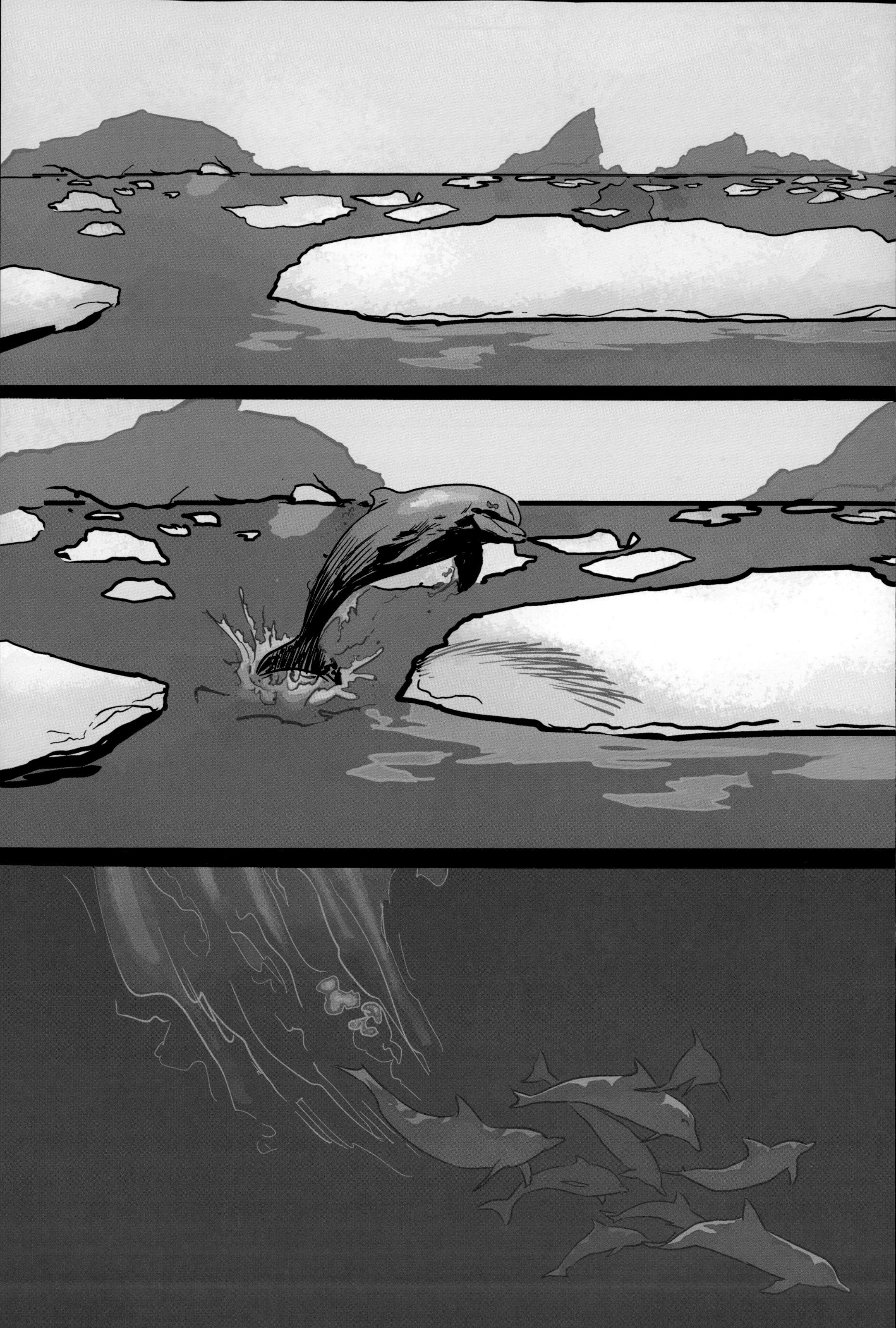

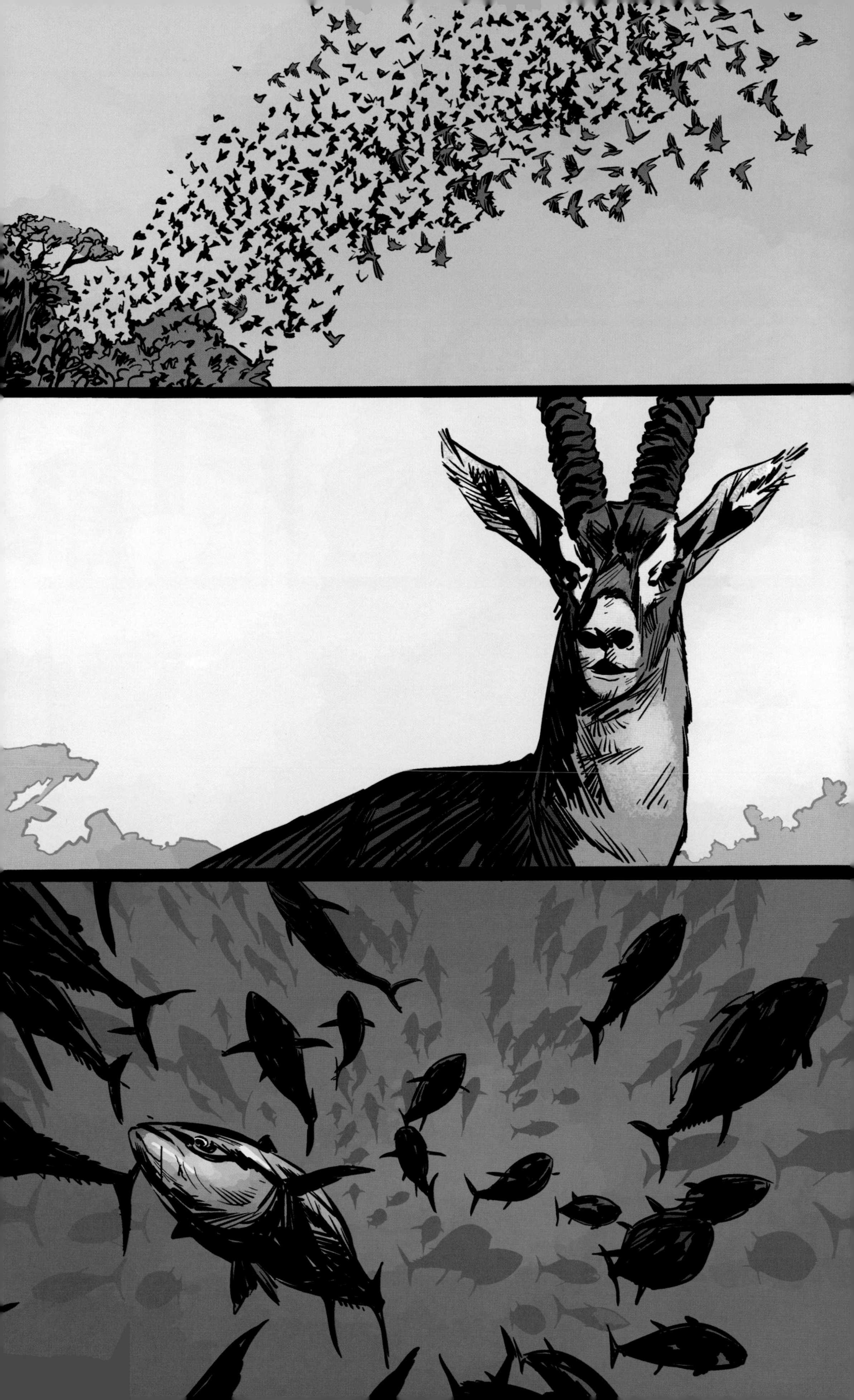

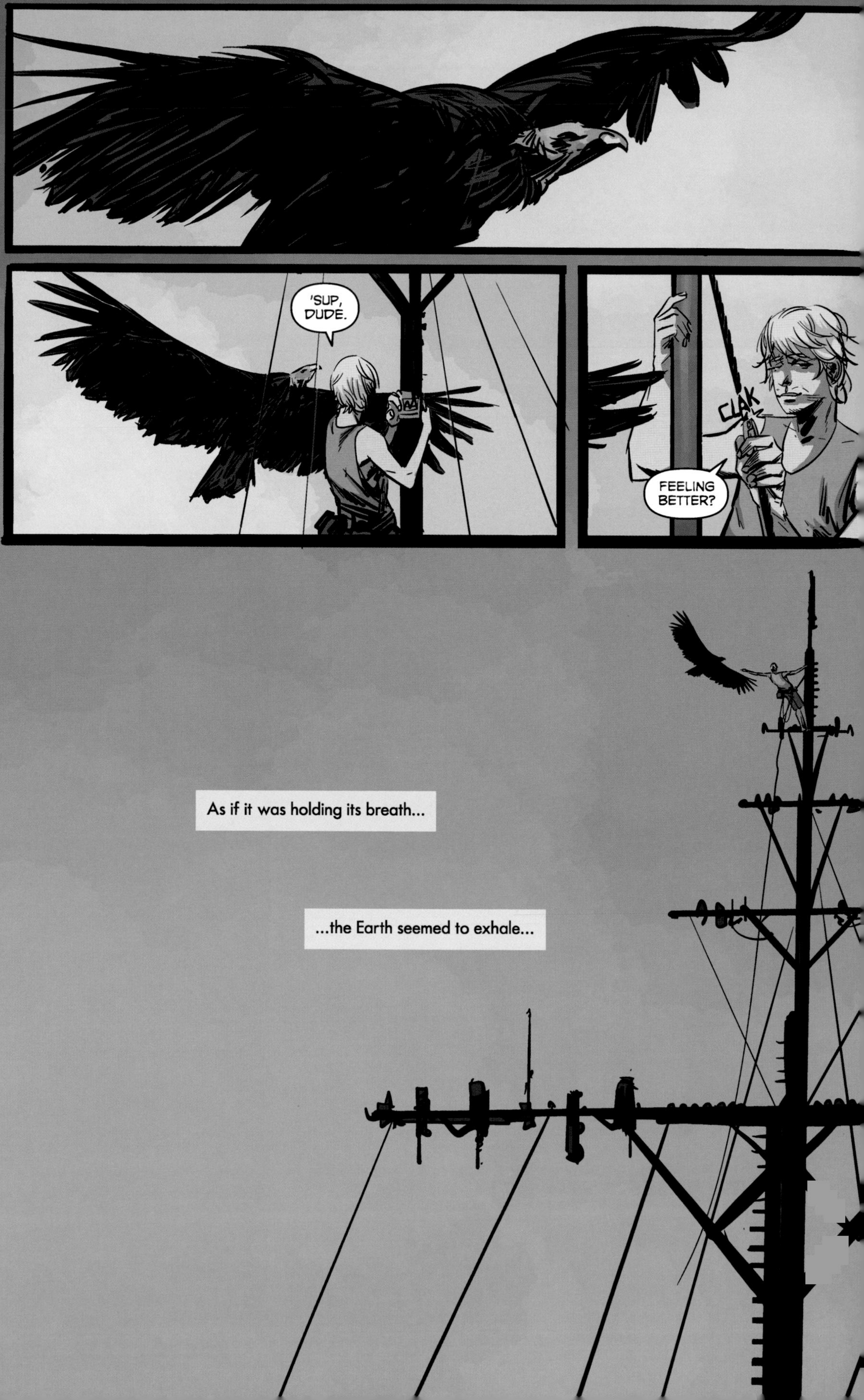
'SUP, DUDE.
CLAK
FEELING BETTER?
As if it was holding its breath...
...the Earth seemed to exhale...

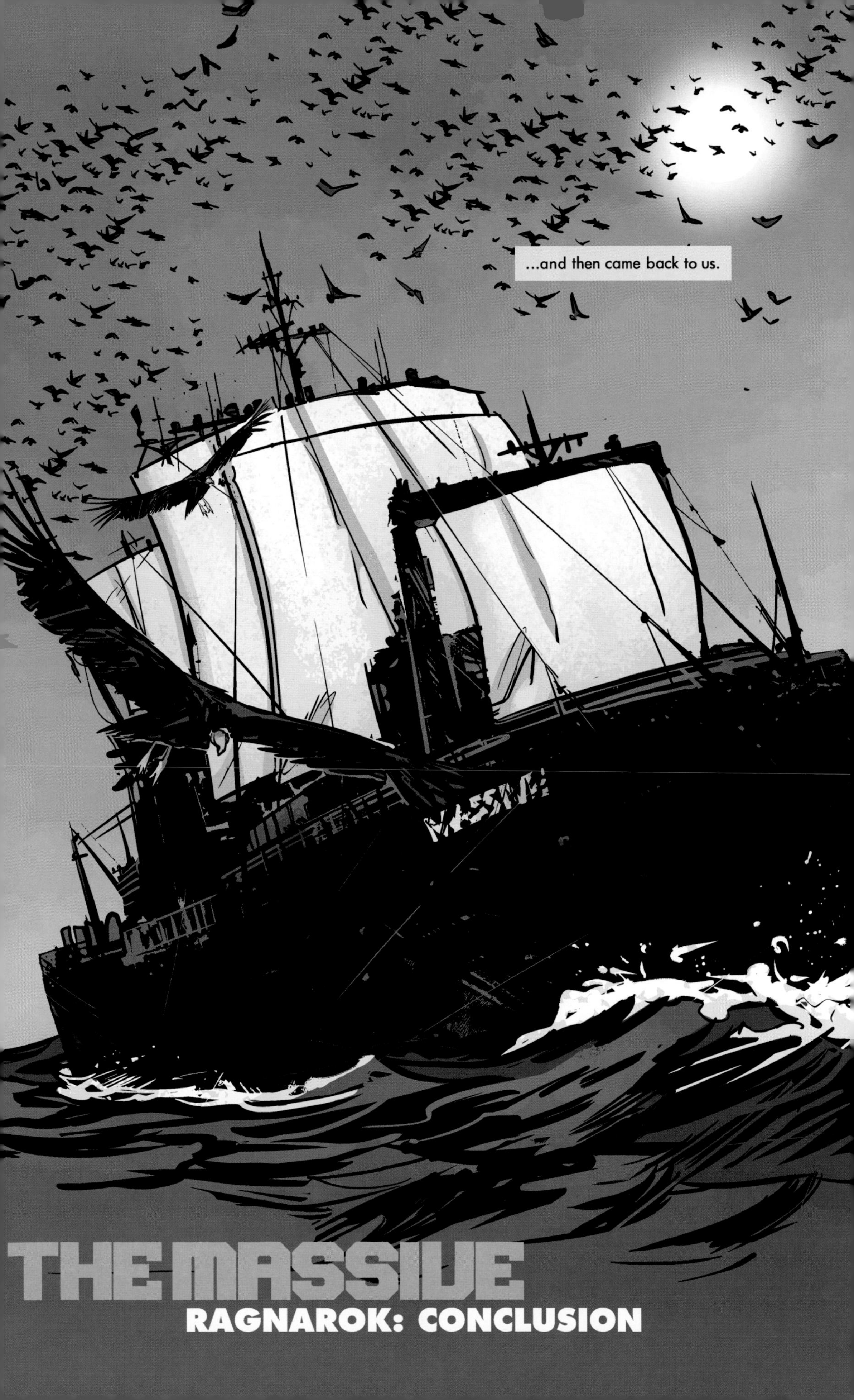

...and then came back to us.
MASSIVE
THE MASSIVE
RAGNAROK: CONCLUSION

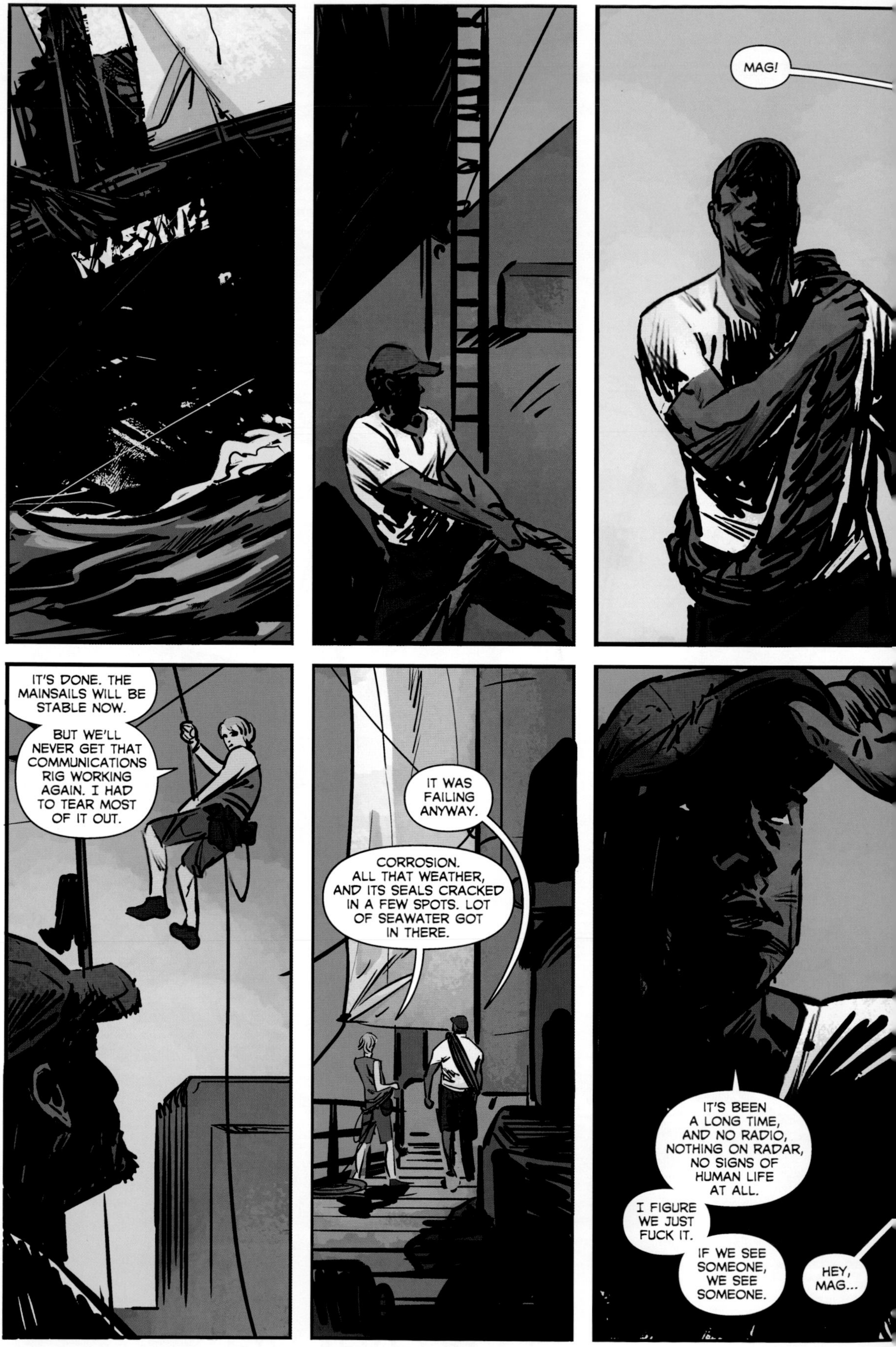
MAG!
IT'S DONE. THE MAINSAILS WILL BE STABLE NOW.
BUT WE'LL NEVER GET THAT COMMUNICATIONS RIG WORKING AGAIN. I HAD TO TEAR MOST OF IT OUT.
IT WAS FAILING ANYWAY.
CORROSION. ALL THAT WEATHER, AND ITS SEALS CRACKED IN A FEW SPOTS. LOT OF SEAWATER GOT IN THERE.
IT'S BEEN A LONG TIME, AND NO RADIO, NOTHING ON RADAR, NO SIGNS OF HUMAN LIFE AT ALL.
I FIGURE WE JUST FUCK IT.
IF WE SEE SOMEONE, WE SEE SOMEONE.
HEY, MAG...

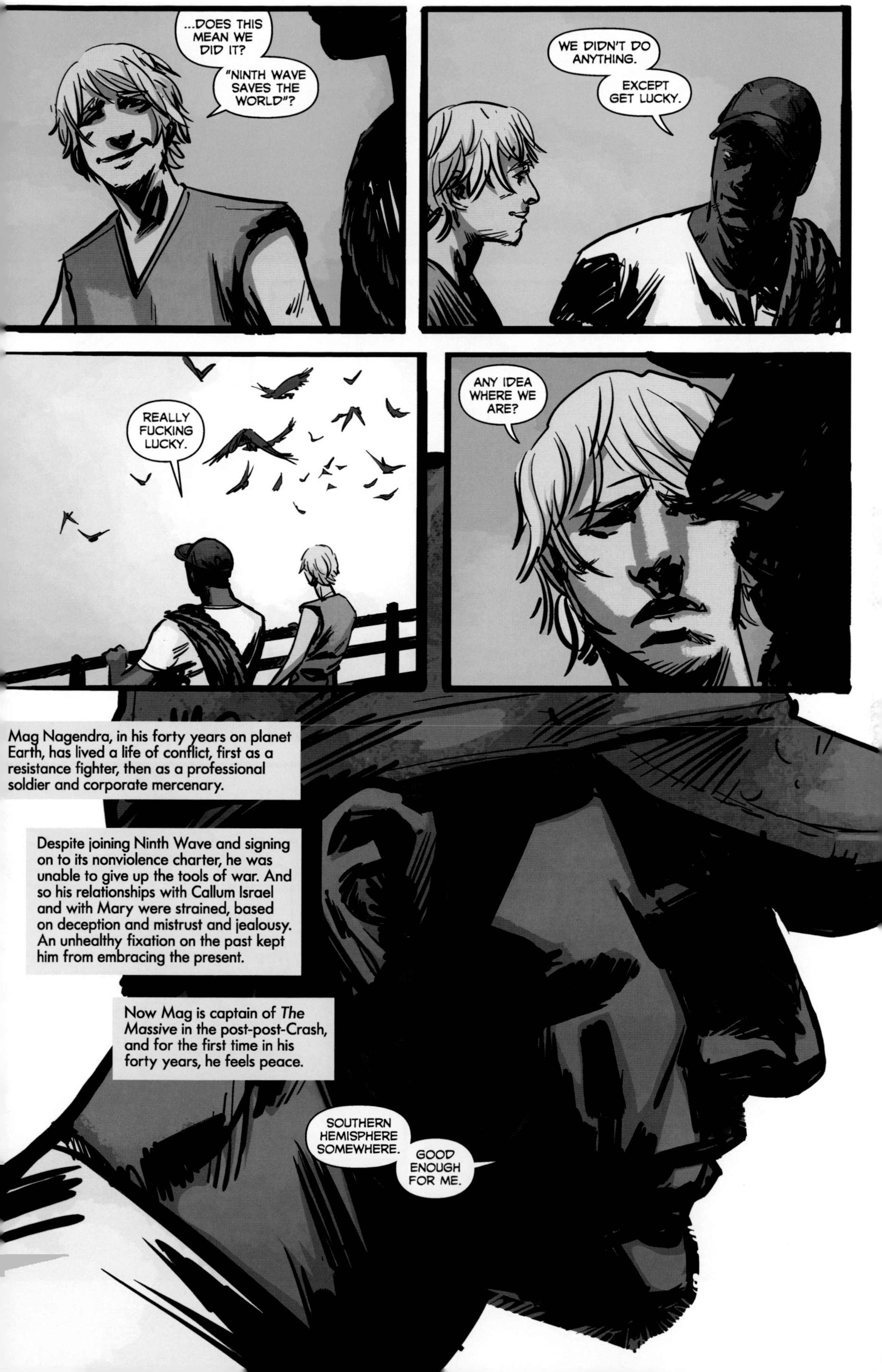
...DOES THIS MEAN WE DID IT?
"NINTH WAVE SAVES THE WORLD"?
WE DIDN'T DO ANYTHING.
EXCEPT GET LUCKY.
REALLY FUCKING LUCKY.
ANY IDEA WHERE WE ARE?
Mag Nagendra, in his forty years on planet Earth, has lived a life of conflict, first as a resistance fighter, then as a professional soldier and corporate mercenary.
Despite joining Ninth Wave and signing on to its nonviolence charter, he was unable to give up the tools of war. And so his relationships with Callum Israel and with Mary were strained, based on deception and mistrust and jealousy. An unhealthy fixation on the past kept him from embracing the present.
Now Mag is captain of *The Massive* in the post-post-Crash, and for the first time in his forty years, he feels peace.
SOUTHERN HEMISPHERE SOMEWHERE.
GOOD ENOUGH FOR ME.

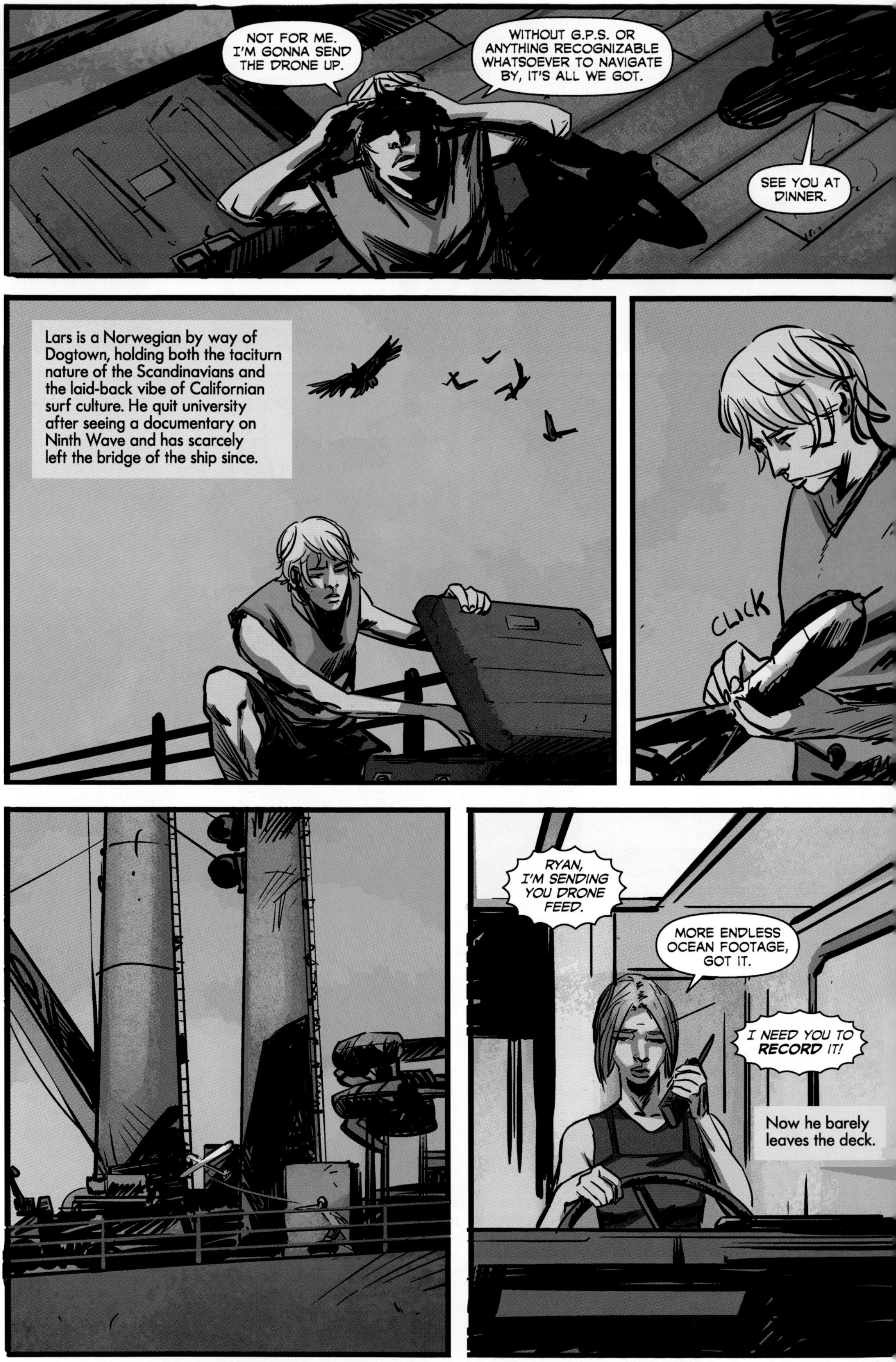
NOT FOR ME. I'M GONNA SEND THE DRONE UP.
WITHOUT G.P.S. OR ANYTHING RECOGNIZABLE WHATSOEVER TO NAVIGATE BY, IT'S ALL WE GOT.
SEE YOU AT DINNER.
Lars is a Norwegian by way of Dogtown, holding both the taciturn nature of the Scandinavians and the laid-back vibe of Californian surf culture. He quit university after seeing a documentary on Ninth Wave and has scarcely left the bridge of the ship since.
CLICK
RYAN, I'M SENDING YOU DRONE FEED.
MORE ENDLESS OCEAN FOOTAGE, GOT IT.
I NEED YOU TO RECORD IT!
Now he barely leaves the deck.

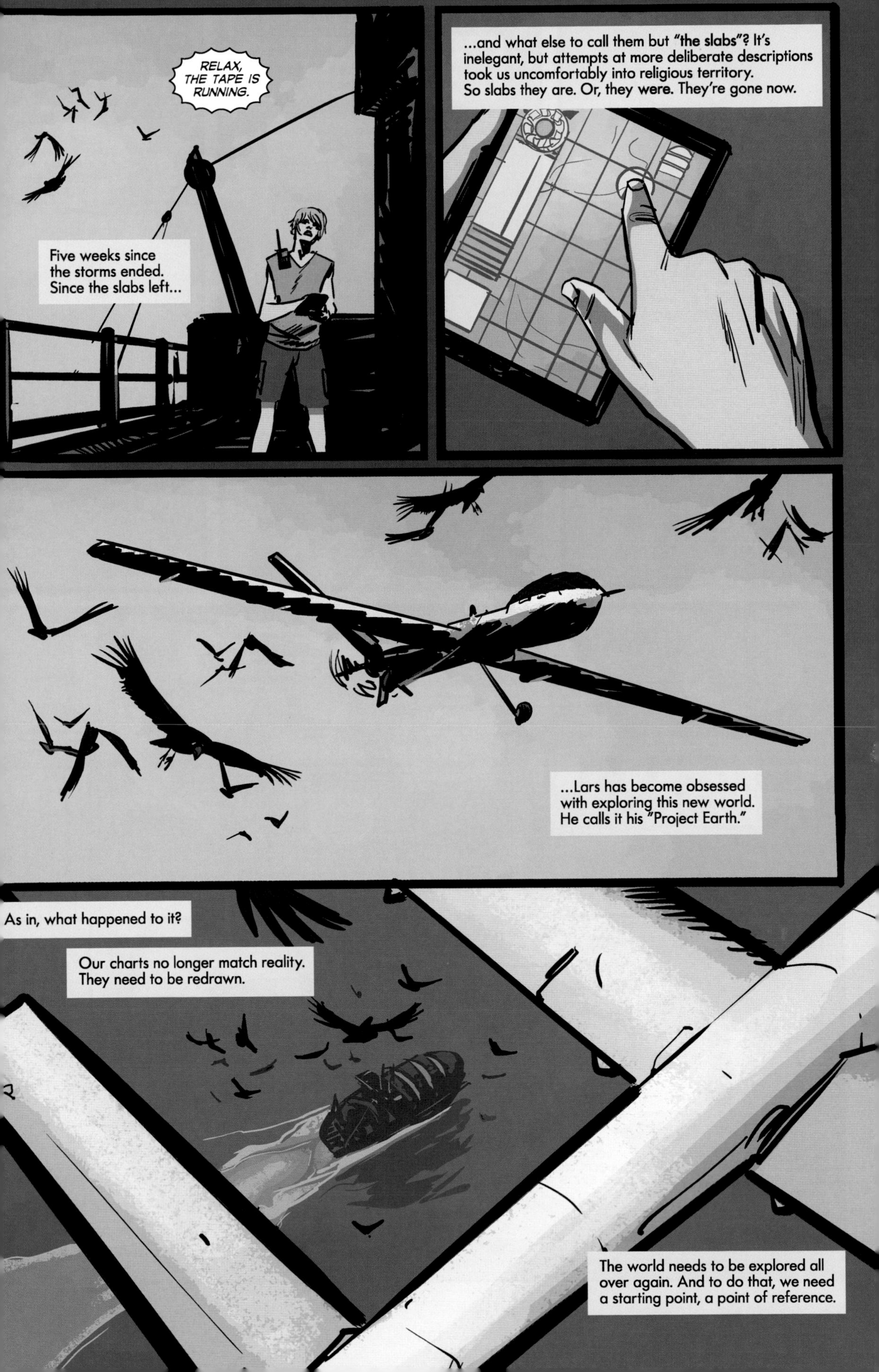
RELAX, THE TAPE IS RUNNING.
Five weeks since the storms ended. Since the slabs left...
...and what else to call them but "the slabs"? It's inelegant, but attempts at more deliberate descriptions took us uncomfortably into religious territory. So slabs they are. Or, they were. They're gone now.
...Lars has become obsessed with exploring this new world. He calls it his "Project Earth."
As in, what happened to it?
Our charts no longer match reality. They need to be redrawn.
The world needs to be explored all over again. And to do that, we need a starting point, a point of reference.

RECOGNIZE ANYTHING?

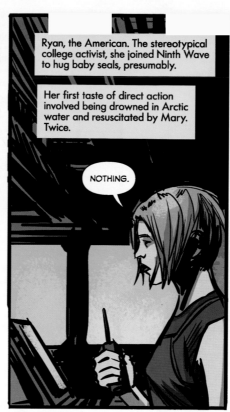

Ryan, the American. The stereotypical college activist, she joined Ninth Wave to hug baby seals, presumably.

Her first taste of direct action involved being drowned in Arctic water and resuscitated by Mary. Twice.

NOTHING.

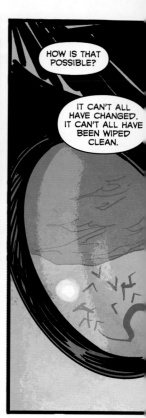

HOW IS THAT POSSIBLE?

IT CAN'T ALL HAVE CHANGED. IT CAN'T ALL HAVE BEEN WIPED CLEAN.

LOOK AROUND YOU, LARS. LOOK AT THE BIRDS. WE'RE HARDLY ALONE.

YEAH, I GUESS.

I'M GONNA KEEP LOOKING FOR A WHILE LONGER.

HE MISSES IT.

MISSES WHAT?

THE OLD WORLD. THE DROWNED WORLD.

THE *FIRST* WORLD.

HE WILL LOOK AND LOOK UNTIL HE FINDS IT.

SOMEONE LIKE MAG, OR YOU, I THINK...YOU LOVE THIS QUIET, PEACEFUL EXISTENCE OF ANIMALS AND NATURE. YOU THINK, *YES*, THIS IS WAY IT *SHOULD* BE.

LARS? HE IS *BORED*.

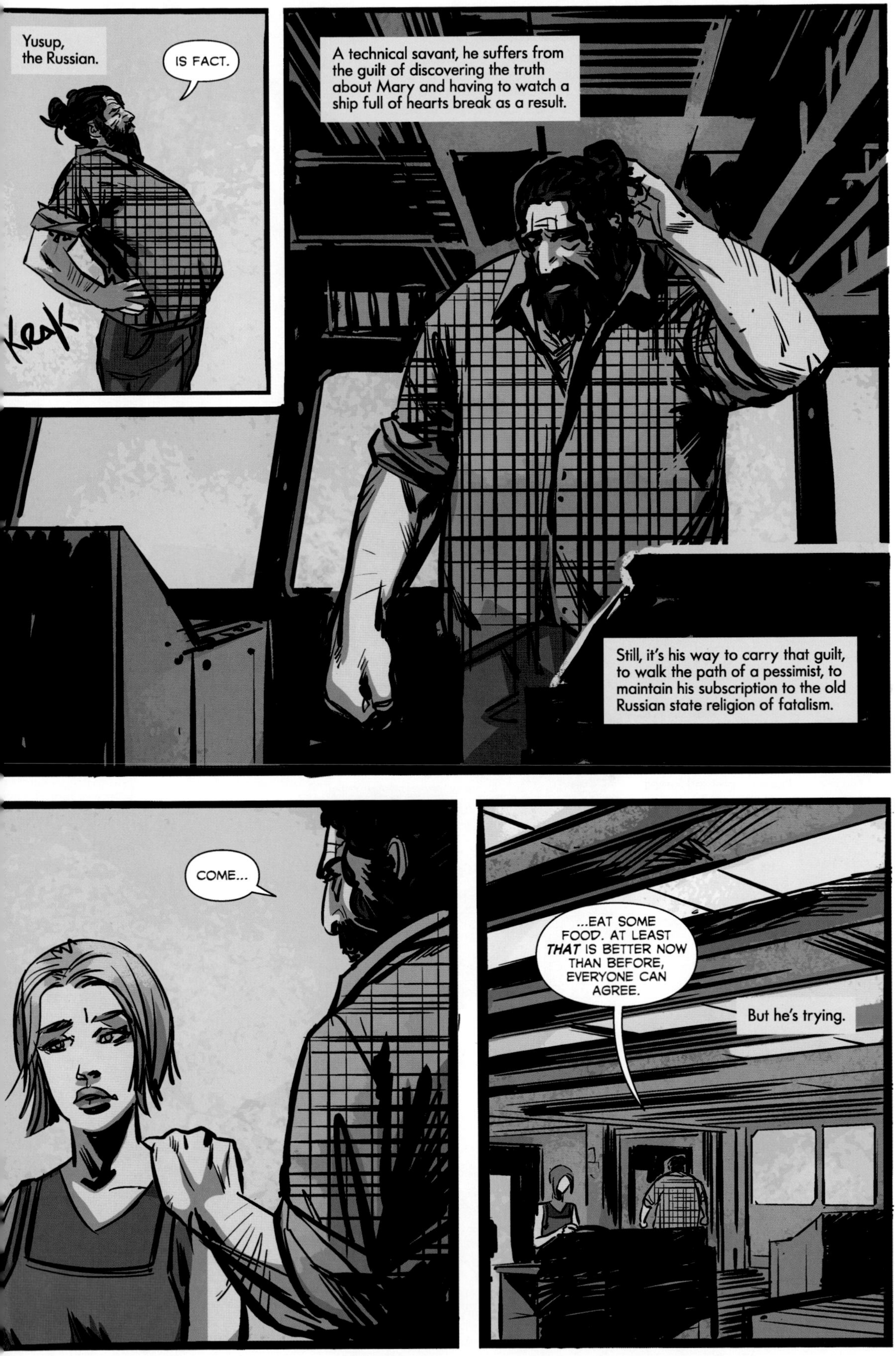
Yusup, the Russian.
IS FACT.
KRAK
A technical savant, he suffers from the guilt of discovering the truth about Mary and having to watch a ship full of hearts break as a result.
Still, it's his way to carry that guilt, to walk the path of a pessimist, to maintain his subscription to the old Russian state religion of fatalism.
COME...
...EAT SOME FOOD. AT LEAST *THAT* IS BETTER NOW THAN BEFORE, EVERYONE CAN AGREE.
But he's trying.

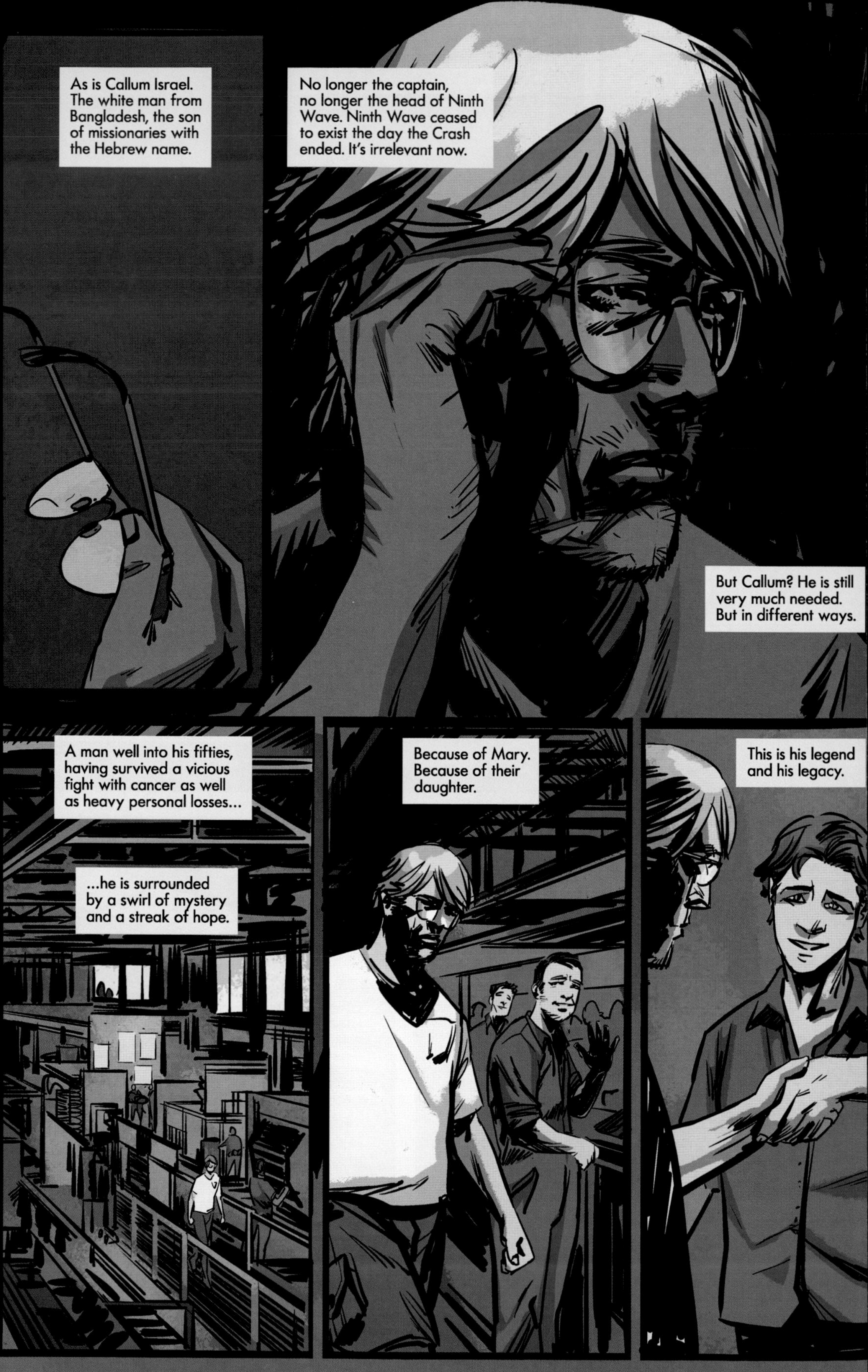
As is Callum Israel. The white man from Bangladesh, the son of missionaries with the Hebrew name.
No longer the captain, no longer the head of Ninth Wave. Ninth Wave ceased to exist the day the Crash ended. It's irrelevant now.
But Callum? He is still very much needed. But in different ways.
A man well into his fifties, having survived a vicious fight with cancer as well as heavy personal losses...
...he is surrounded by a swirl of mystery and a streak of hope.
Because of Mary. Because of their daughter.
This is his legend and his legacy.

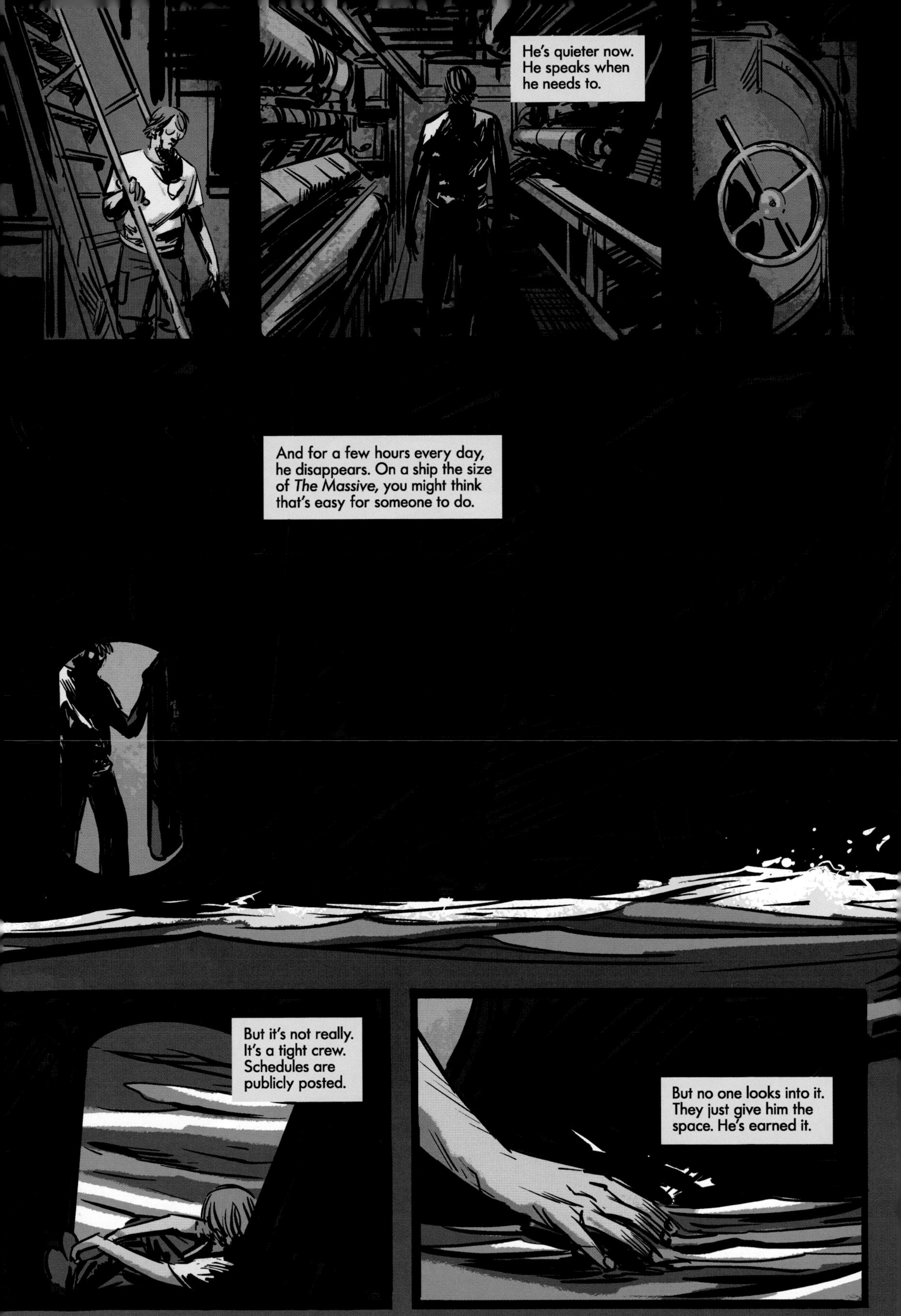
He's quieter now. He speaks when he needs to.
And for a few hours every day, he disappears. On a ship the size of *The Massive,* you might think that's easy for someone to do.
But it's not really. It's a tight crew. Schedules are publicly posted.
But no one looks into it. They just give him the space. He's earned it.

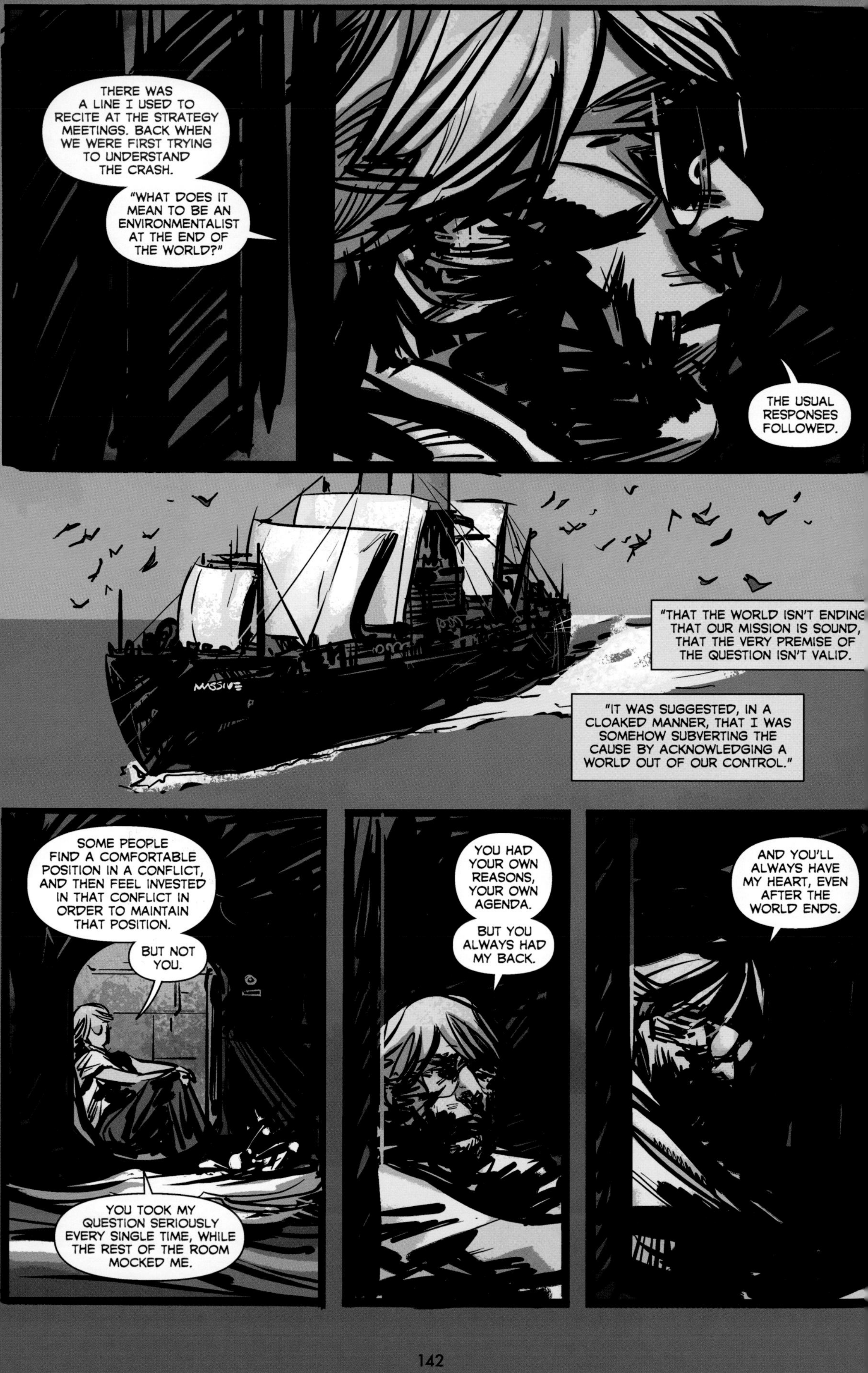
THERE WAS A LINE I USED TO RECITE AT THE STRATEGY MEETINGS. BACK WHEN WE WERE FIRST TRYING TO UNDERSTAND THE CRASH.
"WHAT DOES IT MEAN TO BE AN ENVIRONMENTALIST AT THE END OF THE WORLD?"
THE USUAL RESPONSES FOLLOWED.
MASSIVE
"THAT THE WORLD ISN'T ENDING, THAT OUR MISSION IS SOUND, THAT THE VERY PREMISE OF THE QUESTION ISN'T VALID.
"IT WAS SUGGESTED, IN A CLOAKED MANNER, THAT I WAS SOMEHOW SUBVERTING THE CAUSE BY ACKNOWLEDGING A WORLD OUT OF OUR CONTROL."
SOME PEOPLE FIND A COMFORTABLE POSITION IN A CONFLICT, AND THEN FEEL INVESTED IN THAT CONFLICT IN ORDER TO MAINTAIN THAT POSITION.
BUT NOT YOU.
YOU TOOK MY QUESTION SERIOUSLY EVERY SINGLE TIME, WHILE THE REST OF THE ROOM MOCKED ME.
YOU HAD YOUR OWN REASONS, YOUR OWN AGENDA.
BUT YOU ALWAYS HAD MY BACK.
AND YOU'LL ALWAYS HAVE MY HEART, EVEN AFTER THE WORLD ENDS.

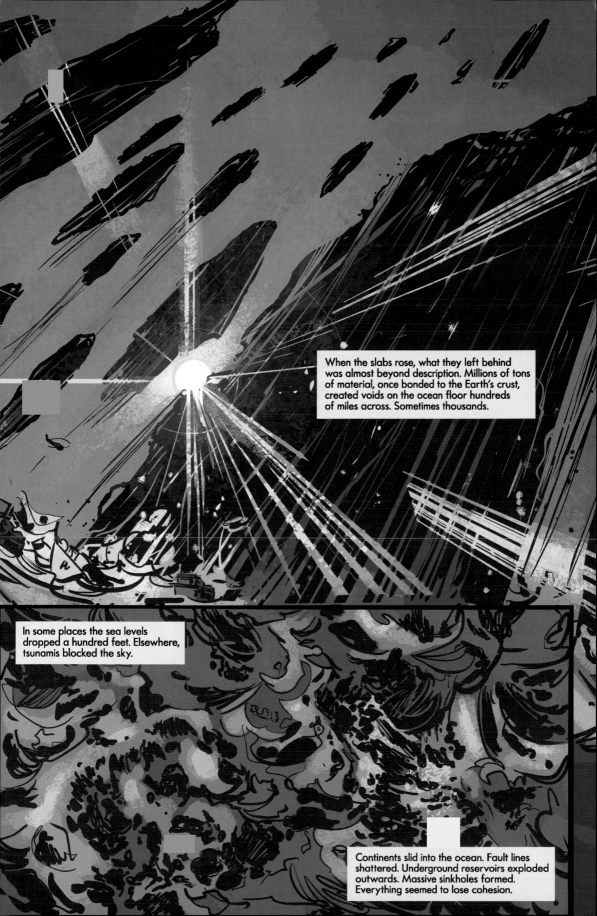

When the slabs rose, what they left behind was almost beyond description. Millions of tons of material, once bonded to the Earth's crust, created voids on the ocean floor hundreds of miles across. Sometimes thousands.

In some places the sea levels dropped a hundred feet. Elsewhere, tsunamis blocked the sky.

Continents slid into the ocean. Fault lines shattered. Underground reservoirs exploded outwards. Massive sinkholes formed. Everything seemed to lose cohesion.

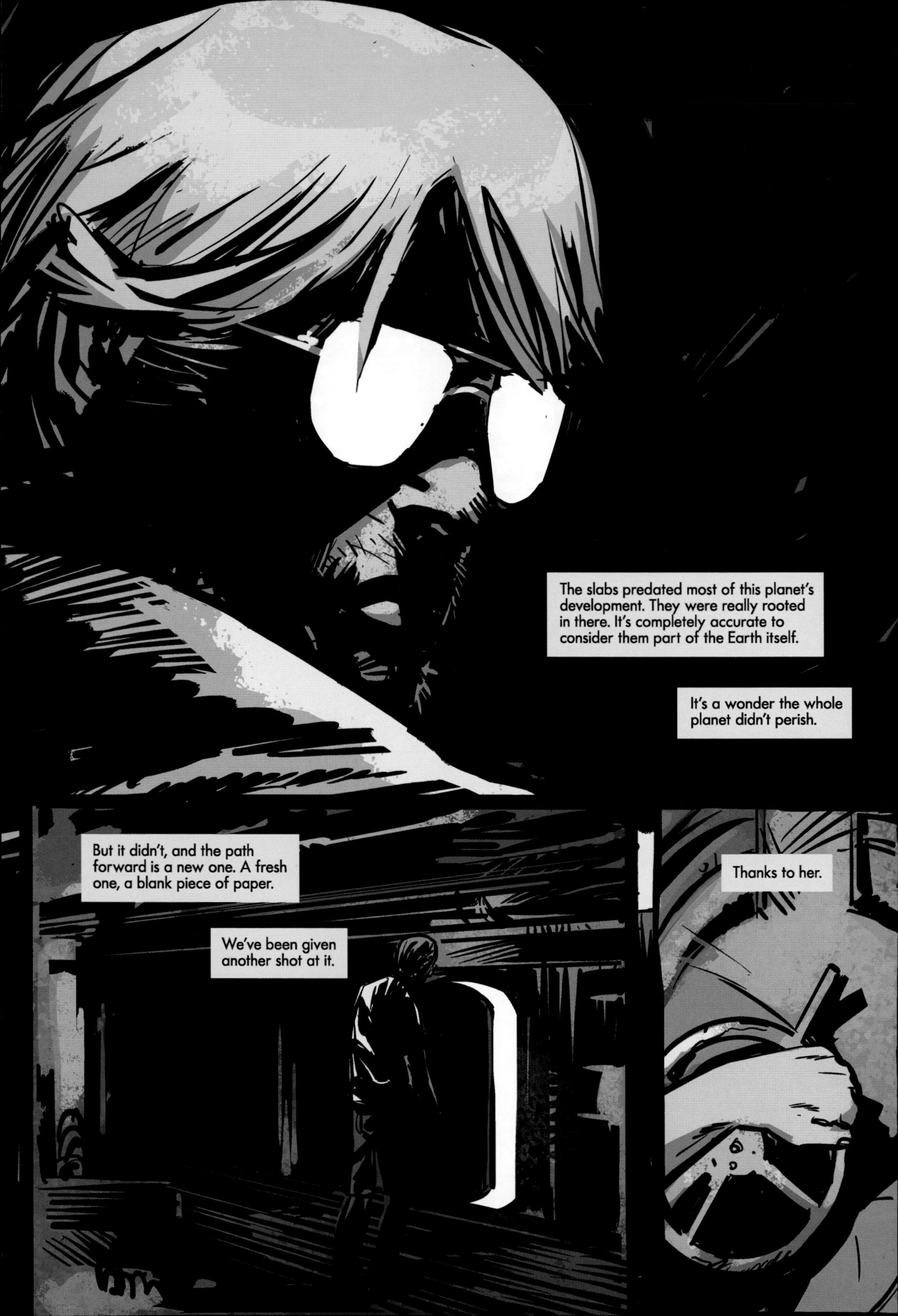
The slabs predated most of this planet's development. They were really rooted in there. It's completely accurate to consider them part of the Earth itself.
It's a wonder the whole planet didn't perish.
But it didn't, and the path forward is a new one. A fresh one, a blank piece of paper.
We've been given another shot at it.
Thanks to her.

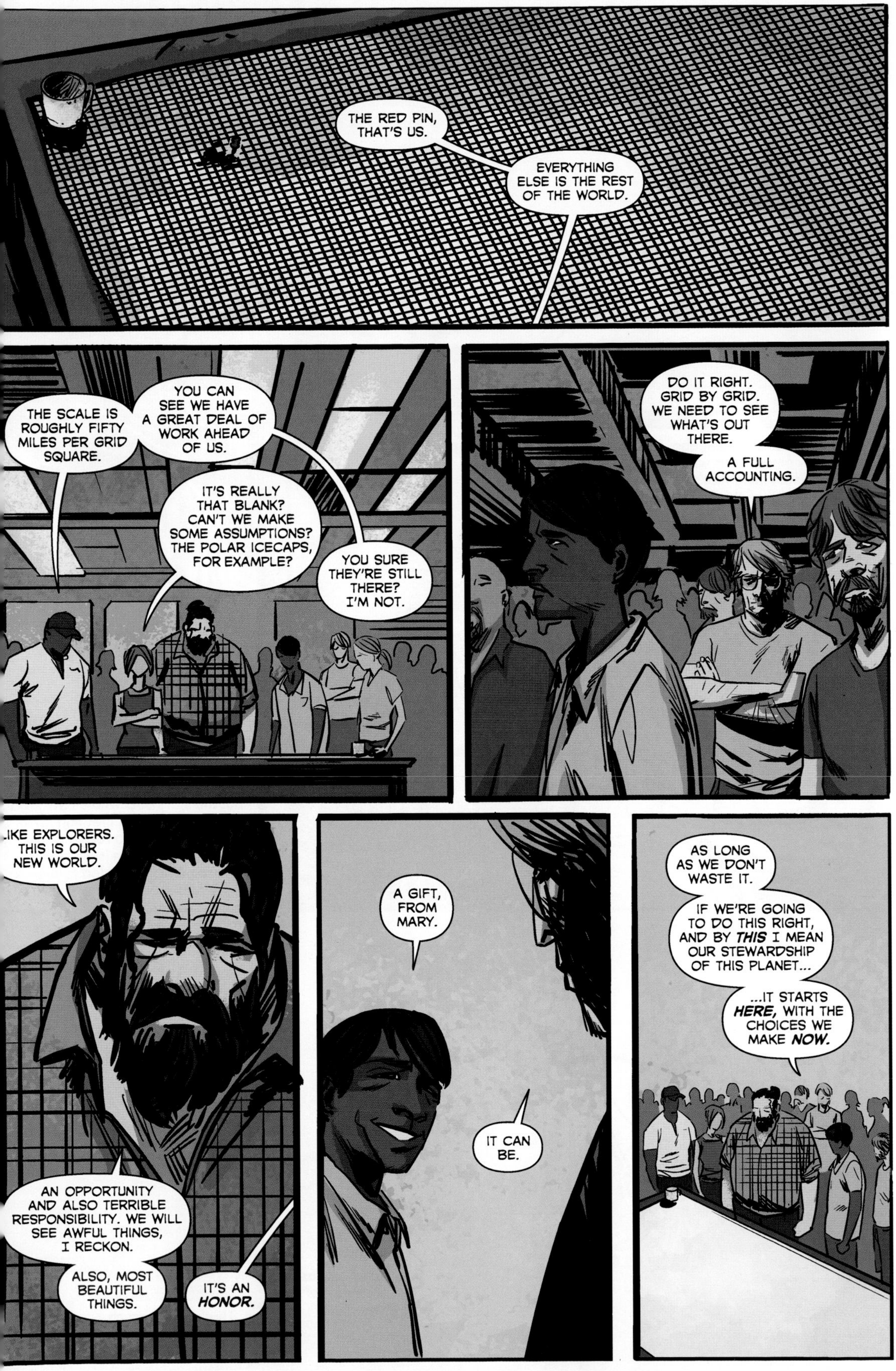

THE RED PIN, THAT'S US.
EVERYTHING ELSE IS THE REST OF THE WORLD.
THE SCALE IS ROUGHLY FIFTY MILES PER GRID SQUARE.
YOU CAN SEE WE HAVE A GREAT DEAL OF WORK AHEAD OF US.
IT'S REALLY THAT BLANK? CAN'T WE MAKE SOME ASSUMPTIONS? THE POLAR ICECAPS, FOR EXAMPLE?
YOU SURE THEY'RE STILL THERE? I'M NOT.
DO IT RIGHT. GRID BY GRID. WE NEED TO SEE WHAT'S OUT THERE.
A FULL ACCOUNTING.
LIKE EXPLORERS. THIS IS OUR NEW WORLD.
AN OPPORTUNITY AND ALSO TERRIBLE RESPONSIBILITY. WE WILL SEE AWFUL THINGS, I RECKON.
ALSO, MOST BEAUTIFUL THINGS.
IT'S AN *HONOR.*
A GIFT, FROM MARY.
IT CAN BE.
AS LONG AS WE DON'T WASTE IT.
IF WE'RE GOING TO DO THIS RIGHT, AND BY *THIS* I MEAN OUR STEWARDSHIP OF THIS PLANET...
...IT STARTS *HERE,* WITH THE CHOICES WE MAKE *NOW.*

"GRID BY GRID."

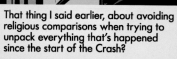

That thing I said earlier, about avoiding religious comparisons when trying to unpack everything that's happened since the start of the Crash?

Still holds. But still...

...it's hard to see this as anything but the start of a whole new world, a whole history. A creation myth. Doesn't have to be religious, but then again, religion is a creation too, something invented to explain the world around us.

From chaos... comes life?

That's pretty much what I see when I look out the window.

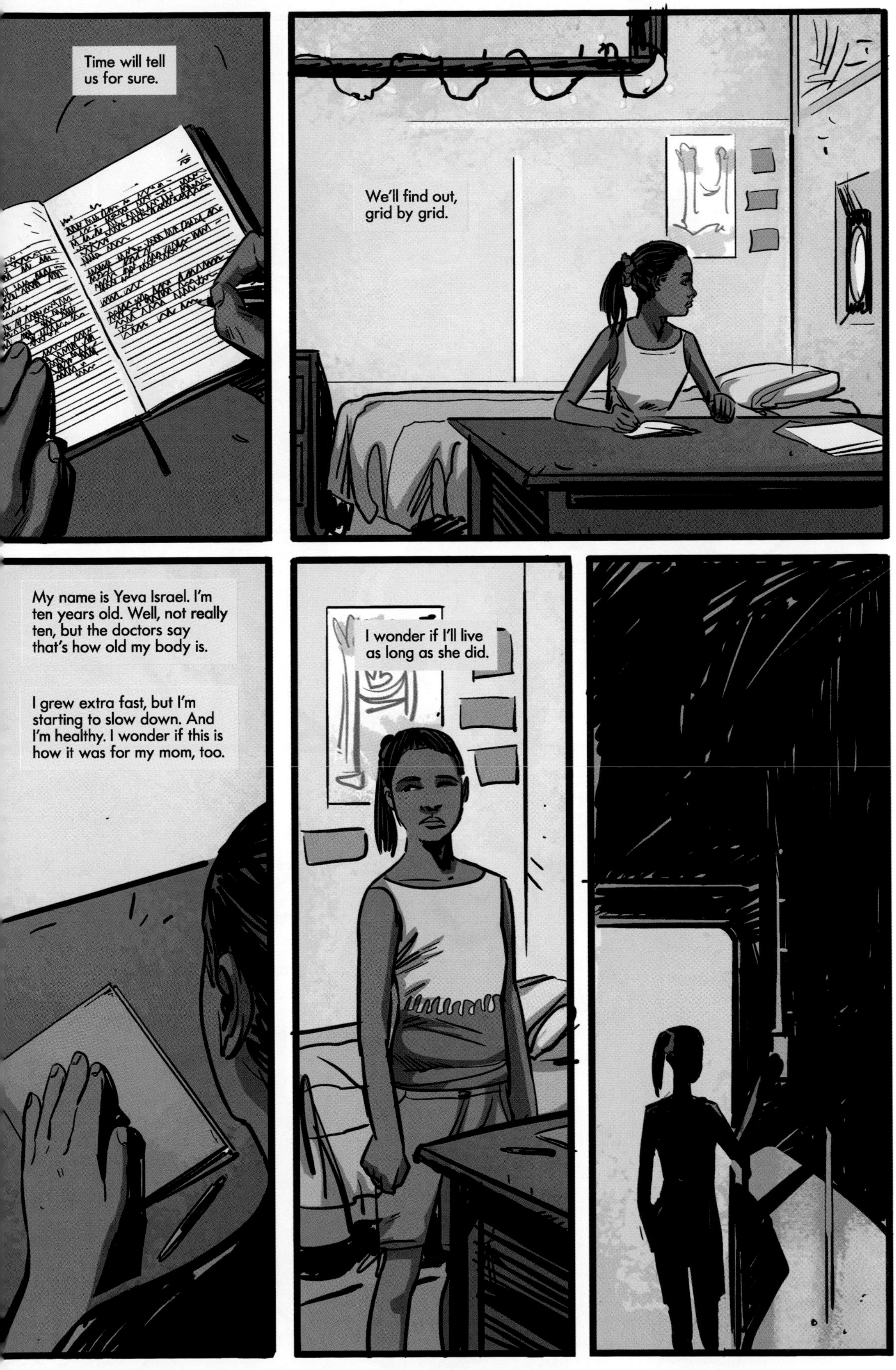
Time will tell us for sure.
We'll find out, grid by grid.
My name is Yeva Israel. I'm ten years old. Well, not really ten, but the doctors say that's how old my body is.
I grew extra fast, but I'm starting to slow down. And I'm healthy. I wonder if this is how it was for my mom, too.
I wonder if I'll live as long as she did.

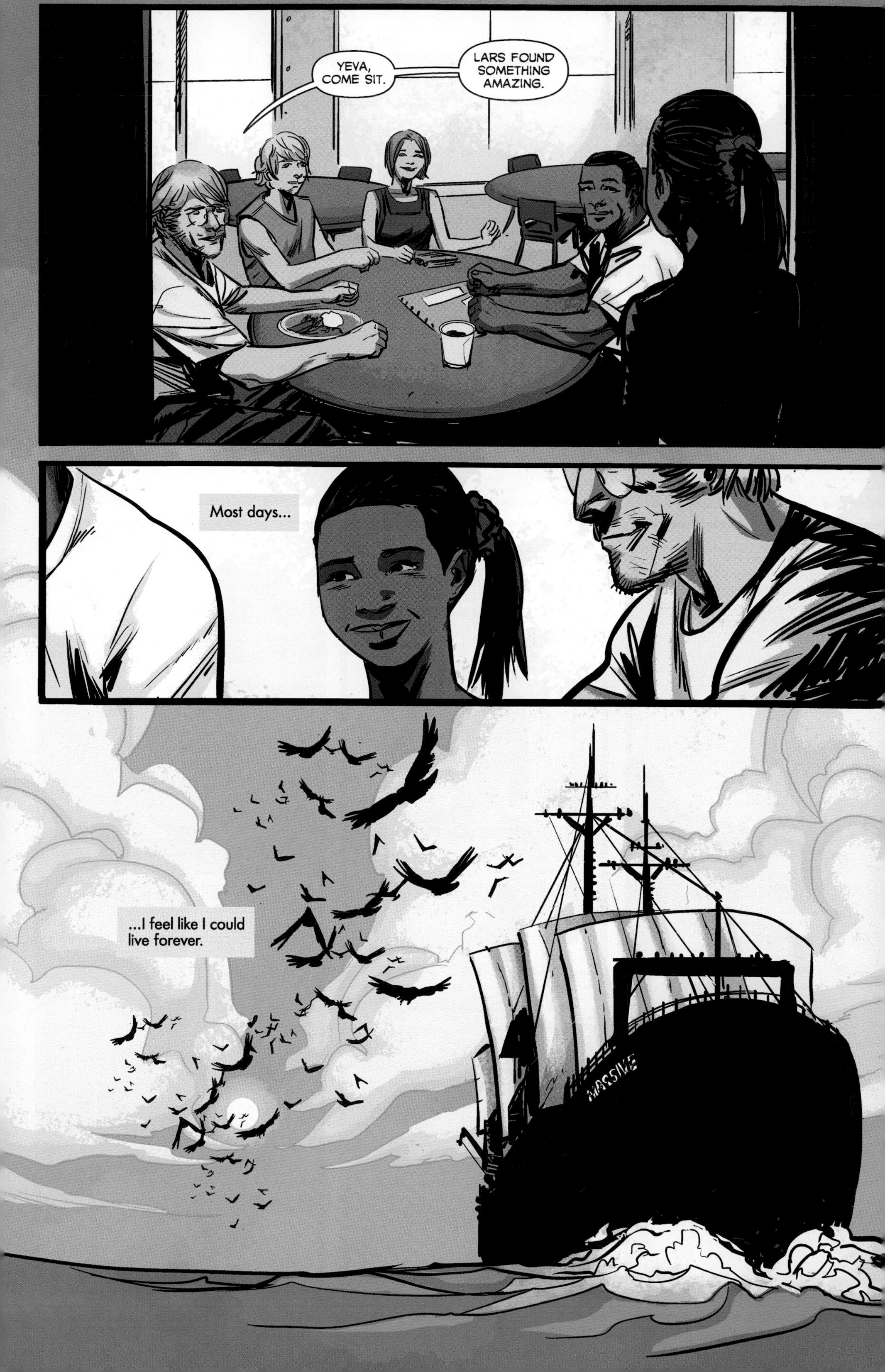
YEVA, COME SIT.
LARS FOUND SOMETHING AMAZING.
Most days...
...I feel like I could live forever.
MASSIVE

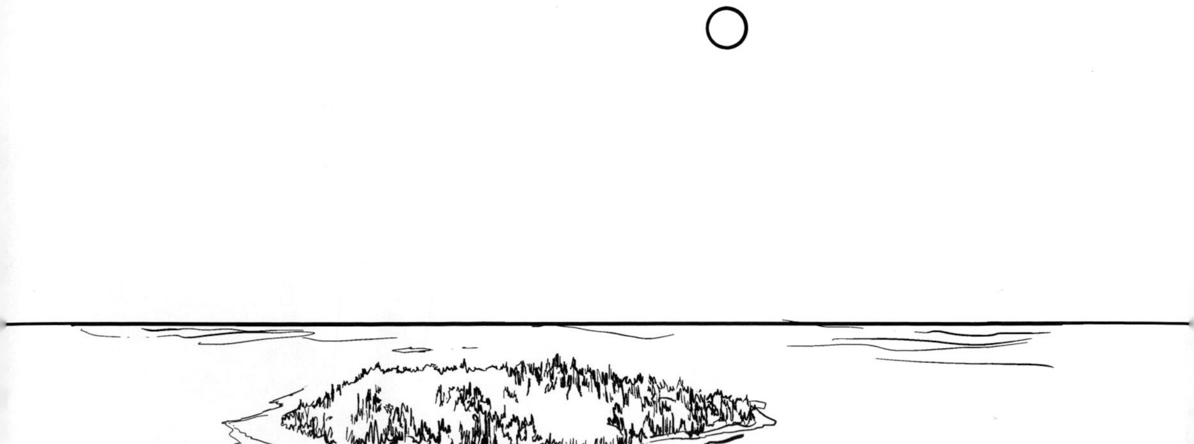

Multiple Eisner Award nominee **BRIAN WOOD** released his first series, *Channel Zero*, to considerable critical acclaim in 1997 and has continued to create hard-hitting original series, such as *DMZ, Northlanders, The Couriers*, and *The Massive*. He's written some of the biggest titles in pop culture, with work on *Star Wars, Conan the Barbarian, Lord of the Rings*, and *The X-Men*. He lives with his wife and two children in Brooklyn, New York.

GARRY BROWN is an LA-based Scottish artist. He is currently working on *Catwoman* for DC. His collaboration with Brian Wood continues in their Image series, *Black Road*. He has also worked for *2000 AD*, IDW, Marvel, and Boom.

JORDIE BELLAIRE is an Eisner Award–winning colorist who is best known for her work on *Manhattan Projects, Mara, Moon Knight, Nowhere Men, Pretty Deadly*, and *Zero*. She lives in Ireland with her cat Buffy.

JARED K. FLETCHER grew up sailing around the waters of his native Rhode Island. After graduating from the Kubert School, he began working at DC Comics as part of their new in-house lettering department. He left to pursue his freelance career as the proprietor of Studio Fantabulous. He spends long days there designing logos and type treatments, art directing covers, cartooning, designing T-shirts, and lettering comic books like *Batman, Ex Machina, The New Frontier, DMZ*, and *Wonder Woman*.

JOHN PAUL LEON is best known for his critically acclaimed work that envisioned and redefined the entire Marvel universe in the maxiseries *Earth X*. He first began working professionally at the age of sixteen, with a series of black-and-white illustrations for TSR's *Dragon* and *Dungeon* magazines. JP has contributed artwork for the *Superman Returns, Batman Begins, Green Lantern*, and *Dark Knight* style guides, as well as a pair of Superman children's books for Meredith Books. He is currently working on a *Batman* miniseries for DC Comics. JP lives in Miami, Florida.

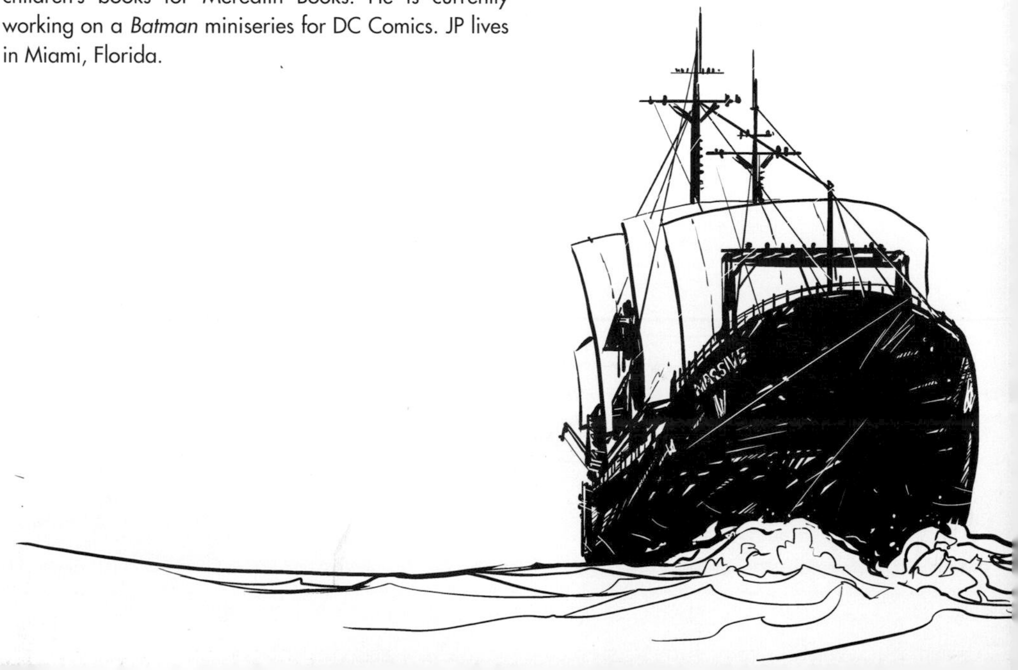
MASSIVE

MORE FROM *NEW YORK TIMES* BEST-SELLING AUTHOR

BRIAN WOOD

"Someone remembered what comics are for. Meet Brian Wood."
—Warren Ellis

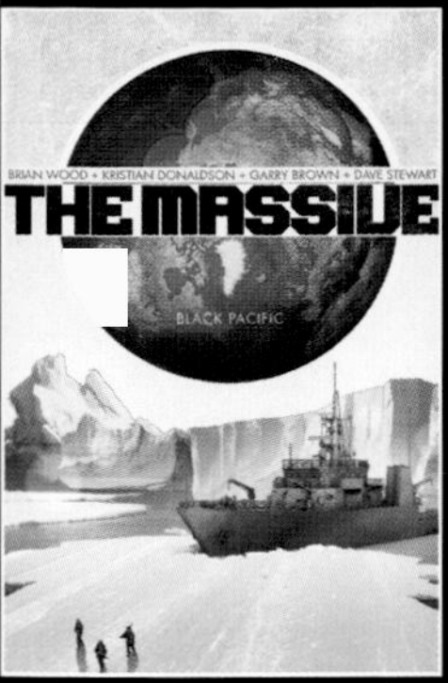
THE MASSIVE
BLACK PACIFIC

THE MASSIVE

Written by Brian Wood, Art by Kristian Donaldson and Garry Brown

In this first volume of Brian Wood's new, sprawling postapocalyptic epic, follow the crew of the *Kapital* from the flooded remnants of Hong Kong to Unalaska, with stops in Antarctica and Mogadishu, as post-Crash ethics and economics are explored across a broken world.

Volume 1: Black Pacific
ISBN 978-1-61655-132-2 | $19.99

Volume 2: Subcontinental
ISBN 978-1-61655-316-6 | $19.99

Volume 3: Longship
ISBN 978-1-61655-446-0 | $19.99

Volume 4: Sahara
ISBN 978-1-61655-508-5 | $19.99

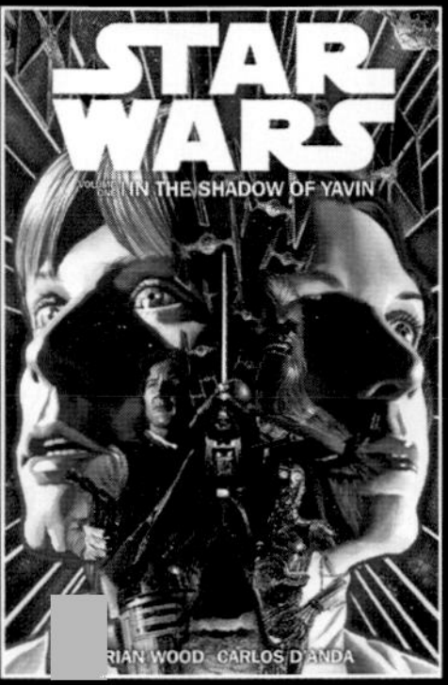
STAR WARS
IN THE SHADOW OF YAVIN

STAR WARS VOLUME 1: IN THE SHADOW OF YAVIN

Written by Brian Wood, Art by Carlos D'Anda, Ryan Odagawa, and Gabe Eltaeb, Cover by Alex Ross

After the destruction of the Death Star, the Rebels are hounded by the Empire. Suspecting a spy in their ranks, Princess Leia forms a secret X-wing squadron—which includes Luke Skywalker—to expose the spy and find a safe home. Meanwhile, Han Solo and Chewbacca are sent on a covert mission!

ISBN 978-1-61655-170-4 | $19.99

THE NEW YORK FOUR

Written by Brian Wood, Art by Ryan Kelly

Worlds collide when four young women begin college at the prestigious New York University. But that freedom comes at a price: roommate drama, mysterious love interests, school troubles, and family conflicts. Welcome to adulthood!

ISBN 978-1-61655-605-1 | $19.99

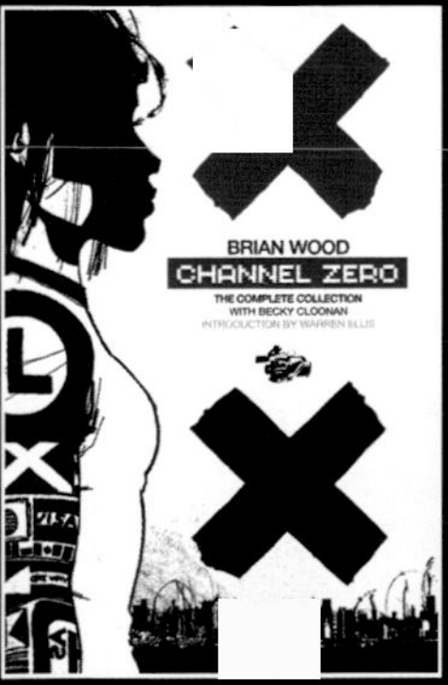
BRIAN WOOD
CHANNEL ZERO
THE COMPLETE COLLECTION
WITH BECKY CLOONAN

CHANNEL ZERO

Written by Brian Wood, Art by Becky Cloonan

A blistering take on media control in a repressive future America! *DMZ* and *The Massive* creator Brian Wood launched an all-out assault on the comics medium in 1997 with *Channel Zero*, an influential, forward-thinking series that combined art, politics, and graphic design in a unique way.

ISBN 978-1-59582-936-8 | $19.99

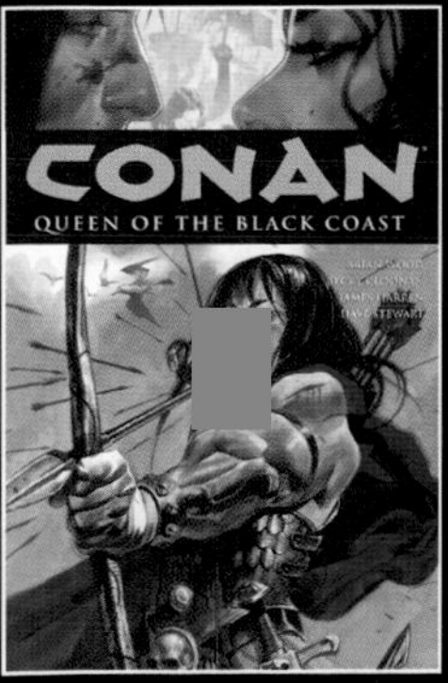
CONAN
QUEEN OF THE BLACK COAST

CONAN VOLUME 13: QUEEN OF THE BLACK COAST

Written by Brian Wood, Art by Becky Cloonan and James Harren

Conan turns his back on the civilized world and takes to the Western Ocean. Finding first danger and then passion in the arms of the pirate queen Bêlit, the Cimmerian begins a new life of pleasure and pillage along the Black Coast, in this epic of romance and terror!

TPB: ISBN 978-1-61655-043-1 | $19.99
HC: ISBN 978-1-61655-042-4 | $24.99

CONAN VOLUME 14: THE DEATH

Written by Brian Wood, Art by Becky Cloonan, Vasilis Lolos, and Declan Shalvey

Conan returns to Cimmeria to track down an impostor destroying villages in his name, only to discover a tragic connection to his own past!

TPB: ISBN 978-1-61655-123-0 | $19.99

AVAILABLE AT YOUR LOCAL COMICS SHOP OR BOOKSTORE! • To find a comics shop in your area, call 1-888-266-4226.
For more information or to order direct visit DarkHorse.com or call 1-800-862-0052 Mon.–Fri. 9 AM. to 5 PM. Pacific Time. Prices and availability subject to change without notice.

CREATIVE GIANTS!

GET YOUR FIX OF DARK HORSE BOOKS FROM THESE INSPIRED CREATORS!

MESMO DELIVERY SECOND EDITION

Rafael Grampá

Eisner Award–winning artist Rafael Grampá (*5*, *Hellblazer*) makes his full-length comics debut with the critically acclaimed graphic novel *Mesmo Delivery*—a kinetic, bloody romp starring Rufo, an ex-boxer; Sangrecco, an Elvis impersonator; and a ragtag crew of overly confident drunks who pick the wrong delivery men to mess with.

ISBN 978-1-61655-457-6 | $14.99

SIN TITULO

Cameron Stewart

Following the death of his grandfather, Alex Mackay discovers a mysterious photograph in the old man's belongings that sets him on an adventure like no other—where dreams and reality merge, family secrets are laid bare, and lives are irrevocably altered.

ISBN 978-1-61655-248-0 | $19.99

DE:TALES

Fábio Moon and Gabriel Bá

Brazilian twins Fábio Moon and Gabriel Bá's (*Daytripper*, *Pixu*) most personal work to date. Brimming with all the details of human life, their charming tales move from the urban reality of their home in São Paulo to the magical realism of their Latin American background.

ISBN 978-1-59582-557-5 | $19.99

THE TRUE LIVES OF THE FABULOUS KILLJOYS

Gerard Way, Shaun Simon, and Becky Cloonan

Years ago, the Killjoys fought against the tyrannical megacorporation Better Living Industries. Today, the followers of the original Killjoys languish in the desert and the fight for freedom fades. It's left to the Girl to take down BLI!

ISBN 978-1-59582-462-2 | $19.99

DEMO

Brian Wood and Becky Cloonan

It's hard enough being a teenager. Now try being a teenager with *powers*. A chronicle of the lives of young people on separate journeys to self-discovery in a world—just like our own—where being different is feared.

ISBN 978-1-61655-682-2 | $24.99

SABERTOOTH SWORDSMAN

Damon Gentry and Aaron Conley

When his village is enslaved and his wife kidnapped by the malevolent Mastodon Mathematician, a simple farmer must find his inner warrior—the Sabertooth Swordsman!

ISBN 978-1-61655-176-6 | $17.99

JAYBIRD

Jaakko and Lauri Ahonen

Disney meets Kafka in this beautiful, intense, original tale! A very small, very scared little bird lives an isolated life in a great big house with his infirm mother. He's never been outside the house, and he never will if his mother has anything to say about it.

ISBN 978-1-61655-469-9 | $19.99

MONSTERS! & OTHER STORIES

Gustavo Duarte

Newcomer Gustavo Duarte spins wordless tales inspired by Godzilla, King Kong, and Pixar, brimming with humor, charm, and delightfully twisted horror!

ISBN 978-1-61655-309-8 | $12.99

SACRIFICE

Sam Humphries and Dalton Rose

What happens when a troubled youth is plucked from modern society and thrust though time and space into the heart of the Aztec civilization—one of the most bloodthirsty times in human history?

ISBN 978-1-59582-985-6 | $19.99

AVAILABLE AT YOUR LOCAL COMICS SHOP OR BOOKSTORE
To find a comics shop in your area, call 1-888-266-4226. For more information or to order direct: ON THE WEB: DarkHorse.com
E-MAIL: mailorder@darkhorse.com / PHONE: 1-800-862-0052 Mon.–Fri. 9 a.m. to 5 p.m. Pacific Time.